Donated by...

**The
Jost-Ore**

FOR THE BIRDS

This is the first of an intended collection of texts published in co-operation with Semiotext(e) Magazine, Silvère Lotringer, General Editor

This English version was prepared by Richard Gardner and edited by Tom Gora and John Cage

Books by John Cage

Silence
A Year from Monday
'M'-Writings '67-'72
Empty Words

FOR THE BIRDS

in conversation with
Daniel Charles

Marion Boyars
Boston : London

Published simultaneously in the
United States, Canada and Great Britain
in 1981 by
Marion Boyars Inc.
99 Main Street, Salem, New Hampshire 03079
and Marion Boyars Ltd.
18 Brewer Street, London W1R 4AS

Australian and New Zealand distribution by
Thomas C. Lothian
4-12 Tattersalls Lane, Melbourne, Victoria 3000

© This version Marion Boyars Publishers, 1981

French Edition under the title *Pour Les Oiseaux*
Editions Pierre Belfond
3 bis, passage de la Petite-Boucherie
75006 Paris
© Belfond 1976

Library of Congress Cataloging in Publication Data

Cage, John.
  [Pour les oiseaux. English]
  For the birds.

  Translation of: Pour les oiseaux.
  Bibliography: p.
  1. Cage, John. 2. Composers–United States–
Interviews. I. Charles, Daniel, maître-assistant.
II. Title.
ML410.C24A33   780'.92'4   81-1642
ISBN 0-7145-2690-8   AACR2

British Library Cataloguing in Publication Data

Cage, John
  For the birds.
  I. Title   II. Charles, Daniel
  III. Pour les oiseaux. *English*
  780'.92'4   ML410.C24

CONTENTS

Note on the Book's History   7

Preface by Daniel Charles   9

An Introduction by John Cage   11

Sixty Answers to Thirty-Three Questions from Daniel Charles   13

A Dialogue with John Cage followed by a discussion   31

Interviews with John Cage   63

   Forward I   64

   Forward II   65

   First Interview   67

   Second Interview   83

   Third Interview   101

   Fourth Interview   121

   Fifth Interview   139

   Sixth Interview   155

   Seventh Interview   175

   Eighth Interview   191

   Ninth Interview   207

   Tenth Interview   223

Afterword to the French Edition   239

A NOTE ON THE BOOK'S HISTORY

For the Birds began in 1968 as a series of interviews published in *La Revue d'esthétique* (Vol. XXI, Nos. 2, 3 and 4; April-December, 1968) by its editor, Daniel Charles, and Editions Klincksieck. They were collected into one volume by Editions Belfond in 1976. Semiotext(e) Magazine and Marion Boyars Publishers obtained permission to publish the book in English in 1978, but it was soon discovered that the original taped interviews – in English – had been lost. This necessitated the very Cagian task of retranslating a translation. Needless to say, the result is not at all a record of actual conversation, but rather our[1] performance (or interpretation) of a John Cage score.[2] A further intermingling of categories that makes John Cage very happy.

For further accounts of John Cage's personal exploits, see the chapter entitled 'John Cage' in Calvin Tomkins' *The Bride and the Bachelors* (New York: Viking Compass, 1965. pp. 69-144), and the collection of pieces, including an excellent bibliography, edited by Richard Kostelanetz and entitled *John Cage* (New York: RK Editions, 1974).

Tom Gora

---

[1]Richard Gardner's translation has been edited by me, Tom Gora, and then again by John Cage. Though tempted to add to the use of brackets (see John Cage's introduction), Cage refrained from so doing, wishing to remain faithful to what appeared in French.
[2]Actually, the score is by Daniel Charles. Their conversations, Cage's letters to him, articles and books Cage sent him were used as material for the composition of something new.

7

A PREFACE BY DANIEL CHARLES

In 1972, once he had finished rereading the text of the Interviews, a task
he considered essential, John Cage prepared a Foreword and Postface.
Concerned with clearly expressing to the reader the reasons and
circumstances behind these Interviews, he asked in addition that I open
the projected book with a preface where I would clarify the pre-
suppositions which I had at the time (the very end of 1970) when I
interviewed him. The same day, he chose the title of the work. This
choice, he told me, was informed merely by the pleasure he got out of a
pun on his own name.

The end of 1976: *For the Birds* is at the printers.[1] I have the feeling,
just as I did five years ago, that these texts comprise a multiple and
unique gloss of Chuang-tze. In any case, the sole aim of my questions
was to bring out what, for brevity's sake, I call John Cage's Taoism. A
page from Octavio Paz recently reassured me that this plan did not at all
escape John and that even the title he suggested points in that direction.
Therefore I shall borrow my preface from the author of *The Bow and the
Lyre*.

'When Chuang-tze explains that the Tao experience implies a return
to a sort of elementary or original frame of mind, where the relative
meanings of language are inoperative, he resorts to a play on words that
is a poetic riddle. He says that this experience of a return to what we are
originally is like "entering a cage of birds without making them sing."
Fan means "cage" and "return"; *ming*, "song" and "names". The sentence, therefore, equally means "to return to the place where names are
superfluous," to silence, to the kingdom of the obvious. To the place
where names and things melt into one: to poetry, the kingdom where
naming is being.'

My desire was and remains that, despite the imperfections for which I
alone am responsible, *For the Birds* may make such a return possible.

Daniel Charles

---

[1]The Belfond French edition, which preceded the English language edition (Translator's
note).

AN INTRODUCTION BY JOHN CAGE

The following text, which I wrote as a preface for an earlier English translation by another translator of part of this book (Semiotext(e), Vol. III, no. 1, pp. 24-35), is, it seems to me, still relevant.

Pour Les Oiseaux finally appeared in Paris in January 1977, but without its author's name, only mine on the cover! Many years before, at the request of the publisher, Pierre Belfond, Daniel Charles and I engaged in many conversations which were recorded on tape. For one reason or another the project of making a book out of this material was shelved year after year. There was too much material, or not enough that was up-to-date, etc. When I eventually read galleys (not of this version but of an earlier one), I found that I did not always recognize myself in a passage ascribed to me. Some tapes apparently had been damaged or lost or inadvertently erased, so that it had sometimes been necessary for Daniel Charles to compose my responses to his questions. Instead of 'correcting' his work, I suggested the use of two different typefaces for my responses. One would indicate that I could hear myself speaking, the other that I couldn't. (In the present printing, square brackets have been used instead of italics to indicate I couldn't hear myself speaking.) This idea was accepted but still the book was not published. In fact, in order to please the publisher, Charles later made a new version, in some cases an abridgement of the earlier one, in others having new material, 'conversations' written by Charles himself, following new articles or letters or tapes of lectures that I sent to him. I made no changes in the final version. When I was asked to suggest a catchy title, I said: Call it *Pour Les Oiseaux*. Though Pierre Belfond accepted this, he asked me somewhat nervously after the publication of the book whether my title was merely a joke. I said: No. I am for the birds, not for the cages in which people sometimes place them.

I was given the opportunity of going over the typescript of the translation of Daniel Charles' book (Charles' name, I am glad to report, appears with mine on the cover of the Italian translation), and making any changes I wished, so that it would sound like me (which now, of course, it doesn't in any sense at all). After a few labored alterations, I found myself reading all the way through, more entertained than I would have been had I been recognizing myself. And then I went back to the beginning and put the word 'stet': that is, keep it as you have it. The ideas, so to speak, have changed their clothes but they are healthy. I decided not to do anything to them. Let them live their own lives. They are certain to change in further unpredictable ways whenever someone takes the time to use them.

John Cage

SIXTY ANSWERS TO THIRTY-THREE QUESTIONS FROM DANIEL CHARLES

SIXTY ANSWERS
to thirty-three questions from Daniel Charles

Schoenberg, whose student you were, said that you were 'not a composer, but an inventor – of genius'.
What have you invented?

Music, (not composition).

What interests you, in certain of your recent works, (I'm thinking of Variations IV), is not determining sounds, but the location where they take place. Why this insistence on space?

It was an attempt to expel music, just as we send children outdoors to play so the grownups may finish what they were in the midst of doing.

Buddha's foot is in the grave. Once born, the baby Buddha cries (we do what we do by means of contradiction): 'I am the World-honored One (not by quality – how, where, what, who, if – just continuity)!'

What you're alluding to with the name music is a game without goal. An absence of finality. The impression of what I call an indirect method. Letting sounds be what they are is, according to you, only possible by bracketting any intention regarding them. You thus hope to act in 'the way Nature operates'. By thus suppressing any expression of the artist's individuality, you imitate Nature, but it's your idea of Nature that runs the risk of presenting a puzzling appearance. After all, the artist as a thinking, desiring, intending individual is also part of Nature.

Or is the world only a 'game without players'? In that case, why do you continue to play?

Subjectivity

What do you think of Leonard Meyer's opinion of your aesthetics: a 'radical empiricism'?

Tenney wrote to say, 'What's needed … is … a radical eclecticism (Ives) … "The duty of every composer" … More power to Fuller … to revolutionary guerillas … to Christian pacifists … to flower children … to hippies … to acid-heads … beatniks, fools in love, agitators … to the black militants … to those who continue to ask questions.'

What we must do is establish a dialogue between man (society, too) and nature (the celestial city is no longer fortified: it has flown off into space).

There are several solutions: loss of interest, flight.

When you perform with Merce Cunningham, you bring music and dance together. For you, these activities are independent. But is that always the case? Aren't bonds of causality naturally woven by themselves where you pretend to see only a simple concomitance?

Xenakis assured me that you returned disappointed from one of your trips to Japan. Is that true? And why?

We separated from each other. Instead of space, it was as though we were dead. There must be times for him, as there are for me, when, looking in my direction and wanting to say hello, he sees me passing by without so much as glancing at him. Saving grace – we were identical. Ergo, nothing is lost.

Is your music a koan?

There is one thing we do not do, and that is to use an answering service. It is of the greatest urgency – even an ethical matter – that we be able to reach one another. Even those who are egotists will change their minds about interruptions (that is, they will become superficially moral): telephone communications received will be the means by which their social credit exceeds a basic economic security (keeping social usefulness in mind).

Does Zen seem to you a 'radically empiricist' activity? By using the conceptual apparatus of William James to elucidate it, doesn't Suzuki seem to you to have empiricized it?

The I-Ching was delighted to be 'computerized' (an increase of advantages) and advised modesty, recourse to ancient wisdom.

You have often made use of chance. Is that the best way to avoid intentions, desires, fancies about getting somewhere, which – according to you – thwart the proper activity of music: to let sounds be what they are?

The world is changing. Why should the artist settle for the task of accompanying that change and a fortiori of instigating it? Isn't it just as legitimate, just as noble, to refuse all change? Or, as Max Picard put it, 'Can't one fully live an epoch while opposing it?' Have you ever had the idea of opposing your epoch? Isn't the plenitude of life also on the side of the permanent, the stable, the unchanging?

'The world is never left without a Buddha.'
'The world in a grain of sand.'

No determination

Even paradox is not a clear situation. Something in *Alice in Wonderland* makes this clear. Sitting down to wait (the Boddhisattva Doctrine), we become fat. When do we begin to smile? Whence come the gifts which surpass what we can bear? And another question: in what brief respite will we already have what someone intends to give us?

Can you point to something which doesn't exist? Take books, for example, that you gather together, but abandon for a while, let's say ten years. Then, you happen upon them in the eleventh year only to discover that you cannot put them down. Where is the arithmetic in that?

The world changes according to the place we place our attention. This process is additive and energetic.

Are you conscious of fighting for any sort of political, social, economic, material liberation? What do you think of the Marxist interpretation of your course of action that was proposed in the past?

We are thinking at the same time as others (sentient, non-sentient) are thinking. We are already intimate with whatever is going to come into existence. No blood. Only relationship.

Anarchy is finally practical. The old structures of power and profit are in the process of dying. The image being born is that of the utilities. We are going to create a world 'which works so well that we can actually go mad in it.'

Isn't chance an open door to violence – to what is violent and naively police-state, sometimes (and according to your own admission) in happenings?

The social situation is critical. The one who does what's already done no longer counts. That something is done means that it is not necessary for someone else to do it. One hand suffices; two is one too many. Hands are not possessive – they belong to the same body.

A completely modern means involves the use of a computer. The yield is voluminous, fascinating.

Since today is Sunday, the day of ignorance, I have no way to improve my mind. Instead I shall soon be outside in the rain getting soaking wet.

Not long ago silence seemed an essential, nearly fundamental element in your music. You only discovered later, it seems to me, that silence 'in itself' does not exist. Is it because of this discovery that you allow (or so it seems to me) less and less silence in your music? Aren't you following the path of Europeanization – of conforming to whatever might be happening whether you like it or not – in continuity?

There are many ways to change your mind. But certainly not by asking why. Once changed, mind includes itself. Unchanged, nothing gets in or out (cf: aperiodicity includes periodicity ... no room *vice versa*). Atomic waste is a problem. Send it to the Sun.

Why is there so much noise in Variations V? *You used to be gentle, tender; how could you have become violent? Already, in* Alice Denham in 48 Seconds *by Al Hansen, you were using a machine gun, or something like it. This presents a moral problem to the eyes and especially to the ears of those who have followed you. Can you free yourself from violence by accepting it, by demanding it, or even by imposing it on a public which is after all perfectly innocent? And yet, you did not like the* Hommage *paid to you by Nam June Paik, in Cologne, when he cut off your tie.*

What is a quiet mind? A mind which is quiet in a quiet situation? Think of Wordsworth, Thoreau. Thoreau's lake had a railroad at one end. Daniel in the lion's den. Time no longer exists. Only quantity. Let's say there are only a few sounds. Let's say they're loud. What shall we do? Jump?

During the discussion she asked a question about education. Answer: people together, without restrictions, in an abundantly effective situation. She asked another question. People who never think of asking: Mother! what shall I do now? She turned around and left the room.

Silence, more than sound, expresses the various parameters (including those parameters which we have not yet noticed). Thoreau said that sounds are bubbles on the surface of silence. They burst. The question is to know how many bubbles silence has on it.

I don't have the slightest idea how it happens. Even if I had an idea (which would have been experimentally demonstrated to help it escape my attention), it would happen anyway.

How do you manage to put up with disciples, influence, etc.?

If we begin with the past and move toward the present, we pass from pleasure to irritation. Do you know what's happening? The Hindu mind is moving. It will soon be able to handle computers, cybernetic machines, I don't know what else, better than other minds know how to.

You are probably less responsible than generally believed for the increasing refinement and facility which your undertakings have supposedly engendered, as they were produced despite you. Still, thanks to you, not only sounds but also people are usefully revealed for what they are: sub-sounds, and sub-people. You force both sounds and people to free themselves from what they are not. Through your intervention, people may eventually become people again, and sounds may eventually become sounds again. But would you agree that there has been a serious decline in this perception dating from post-Renaissance art in the West?

Do you seriously think that non-Western arts have been sheltered from a similar decline through the ages?

When you leave a reception, after you say good-bye to the host, you seek out the hostess to thank her. The family idiots, whom at one time you might also have thanked, are unfortunately no longer kept at home.

You are right: it couldn't be otherwise. Innocent vision. But we have a gift for making things ugly. Someone all alone will always darken the corner where he is without any trouble at all. When Gandhi was asked what he thought of Western civilization, he said: 'it would be nice.'

You have always had a certain taste for asceticism or self denial. Beethoven, the vibraphone, bel canto, *jazz, the radio, you have little by little included all these elements, which you don't like, in your music. It was a way to 'open your ears (and ours, too)'. But harmony, counterpoint, serialism – everything that remains and that you don't like either – shouldn't you approach them in a similar manner, with an 'open' ear? When you say that 'Beethoven now is a surprise as acceptable to the ear as a cowbell' – hasn't there always* also *been that way of listening to him?*

**D
u
c
h
a
m
p**

What do you think of Marcel Duchamp today?

And Rauschenberg?

Why do you attach so much importance, in your published texts, to typography?

As I was coming into the house, I noticed that some very interesting music was being played. After one or two drinks, I asked my hostess what music it was. She said, 'You can't be serious?'

Why did you devote a theoretical study to the works of Virgil Thomson?

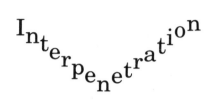

There are those who get sick from resting. Myself ... I'd go to India. Human beings living with animals. Graves said, imagine you're dreaming. I told him to extend his visit to the limit, and then to stay another day.

What do you think of Flower Power?

It was dangerous. It still is. We're continually being warned. Moreover, although we gave our lives, our actions seemed superficial. That is, we were leaving rather than returning. The premise was that opposites are intimately connected. If we were to start over again, we would begin with something more (a constellation of ideas).

The mountains where I live are old. They have lost their peaks.

McLuhan and Fuller are generally mentioned as your masters in thought. What do you admire about them?

We are doing what no one else doe . Economy. (We do not believe in 'human nature'). We are nouveaux riches. Be 'ond that, we are criminals. There, against the law, we speak the truth. For this rei son, we exploit technology. Circumstances determine our actions.

At times you have opposed Satie and Webern, whose works are based on duration, to Beethoven, who composed, as you maintain, according to harmony. But isn't harmony also in time, a function of time, and, because of that, also itself duration?

Music is only a word. It doesn't exist as a separate, pure activity. It hardly has any autonomy. Yet, you have no compunction about saying that 'everything we do is music.' Why?

There are two ways to fall down a mountain. One is to slip while you are climbing up. The other is natural. Once you have reached the summit and begin to go down, you gain speed.

Reading Thoreau's *Journals,* I discover all the ideas I've ever had that are worth their salt. (Oppressive laws were made to keep two Irishmen from fighting in the streets.)

People use words in different ways, and I'm not a scholar. I know what I mean when I say something or when I write something. But sooner or later I happen to forget what I had in mind. In general I find what others say or write to be poetic. In order to avoid misunderstanding, we begin our conversations with definitions. So tell me, what was your question?

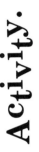

The door opened. He entered, turned on the light, sat down, died. The light is still on. No one turned it off.

Feldman accuses you – in a friendly way, I trust – of not acting, in certain of your recent works (or non-works) as you say you are acting. Despite your refusal to consider music as an autonomous art, you conduct yourself as a musician. You want your scores to be executed accurately. There is some of the artisan in you … I'm thinking of the way that you had of distilling a percussion section from your Atlas Eclipticalis, *at the time of the* Museum Event *at Saint-Paul-de-Vence … And then, in your concerts, there are ultimately more sounds or noises than in the daily life of a lot of people, whether their life is silent or not. I wonder whether your music is really connected with life, or whether it doesn't remain, despite your efforts, music. What you are delivering is still art, even if, in theory, you are, for once and for all, abolishing the distinction between art and non-art.*

Satie was furious that people kept quiet in order to hear his Furniture Music. Do you ever have similar feelings?

I believed that he was putting all his eggs into one basket. Probably he did that in order to have ideas. In fact he is very serious. Even light-hearted.

Looking out of other windows.

Criticism is not the time to think. Think ahead of time.

I would be happy, I've said, if they didn't use strobe lights (although I loved the light which made white so luminescent).

What we have to do (Fuller) – like everything else, it is provocative – is arrange the world in such a way that every-one will have what he needs: food, clothing, shelter, trans-portation, means of audio and visual communication, electric-ity, water, health, and long life. This is a project which doesn't permit error. Now, errors are deadly. The machine isn't work-ing! How did that come about?

Would you accept a qualification of your music as 'informal' (in Adorno's sense)?

So as to continue connecting me with 'my' work? Don't you see that I am a human being and that my work isn't? If, for example, you were to decide to kick me and my work, you would have, wouldn't you, two actions to perform and not just one? The more I leave my work, the more productive it becomes. (cf. the earth, modern agricultural methods).

When someone says 'I don't think', he means that he prefers to continue thinking rather than reaching a conclusion. Observations are made, but they are sent to different regions of the brain.

We interrupt our flights by spending the night in airport motels. No one knows where we are.

If, by 'experimental music' we must understand a music in which no one, and especially not the composer, can foresee what is going to happen, doesn't some of your music, which is 'indeterminate with respect to its performance,' ultimately arise from a certain quietism? How can you foresee that life will be 'so excellent' once sounds have again become what they are?

You're missing the main point. We don't arrange things in an order (that's the function of the utilities). Quite simply, we are facilitating the processes so that anything may happen.

Let's say I said 'this' was 'that'. It would be of no use to you. Things must enter into us. (He said that he had never heard my music. Reply ... you haven't missed a thing.)

When you say that contemporary music is neither that of the future, nor that of the past, but only the music present this very moment, it seems to me that, among the three dimensions usually distinguished in time — past, present, future – you privilege the middle one. But is only thinking the present – or if you prefer, the moment – sufficiently thinking time? What happens to memory, then? Utopia? Musical memory, musical utopia?

Isn't the instant a myth?

We don't mention time any more. We don't know where we are. Here, then there. Once on the ground (the pilot refuses to fly), we rush into the woods, make important discoveries (*Tricholoma equestre*). In clear weather we stop along the airport road, finding *Pleuroti*, *Collybiae*.

The unassisted senses only allow us to see about five per cent of what exists. By means of micro-this, micro-that, tele-this, tele-that, we explore the rest. Since despite our poverty we have a sense of the abundance which is ours, can't we suppose with some degree of certainty, now that we have more than we can use, that no matter what, no matter where, no matter when, may be had by no matter whom?

The present moment is zero o'clock. It easily becomes more or less. This is not true for what has not yet happened. (Seeing the second of two like objects, we no longer manage to remember the first.)

Silence: people having confidence in one another.

Quoting Meister Eckhart, you make allusion to the Ground. *How can something – music, actions, in short, theater – come forth from this* Ground?

Meister Eckhart spoke to us about the simplicity of the soul. But nature is complicated. We should rid ourselves of the soul or teach it to deal with an innumerable number of things. Likewise, the ego, its dreams, its value judgements. (Perhaps we will manage to get there.)

What he said was one thing, another what I understood.

We were at opposite ends of the hall. We left our separate rooms, and now we are in the hall itself. Now incompatible ideas are working together to produce an increase in the quantity and kinds of art which were already 'surprising, and productive of joy'.

Do you know of Angelus Silesius?

Because he got his hands dirty, it is possible for us to live. (We also are trees.) That I am thankful doesn't cost him any time. Coming back from the pilgrimage, they told us the roof was leaking. So what, our heads are worn out. (His ideas can get in.) He is as serious and frivolous as Chaos. When does the tempest begin?

You are fond of spiritual virtuosity. Only that virtuosity, as Dick Higgins observes, is still just that, virtuosity. What do you think about that?

We are drawing closer to one another. Soon we will be able to touch. We were separated too long. Let's not forget the others who are not yet free to join us: those who are mad, those whose skin color is different from ours, those who style or wear their hair in an unconventional manner; the people in prison, at war, in school, in useless occupations. Put the very young and the very old together. They're interested in each other.

John Cage

A DIALOGUE
WITH JOHN CAGE

followed by a discussion

Structure and material: method and form
Works from his youth
Prepared piano
Function of silence
Application of Zen to music
Beyond expressivity: use of chance
Liberation of time
The *I Ching*
About some accidents
On relationships
What remains of organization
Instant, duration, repetition
Against the ego
Electro-acoustic techniques and 'live electronic music'
Importance of space
Musicircus
On the proper use of happenings
Anarchy and the utilities
On some recent concerts
Against politics
Discussion

The following is a summary of the interview-discussion between Daniel Charles and John Cage, held on Tuesday, October 27, 1970, at 2.20 pm, in the Museum of Modern Art of the City of Paris, within the framework of the *John Cage Days* organized by the International Music Weeks of Paris, under the direction of Maurice Fleuret. The recording conditions did not, however, permit the transcription of the entire discussion; two or three questions, and John Cage's corresponding replies, had to be sacrificed because they could not be understood.

DANIEL CHARLES: *I would like to focus on some of the theoretical problems posed by the progressive stages in your composition. If you are amenable, I shall begin with the development of certain concepts you forged during the epoch when you wrote your first works. Would you then define for us* structure, method, form, material — *all of which have had at a certain time the greatest importance for you?*

JOHN CAGE: When I was studying with Schoenberg, I was first of all struck by the idea he had devised of musical structure. In his eyes, tonality represented the means of arriving at this structure. And this structure was the division of a work into parts. When one uses tonality, structure depends on cadence because cadence alone permits the definition of the parts of a musical work.

D.C.: Do you still hold to this conception of structure?

J.C.: No, of course not. I began by accepting it, but only because I was no longer structuring according to tonality, but according to time.

D.C.: Why?

J.C.: Because I wanted to include the world of noises in a musical work.

D.C.: Then, you rejected the tonal system from the beginning?

J.C.: Yes, because noises have nothing to do with cadences.

D.C.: And, by the same act, you avoided remaining within a 'cultural' definition of structure.

J.C.: Yes. I was obliged to re-examine the notion of musical material.

D.C.: Can you specify the link between structure and material?

J.C.: Structure or material can be linked or opposed to each other.

D.C.: They are two notions forming a couple?

J.C.: Exactly.

D.C.: What do you mean by method?

J.C.: I had noticed that when Schoenberg put the dodecaphonic series to work, he was concerned with the movement from one sound to another. That's not a question of structure, but what I call method. Method consists of taking one step after the other, the right then the left. You can walk like that with the twelve tones, can't you? Or even with counterpoint. Schoenberg's course was essentially methodical. So we have spoken of structure, material, and method ...

D.C.: *That leaves form.*

J.C.: At that time, I considered form as the aspect of mystery in which the life of an organism sometimes cloaks itself. If you attempt to organize it, you kill it. Likewise, when you imitate someone else's form, you enter a little bit into the other's life. A little bit, but not completely. You don't really *possess* that life.

D.C.: *Form is unique, it does not repeat itself.*

J.C.: It's better if that's the case.

D.C.: *You mentioned the possibility of a relationship between structure and material. Can other relationships be established at the heart of a musical work?*

J.C.: Structure and method seem to me linkable through love of organization ...

D.C.: *Or capable of challenging that love of organization ...*

J.C.: ... that people say we have. The choice of material, on the contrary, and especially of form, must and can be free. It seemed obvious to me that you could organize material but not form. And you can't improvise structure. Such are, or rather, such were the ideas that I had in the Forties.

D.C.: *Up until 1950?*

J.C.: I began not to believe in them any longer, not to be interested in them any more, around 1948-1949. But until then, I thought that three of the four components could be improvised, form, material, and method, and that three could be organized, structure, method and material. And the two in the middle, material and method, could be either organized or improvised.

D.C.: *But a musical work can lack one of the four components. For example,* Metamorphosis, *one of your twelve-tone pieces for piano which adheres to the rigor of a certain method. Can we say that this piece has a structure?*

J.C.: Certainly not.

D.C.: *With a method, but without a structure, could it have been a 'music of the heart'?*

J.C.: Let's simply say that it's music *without structure! (Laughter.)* In that work I had divided the row into static cells. They can be heard, *tatata, tatata, tatata* ... And I used a series as the basis of the work so as to know from which note I could begin to repeat this or that cell.

D.C.: *The series concerned no one but you, the composer; it had only a mnemonic function.*

J.C.: What is heard is not the series; but the series is at the basis of what is heard.

D.C.: *Yet it is the series which allows the sounds to spring forth, to arrive.*

J.C.: But they are not themselves.

D.C.: *If the sounds are not themselves it's because they depend on some other solicitation — perhaps intellectual.*

J.C.: There is no structure and method here is on the side of intelligence.

D.C.: *Would* Metamorphosis *then be an* exaggeratedly *intellectual work? Would you agree to recognizing in it what you later called a 'Frankenstein monster'?*

J.C.: Yes indeed! And the repeated cells are *boring as hell! (Laughter.)*

D.C.: *Would you give us some details on material? Would you speak about the* Bacchanale, *for example, since it's the first of your works to involve the prepared piano. A giant myth has enveloped that prepared piano. You yourself noted that music critics hardly ever bothered to find out exactly what was in the piano once you had finished preparing it. Sometimes, in addition to what you really put in it, they mentioned forks, pens, other items ...*

J.C.: *(Laughter.)* And even snow!

D.C.: *Would you describe for us the circumstances surrounding your invention?*

J.C.: The theater where Syvilla Fort's dance was to be performed had no room for a percussion orchestra ...

D.C.: *At that time, you conducted an orchestra, an orchestra, that is, of drummers?*

J.C.: Yes, and I had problems with the halls! That time, we arrived at the solution just three or four days before the performance.

D.C.: *You said to yourself, it's not the theater that's to blame, nor is it my fault, it's the piano.*

J.C.: Yes.

D.C.: *You decided to place non-pianistic objects inside the piano?*

J.C.: Yes, to place in the hands of a single pianist the equivalent of an entire percussion orchestra.

D.C.: *A principle of economy.*

J.C.: With just one musician, you can really do an unlimited number of things on the inside of the piano if you have at your disposal an 'exploded' keyboard.

D.C.: *And your taste for material led you to 'explode' not only the keyboard, but also, for the benefit of form, everything that is structure?*

J.C.: In the specific case of the *Bacchanale*, I simply followed the structure of the dance.

D.C.: *In what way?*

J.C.: I took a metronome and a chronometer, and I asked Syvilla Fort for the measures of the dance; having taken its measurements, I was able to write the music.

D.C.: *Directly?*

J.C.: Yes, based on the structure of her dance. The music composers for Hollywood films proceed no differently.

D.C.: *And after the* Bacchanale?

J.C.: I pursued this enlargement of material.

D.C.: *Thus you introduced something other than wood into the piano. Metal ...*

J.C.: And also rubber. In *The Perilous Night*, there is more than wood; but the wood that plays is bamboo! *(Laughter.)*

D.C.: *Why?*

J.C.: My mother had the idea that the effect would be better if I put natural things into the piano! *(Laughter.)*

D.C.: *Let's go back to your definition of material. You once characterized your music as relying simultaneously and equally on sounds and silences.*

J.C.: Yes, my piano solos, especially, take silence seriously ...

D.C.: *When I listen to them, I think of certain Japanese pieces for the* koto, *where the attacks are isolated, carefully distributed in the silence. Were you — or are you — going so far as to consider the sequence silence-*

sound-silence as constituting the essence of this music?

J.C.: Every time there is, as in the works you're describing, a time structure, you can *divide* that time and introduce into it, as material, silence. I attempted to do as Satie or Webern had done: to *clarify structure*, either with sounds or with silence.

D.C.: *In this you are moving away from the traditional conception of silence. Your silence has nothing to do with that of the classical musician, who says to himself, 'let's rest in the meditation that follows our auditory perception of a sound.'*

J.C.: I didn't see why it was necessary to give preference to sounds.

D.C.: *You mentioned Webern — you followed his example.*

J.C.: Certainly, but not in the same way as the 'post-Webernians'.

D.C.: *What do you mean?*

J.C.: They only sought in Webern what related to their interest in control.

D.C.: *While you were especially sensitive to what the German critic Heinz-Klaus Metzger described as 'the irrepressible cough which seizes the public every time it hears a silence in Webern'* ...

J.C.: Yes, I've found myself to be very sensitive to all those people who cough ... *(Laughter.)* That's true.

D.C.: *Taking silence seriously, not giving preference to the* musical *sound is thus also* enlarging *the sound itself.*

J.C.: It is refusing to see it made subservient to what is commonly described as 'musical'.

D.C.: *You integrate the sounds of people coughing with the sounds of your music* ...

J.C.: That is, what others call 'silence.' I can exchange the sounds and the silences.

D.C.: *And in so doing, you upset music!*

J.C.: 'Music', as you put it, is only a word.

D.C.: *Would you say that what people continue to call 'silence,' by force of habit, belongs in reality to another domain? Or does silence indeed arise from this* same *domain: music?*

J.C.: It's already sound, and it's sound all over again. Or noise. It becomes sound at that moment.

D.C.: *Your work carries along with it the musicalization of what was not musical to begin with and which becomes* your *music.*

J.C.: Yes, but remember that this process took years.

D.C.: You start from a criticism of language, since language talks about silences and there are never any silences. If silence does not exist, no one can possess it. If sound and silence are at once opposites and the same, *can anyone possess sounds? Is that indeed what you said to yourself?*

J.C.: Yes, and so you understand how I was led to rethink structure. If silence does not exist, we have only sounds. But at that moment, you begin to realize that there is no more need for structure. Little by little, I gave up structure altogether.

D.C.: Is that realizing what Suzuki, who introduced you to Zen, calls non-obstruction?

J.C.: Yes, the sound no longer comprises an obstacle to silence; silence is no longer a screen with regard to sound.

D.C.: It would then be false to think that Zen sets an end, a stop, a goal for itself — which would, for example, be the state of illumination in which all things reveal themselves as nothingness.

J.C.: This nothingness is still just a word.

D.C.: Like silence, it must cancel itself out.

J.C.: And consequently we come back to what exists; to sounds, that is.

D.C.: But don't you lose something?

J.C.: What?

D.C.: Silence, nothingness …

J.C.: You see quite well that I'm losing *nothing*! In all of this, it's not a question of *losing*, but of *gaining*!

D.C.: Coming back to sounds is thus coming back, short of any structure, *to sounds 'accompanied' by nothingness.*

J.C.: And the return moves towards something completely natural: men are men once again, and once again sounds are sounds.

D.C.: Had they ever stopped being sounds?

J.C.: Certainly not! But Zen demonstrates this better than we can.

D.C.: Your course of action depends on Zen then.

J.C.: No, not entirely. There has not been just Zen.

D.C.: Nonetheless, don't you owe the essential part of these ideas to your teacher Suzuki?

J.C.: As soon as I began to study oriental philosophy, I introduced it into my music. People then were always pretending that a composer had to have something to say. So, what I was saying was nothing more than what I had then understood about oriental philosophy, first that of Sri Ramakrishna, the philosophy of India. Zen didn't come until later. I actually did have Suzuki as a teacher.

D.C.: *In the beginning, were you concerned, for example in your music of the years around 1945, with* expressing *something?*

J.C.: Yes, I thought that music should 'communicate.' For example, the *Sonatas and Interludes*, that Gérard Frémy performed so marvelously yesterday,[1] attempted to represent in music certain ideas of Sri Ramakrishna and the aesthetic principles of India.

D.C.: *How did you get from there to* non-obstruction *and* inter-penetration, *in Suzuki's sense; as it were to* interchange *silence and sound?*

J.C.: I wrote a *Concerto for Prepared Piano and Chamber Orchestra*. I made it into a drama between the piano, which remains romantic, expressive, and the orchestra, which itself follows the principles of oriental philosophy. And the third movement signifies the coming together of things which were opposed to one another in the first movement.

D.C.: *That agreement reconciles sound and silence?*

J.C.: But without yet *interchanging* them. Nor is there any *interchange* between sound and silence in a number of other works, like the *String Quartet*. It was with *Sixteen Dances* that I entered – with confidence – the domain of chance. In fact, Merce Cunningham had prepared sixteen dances – and he had, at that moment, ideas very similar to those developed by my *Sonatas and Interludes*. That meant that he wanted a music which would express emotions. So I wanted to see if I could fulfil a commission for 'expressive' music while at the same time making use of chance operations.

D.C.: *You were worried about fulfilling this commission?*

J.C.: Yes, and I figured if it were possible for me to do it, that would mean that I would be able to continue work with chance, wouldn't it?

D.C.: *Why chance?*

J.C.: We talked about silence as the entirety of unintended sounds. Interchanging sound and silence was to depend on chance.

[1]Concert on Monday, October 26, 1970, at 4.30 pm at the Museum of Modern Art of the City of Paris

D.C.: Yes but, ultimately, nothing was really contingent on you any more. You withdrew your piece from the game. People have often criticized you for that, since strictly speaking, you stopped being the composer. Yet, wasn't there some mystification in that profession of irresponsibility?

J.C.: But if the work I was doing in this state of irresponsibility was accepted by someone else, by somebody who had commissioned the work and who had a need for it, that would mean that it had become perfectly possible without demeaning anyone's honor at all to trust in chance — isn't that so?

D.C.: That reminds me of an episode from your youth. When you were a student at Pomona College, they gave you grades; and your grades were excellent, even when you hadn't worked!

J.C.: There was, strictly speaking, no relation between my work and the grades I received.

D.C.: Did you feel some sort of injustice?

J.C.: No, I didn't resent it, I noticed it. As with chance. It was enough for me to notice that, with or without chance, the result was no different.

D.C.: Is there some relationship in your music between the idea of chance and your conception of time?

J.C.: As long as there is structure, as long as there is method, or rather, as long as structure and method exist by referring back to the mental, to intelligence, time is possessed — or rather people imagine that they possess time.

D.C.: And we must submit to the measurement of time.

J.C.: If you liberate yourself from the measurement of time, you can't continue to take structure completely seriously.

D.C.: Or else you take it seriously in the sense that, yesterday evening, the five superimposed works[1] brought it into play: your lecture 45' for a Speaker maintains it, in the end, only nominally. The structure exists but only as the title of a score.

J.C.: Yes, the structure is still there, but it doesn't have as much importance. And beginning at that moment when it no longer has control, you can get the idea of doing without it.

D.C.: You structure, or, more precisely, destructure *your works in a manner far removed from what the contemporary music world practices in general.*   ·

[1]Concert of Monday, October 26, 1970, at 6.30 p.m. at the *Théâtre de la Ville*: simultaneous performance, by five members of the G.E.R.M. (P. Marietan, director), of *26' 1.1499" for a String Player, 27' 10.554" for a Percussionist, 31' 57.9864" for a Pianist,* and *45' for a Speaker.*

J.C.: But there are now many composers who do what I do!

D.C.: *Of course. Nonetheless, in the Fifties and Sixties you were, if not the only, at least one of the very first, along with Morton Feldman and Christian Wolff ...*

J.C.: I apologize for having been the oldest! Earle Brown joined us later.

D.C.: *Is* structuring – *or* destructuring – *still, according to you, a way of organizing music according to time?*

J.C.: Yes, time seems to me to be the radical dimension of all music.

D.C.: *But you only rejected structure in order to 'liberate' that basic dimension: time?*

J.C.: That's it.

D.C.: *Then would you talk about this* liberation of time through chance operations, *as you have used them?*

J.C.: There was the Chinese book of oracles, the *I Ching*. But before the *I Ching*, I worked with the magic square.

D.C.: *How did you use it?*

J.C.: Instead of numbers, I put sounds, groups of sounds, in the square. That's how I wrote *Sixteen Dances*, as well as the *Concerto for Prepared Piano* which we mentioned earlier.

D.C.: *And how did you come to seek the advice of the* I Ching?

J.C.: Christian Wolff arrived one day wanting to study composition with me. He was quite remarkable, and I believe I learned more from him that he did from me ...

D.C.: *Was he the one who introduced you to the* I Ching?

J.C.: Yes, and this is how. I didn't make him pay for his lessons. Well, his father was a publisher. To thank me, Christian brought me books published by his father. One day, the *I Ching* was among them. On seeing the *I Ching* table I was immediately struck by its resemblance to the magic square. It was even better! From that moment on, the *I Ching* has never left my side.

D.C.: *You used it even outside of music?*

J.C.: Yes, indeed!

D.C.: *For your daily life?*

J.C.: Every time I had a problem. I used it very often for practical matters, to write my articles and my music ... For everything.

D.C.: You have managed, however, to be unfaithful to the I Ching ... *when for example, you composed according to the imperfections in a sheet of paper.*

J.C.: Yes, for my *Music for Piano*. In Darmstadt, one of my students even asked me what he should do faced with a sheet of paper without imperfections.

D.C.: But why did you adopt this process of 'paper accidents'?

J.C.: Using the *I Ching* required an enormous amount of time when I began. For each aspect of each sound, for each parameter, if you wish, which I decided to submit to chance, I was required to toss three coins six times.

D.C.: To make hexagrams?

J.C.: Yes, it took a considerable amount of time and extreme precision. That was how I composed *Williams Mix*. One day, while I was busy working on it, the telephone rang, and a dancer asked me to write some music for her immediately, for a performance. So I said to myself that I had to find a way to work which would be quick, and not, as was most often the case, exaggeratedly slow any more. Certainly I intended to continue working on *Williams Mix* and other pieces as I had started out doing, by consulting the *I Ching* as usual. But I also wanted to have a very rapid manner of writing a piece of music. Painters, for example, work slowly with oil and rapidly with water colors. Well, while reflecting on this problem of the speed of writing, I looked at my paper, and I found my 'water colors': suddenly I saw that the music, all the music, was already there. *(Laughter.)*

D.C.: And you perfected this process.

J.C.: Yes, by superimposing transparencies, each with its own lines or points, I was able to combine the imperfections, multiply them by each other.

D.C.: That explains the complexity of certain types of notation for your Concerto for Piano and Orchestra, *in 1958.*

J.C.: And also for my *Variations*.

D.C.: The first time you open this kind of score, you can't help being struck not only by the unusual character of many of the graphisms, but also by the proliferation of chance operations, and the possible ways of using chance 'legible' in those graphisms.

J.C.: And you can say in particular that if you look at a blank sheet of paper – Mallarmé's white page – you can compare it to silence. From the slightest spot or mark, from the slightest hole, from the smallest defect, or from the smallest smudge, you know there is no silence. 'Mallarmé's vertigo' is useless!

D.C.: Are there any accidents always and everywhere?

J.C.: Certainly!

D.C.: And your Concert for Piano *is a gigantic repertory of possible accidents ...*

J.C.: But you have to consider that aspect of my discovery of accidents in terms of my studies under Schoenberg as well. For him, there was only repetition; he used to say that the principle of variation represented only the repetitions of something identical.

D.C.: Of a cell, a row?

J.C.: Yes. If there is variation, you can change an element – you can always change something – and the rest still stays as it is. And that cancels out the variation. But I introduced into this opposition ...

D.C.: The repetition/variation duality?

J.C.: Yes, I introduced into, or beside, this Schoenbergian idea of a repetition-variation double, another notion, that of something *other*, which cannot be cancelled out.

D.C.: What other *are you talking about?*

J.C.: An element that has nothing to do with either repetition or variation; something which does not enter into the battle of those two terms, and which rebels against being placed or replaced in terms of ... That term is chance.

D.C.: Is that how chance must be defined?

J.C.: There can be, there must be, several events which unfold at once, or else successively, without connection. If you accept this point of view, then you are no longer involved with either repetition or variation.

D.C.: You are in the midst of disorganization. Does that mean that you are in the midst of chaos?

J.C.: I discovered, while simply walking in the forests looking for mushrooms, that it's easy to see a structure in certain species of mushrooms. A particular structure – or a particular art! And from there you go on to value structure and organization as very important. But if you observe everything, all day long, all the experiences you have, you can't talk about organization any more! So art or structure get blurred ...

D.C.: At a certain level there may well be organization; but if you change your measuring means, there is no more organization.

J.C.: Yes, but it is not the same as in the sciences. You can modify focal distance, but then you discover that you haven't gained any more exactitude. You can choose a more extreme level of precision but it's still blurred. It's always blurred. As if the measuring means were constantly shifting ... That's my *Concert for Piano*! A walk in the forest ...

D.C.: *Sort of like the film entitled 'John Cage' shown yesterday:*[1] *the images were never in focus ...*

J.C.: Well, with my increasing involvement with chance and ... the passing of the years, you can see how all these ideas we mentioned, structure and method, and even material, all that has vanished.

D.C.: *A poetics of self-effacement.*

J.C.: It disappears, it goes away. Yes. But at the very instant that it all goes away, you can also say that it's all there.

D.C.: *This feeling — the simultaneity of the presence and absence of all things — never seems to leave you.*

J.C.: We were already talking about that with regard to Zen.

D.C.: *Can we compare this idea of presence-absence with the assertion of one of your biographers who states that your interest in mushrooms comes from or depends on the fact that, in an English dictionary,* music *and* mushroom *are close to each other? They are* present *to each other, and yet, are not connected. So much so that you can say that they are* absent *from each other.*

J.C.: Yes, you can equally see in this how chance includes interpenetration and non-obstruction.

D.C.: *The closest* is *the most distant. But that only happens in dictionaries ...*

J.C.: Or in my music? No, it happens everywhere and always! Think about that commission that Merce Cunningham gave me, and to which you said I responded irresponsibly. Accepting chance like that makes prejudices, pre-conceived ideas, and previous ideas of order and organization disappear! Do you believe anything at all is lost? Certainly not, nothing is lost! When I fulfill a commission through chance (which is not a response ...) it neither wounds nor wrongs anyone in the end.

D.C.: *Except you. You're losing your will.*

J.C.: That's not so serious! And it's only if I act like that with mushrooms that it can kill me ... *(Laughter.)* So, I studied mushrooms conscientiously, to bring about a balance!

[1]Film shown on Monday, October 26, 1970, at the *Cinémathèque française* of the Chaillot Palace.

D.C.: You consciously oscillate between life and death ...

J.C.: As we all do!

D.C.: But by avoiding poisonous mushrooms, you admit that life is preferable, but only at the price of accepting a certain organization. You don't completely refuse structure.

J.C.: I only keep that amount of organization that is useful for survival. That means that I assign organization to the place that it should have. Men generally act otherwise. They organize everything endlessly! And in particular useless things – music, for example ... Thus they forego organizing what should, on the other hand, be organized: the utilities.

D.C.: According to you, it must be possible, without organizing time, without being assured of it, to let it be as it is.

J.C.: Yes but you need to bring together many events, each of which has its own time and lives it own life ...

D.C.: ... And consequently don't obstruct each other, but can ultimately interpenetrate one another. Suzuki's two key ideas again!

J.C.: Yes.

D.C.: I can see that quite well; but, at the same time, I wonder if Western man can reach that.

J.C.: Why should East and West stand in each other's way? Haven't they begun to interpenetrate?

D.C.: In that case what you're doing is converting Western man to a dimension of time which is the instant? *Aren't you risking forgetting everything the West displays — both in its music and in its conception of time — in terms of duration and future?*

J.C.: But the instant is always a rebirth, isn't it?

D.C.: Are we *the ones who are reborn?*

J.C.: Us? We're not there anymore ...

D.C.: So you take exception to what Nietzsche envisioned under the label eternal return?

J.C.: I would say that there is only *eternal rebirth*. Only that.

D.C.: But couldn't we then accuse you, as Leonard Meyer did, of sacrificing a value of duration essential to Western classical music?

J.C.: Do you mean to suggest that there would be a reason to *keep* anything?

D.C.: You're relying entirely on the instant; but time is a sum of instants, isn't it?

J.C.: The time you have in mind is still a construction, an intellectual organization. We must stop short of that.

D.C.: Is that really possible anywhere but in Buddhism?

J.C.: It is very difficult to discuss it because the experience of life is different for each one of us. But we seek to make each one feel, in his own way, his own experience.

D.C.: You reject the idea of a constructed duration. Why, in that case, did you insist on having Satie's Vexations *in New York's Pocket Theater include the eight hundred forty* Da Capos? *The whole thing lasted eighteen hours and forty minutes. You were prepared for everything except the extraordinary impression that this repetitive music produced ... You said that you set in motion something absolutely novel and unexpected. Do you think that Satie's music, arranged according to a strictly repetitive construction of time, contained this something within itself? In spite of the repetitions?*

J.C.: Why certainly! Perhaps the best thing would be to quote these words of René Char: 'Each act is virgin, even the repeated one.'

D.C.: Is that how we must understand what you said when we were talking about Schoenberg, that we must leave the circle of repetition and variation?

J.C.: That is quite precisely what comes into existence with *Vexations*.

D.C.: Now concerning what you said was possible in the framework of a totally predetermined music, can this emerge a fortiori *from indeterminacy?*

J.C.: I believe so.

D.C.: Do the eight hundred forty repetitions of Satie's musical text finally lead to an indeterminacy comparable to your indeterminate *musical compositions?*

J.C.: Yes! I know quite well that, from another point of view, there is repetition, but remember what I said about *indeterminacy*: you can't repeat anything exactly – even yourself! And when you have many pianists, as was the case ...

D.C.: You end up with a 'collection of extreme differences,' as you said about your Concert for Piano.

J.C.: That leads to an experience with so many variations that the dimension of *resemblance* disappears.

D.C.: As well as any impression of boredom?

J.C.: Only if we decide to do something other than get bored! For we are the ones who make ourselves bored. In the experience of *Vexations*, as in the works of Riley or La Monte Young, boredom takes over only if we arouse it in ourselves. That's why I said a while go that *we are no longer there*. There is no more boredom as soon as there is no more ego. We have in common this particular need to break with our ego. Then everything is endlessly reborn. And there is no longer the slightest bit of boredom!

D.C.: I would again raise the objection, however, that an experience involving the suppressing of the ego seems hardly accessible to Westerners.

J.C.: But what you call the West is already not the West anymore. Everything is changing.

D.C.: Let's talk about your relationship to technology. I think I can discern in you a logic, a continuity in this domain, from the prepared piano, through electronic instruments and, more recently, computers. The first 'electronic' work ever created was yours — this is too easily forgotten — and it must date from 1938 or 1939 ...

J.C.: There was a radio studio in Seattle, Washington, the very city where I first performed my *Bacchanale*. And in that studio, I was able to assemble an orchestra of percussion instruments and prepared piano, with the addition — which I immediately accepted — of turntables for recordings of 'technological' sounds. The speed, and thus the frequencies, of the records chould be changed. And I mixed these two kinds of sound sources in the studio.

D.C.: How were you able to separate your activities as an 'experimental' musician from what the Western studios were beginning to develop, a music that took the form of a recording from the beginning?

J.C.: I had the idea of making that music alive and flexible. I noted that people who listened to tape music never failed to fall asleep!

D.C.: They couldn't manage to free themselves from their ego?

J.C.: Ask them ...

D.C.: You composed Cartridge Music *like that, a score using cartridges (the elements in which needles are put to play a record) performed on stage in front of the audience. But if you ever tape recorded* Cartridge Music, *wouldn't you end up with a work just as 'determined' as those soporific tapes from the European studios? Why did you yourself record it?*

J.C.: You could say that there's a contradiction here! Well, yes ... in the recording we superimposed four different performances. Think about it: four distinct performances. You can't do this in a concert hall. In other words, we, David Tudor and I, used the facility of recording to achieve something otherwise impossible.

D.C.: *If it is a contradiction, it is ...*

J.C.: A good contradiction.

D.C.: *Or research?*

J.C.: That's it: research. I call that 'experimental' music: the kind where you do research ... but without knowing what the result will be. Otherwise ...

D.C.: *Otherwise?*

J.C.: Otherwise it's too easy!

D.C.: *Then it's not illicit to listen to a recording of* Cartridge Music?

J.C.: Not at all. But I should like to make it clear that I do not have *any* records in my home ... *(Laughter.)*

D.C.: *Records, according to you, are nothing more than postcards ...*

J.C.: Which ruin the landscape. David Tudor and I thought that superimposing four performances by two musicians, which makes eight actions at once, could turn out to be heavy. And what surprised us the most was that the whole thing remained light ... No, it never became heavy!

D.C.: *Then that complexity would be in the image of life?*

J.C.: Certainly. Did I tell you that one day someone had me listen to some music without telling me whose it was? And I approved of it. Obviously, the composer had not told the sounds what they had to do.

D.C.: *You were the first to* theatricalize *tape music.*

J.C.: The need for theater was recognized by several artists. You know, when I think I have discovered something, I always notice that someone has already thought of it ...

D.C.: *This 'theatrical' aspect of your activity is probably connected with your collaboration with Merce Cunningham's Ballets. But didn't that cause problems? For example, have you ever fought against the dancers you were supposed to work with?*

J.C.: Certainly not with Merce Cunningham in particular.

D.C.: *However, his ideas have often been different from yours. You have never feuded with him?*

J.C.: Of course not! We had structures to share, didn't we?

D.C.: *Yes, but when you abandoned structure, didn't he himself keep structure as a requirement?*

J.C.: Not always. His works became increasingly flexible.

D.C.: *And, as for you, you considered it indispensable that a completely different musical work be juxtaposed with a given ballet.*

J.C.: Yes, if possible, without any connection.

D.C.: *Moreover, your 'indeterminate' works were supposed to take space into consideration.*

J.C.: It was a question of avoiding all fusion between sounds; and to do this, the musicians had to be situated as far away from each other as possible. My concern was to avoid having to deal with some sort of *spatial object*, and thus, likewise, a *finite temporal object* with a beginning, a middle, and an end. That could go well with the extreme extensions of the dancers' space, as Merce Cunningham imagined them; and it was at the same time something else altogether.

D.C.: *So you invented, or reinvented, a certain spatialization of music. But wasn't it Charles Ives who first gave you that idea? Or, on the contrary, did you one day, by yourself, sense the need for it?*

J.C.: In fact, it arose from an experiment by David Tudor and me, with those two pieces for piano that we heard yesterday superimposed on the three others in the G.E.R.M. concert.

D.C.: *These two pieces were commissioned of you as a single work?*

J.C.: Yes, and I used the same structure for both of them but with completely different results.

D.C.: *Why this difference?*

J.C.: The problem was to provoke disparity between the two pianos, because in Donaueschingen they had given us a tiny little rehearsal room with two pianos right beside each other, which is normal when you're playing two pianos. We prepared the pianos and began to play. Well, it was impossible to hear anything at all clearly, since the microtonal frequencies ran together and their complexity even destroyed our ability to hear them. Each of the two pieces neutralized the other. Then, for the concert, we decided to separate the two pianos very conspicuously. I must point out that this evening, in the *Musicircus*,[1] we'll do just the opposite ...

[1] Concert on Tuesday, October 27, 1970, at 6.30 pm, in Pavilion 9 of the Halles de Baltard.

D.C.: *It will be a* Reunion,[1] *an interpenetration without any concern about obstruction?*

J.C.: In a *Musicircus,* you have the right to bring together all kinds of music which are ordinarily separated. We're no longer worried about what there is to be heard, so to speak. It's no longer a question of aesthetics.

D.C.: *Since you're talking about the* Musicircus, *I would like to ask you about your relationship to happenings. You invented them ...*

J.C.: I had read *The Theater and Its Double*, by Antonin Artaud. It gave me the idea for a theater without literature. Words and poetry may, of course, always enter into it. But the rest, everything that is in general *non-verbal*, may enter into it as well. We have to avoid one thing too directly supporting another: for example, the text supporting the action. Well, we performed this at Black Mountain College in 1952. We arranged the spectators' seats into four large triangles whose points were oriented towards the center. Circulation remained free between the triangles and in the center; that allowed us to make the action fluid around the public. The idea was also to permit people in the auditorium to see each other. Art should introduce us to life ... Well, in life we see each other! I do productions like that one as often as I can. But the principle of the *Musicircus* is profoundly different and likewise interests me very much. It is a principle of a flexible relationship, of a flexibility of relationships.

D.C.: *What do you mean by that?*

J.C.: Interpenetration must appear *through* non-obstruction.

D.C.: *You never envision dissociating the two?*

J.C.: No, the public must be exposed to these two movements simultaneously.

D.C.: *Let's get back to the happenings. Those not produced by you continually run the risk of being bound to a single center, under most circumstances, that of the organizer ...*

J.C.: While in my own happenings, everyone must be in the center.

D.C.: *In the* Musicircus, *can there be an organizer?*

J.C.: Yes, but it is better if there are several!

D.C.: *And you didn't organize anything. Someone else organizes, but the essential thing is the collecting together, which you have only suggested.*

J.C.: Yes.

[1] Title of a work by John Cage, David Tudor, David Behrman, Gordon Mumma, Lowell Cross, and Marcel and Teeny Duchamp.

*D.C.: Is the fact that there is someone else who organizes without impor-
tance?*

J.C.: No, why?

*D.C.: Don't you run the risk of creating a new centering, as in the
happenings, other than your own?*

J.C.: No, in music, there can be much organization or a lot of disorganization — everything is possible. In the same way, the forest
includes trees, mushrooms, birds, anything you wish. Although we can
still organize a lot and even multiply organizations, in any case, the
whole will make a disorganization! *(Laughter.)*

D.C.: You wish to reach and make others reach anarchy.

J.C.: Yes, certainly.

*D.C.: A few days ago, we were talking together about anarchy, and you
said: 'What I want is a practical, or practicable, anarchy ...'*

J.C.: Exactly.

*D.C.: Then your anarchy is not like everybody else's. You would accuse
those who want anarchy at any price of nurturing the project of an*
impracticable *anarchy. What do you mean by that?*

J.C.: An *impraticable* anarchy is one which provokes the intervention of
the police.

*D.C.: So, then, you would limit yourself to injecting a little disorder into
what is allowed. You would respect the moral and social order!*

J.C.: It's a little more complicated than that. If the object is to reach a
society where you can do anything at all, the role of organization must
be concentrated on the utilities. Well, we can achieve this even now with
our technology.

D.C.: What do you mean by 'utilities'? The bath-tub, the telephone?

J.C.: Yes, and first of all, water, air, food, cl ... you know perfectly well
what I mean! *(Laughter.)*

D.C.: That is a way of letting order rule!

J.C.: Not at all, because first of all everyone must have access to what he
needs to live, and the others mustn't try to deprive him of anything
whatsoever. That is not what people usually call 'order' ...

*D.C.: You often refer to McLuhan and Buckminster Fuller and you
sometimes mention the bonds which attach you to Thoreau.*

J.C.: Yes, there is a sense of utility with McLuhan and Fuller. And there
is utility with Thoreau, I believe.

D.C.: If I may get back to music, was it because you were thinking about the 'utilities' that you mixed or combined Satie and Thoreau in the Song Books?

J.C.: Several years before the *Song Books*, I had already made this point without thinking much about it in one of my *Diaries*.

D.C.: One of those that you published in A Year from Monday?

J.C.: Right. In that *Diary*, entitled *How to Improve the World (You Will Only Make Matters Worse)*, I said that the relationship between Thoreau and Satie must be recognized and explored. But, strictly speaking, I didn't know what that meant when I wrote it. It came to me all by itself, in what I was writing ...

D.C.: And how did it emerge again?

J.C.: I remembered it when I received the proposal to write the *Song Books*; I found it rather interesting to develop that motif in a musical work that apparently had nothing to do with those problems.

D.C.: With the Song Books, *you provided new and copious evidence of what you mean by the word 'accident.'*

J.C.: And especially of my admiration for Satie and Thoreau!

D.C.: Yesterday evening we listened to those Song Books.[1] *I would like to know what you thought of what the* Rozart Mix *people did during the performance itself. You had your back turned and were typing. So you couldn't see the large sign pointed at the audience which read 'Get up and exchange places with each other.' They didn't do very much. Little by little and respectfully, they came up on stage. Pierre Mariétan was still conducting the* Concert for Piano and Orchestra. *But the audience began talking and walking around. Did that destroy what you had wanted to do?*

J.C.: Oh, no! It didn't destroy anything! It produced something else. For me, the phenomenon was fairly comparable to what I have sometimes seen in the United States when certain of my works were being performed. The audience moves around without being told to do so, don't they? So it was quite acceptable. Certainly nothing with which we were experimenting required that this happen, but I am not at all *against* such an action.

D.C.: Your attitude is always one of acceptance.

J.C.: I try never to refuse anything.

[1] Concert on Monday, October 26, 1970, at 8.30 pm in the Théâtre de la Ville in Paris, which included the simultaneous performance of *Song Books, Rozart Mix*, and *Concert for Piano and Orchestra.*

D.C.: What you refuse to do is to be exclusive, that is, to want *something.*

J.C.: I can want something, but only if I find myself in a set of circumstances where nothing I decide seems to me to concern others.

D.C.: Can you be more specific?

J.C.: When I eat in a restaurant, I can choose chicken instead of steak[1] without really bothering anyone! *(Laughter.)*

D.C.: How can you reconcile this conscious position of non-will, this quietism, with what you had the courage to write in the preface to **A Year from Monday?** *In that text, you asserted that henceforth you intended to develop outside of yourself, outside of your ego, that spiritual virtuosity which until then you had cultivated within yourself. You came out in favor of a politics of emancipation or liberation.*

J.C.: But people say that my music is not music, don't they? Well, if they can say that, why shouldn't they also say that my politics are not politics? *(Laughter.)*

QUESTION FROM THE AUDIENCE: *What is your relationship to contemporary American writers?*

J.C.: In writing my 'literary' texts, I essentially make use of the same composing means as in my music. So there is not really much connection between the writers and myself. However, an Egyptian professor, Ihab Hassan, who taught literature at Wesleyan University where he was Dean of the College of Letters, and who is now at the University of Wisconsin, has been working on the relationship between current trends in literature and what I am trying to do. In fact, I worked with the painters Rauschenberg and Jasper Johns, and later Duchamp, but never with poets – not even with Ginsberg, whom I know, but not very well.[2]

QUESTION: *What were your reactions to the inflatable theater set up in the Maeght Foundation in Saint-Paul-de-Vence, where the last performances you produced with Merce Cunningham took place?*

J.C.: First we received the layout of the theater. But what according to the layout was supposed to be flexible turned out not to be so at all. And it was nearly impossible to work. During the day the dancers were burned up, and in the evening, in front of the audience, they were freezing! I am completely against that theater as it is. The plans were more interesting.

---

[1] Since 1977 I follow the macrobiotic diet. (John Cage; footnote of 1980.)
[2] I have a real admiration for the work of Jackson Mac Low and Clark Coolidge, as well as for any poet who attempts to liberate language from syntax. (John Cage: footnote of 1972.)

QUESTION: *You seem to hold fast to your mask of impassivity and to profess a rejection of all the emotions. Why?*

J.C.: Emotions, like all tastes and memory, are too closely linked to the self, to the ego. The emotions show that we are touched within ourselves, and tastes evidence our way of being touched on the outside. We have made the ego into a wall and the wall doesn't even have a door through which the interior and exterior could communicate! Suzuki taught me to destroy that wall. What is important is to insert the individual into the current, the flux of everything that happens. And to do that, the wall has to be demolished; tastes, memory, and emotions have to be weakened; all the ramparts have to be razed. You can feel an emotion; just don't think that it's so important ... Take it in a way that you can then let it drop! Don't belabor it! It's just like the chicken I ordered in the restaurant: it concerns me, but it's not important. And if we keep emotions and reinforce them, they can produce a critical situation in the world. Precisely that situation in which all of society is now entrapped!

D.C.: *You've taken a vow of indifference.*

J.C.: I am willing to have emotions, but without being a slave to them.

D.C.: *Can we really free ourselves from emotions?*

J.C.: As far as I'm concerned, I am trying to release myself from them. And I discovered that those who seldom dwell on their emotions know better than anyone else just what an emotion is. This is true of the aesthetic thinkers of India; they have considered all nine emotions and know that the most important is tranquility ...

D.C.: *Yes, but we are not Easterners ...*

J.C.: We no longer know the exact definition of sadness or of heroism! In ancient times India defined sadness as the result of the loss of something cherished or the gain of something undesired. Well, during a discussion with a philosopher from Yale University, I realized that in the West people give only a part of that definition. Likewise, we have lost the meaning of heroism. Heroism doesn't consist in brilliantly combatting someone else. It is not a question, as Nixon undoubtedly believed, of winning battles ... What is heroic is *to accept the situation in which you find yourself.* Yes!

QUESTION: *Don't you think, however, that the structure of the individual, as opposed to the structure of each species of mushroom, is in part determined by the emotions through which he has passed?*

J.C.: Perhaps. But today, we must consider the *ecology* even more than the individual. It is not simply by observing the individual, but by reintegrating individuals into nature, by opening the world to the individual, that we will get ourselves out of this mess. Instead of continuing, as in the past, to separate ourselves from each other, instead of being proud of our petty emotions and our little value judgements, we must open ourselves up to others and to the world in which we find ourselves. We must open up the ego, open it up in the way Satie or Thoreau did! Open it up to all our experiences.

QUESTION: *And according to you, those experiences do not include the emotions?*

J.C.: I see that you're still on the level of *object*, while I am talking about *process*!

QUESTION: *But I certainly have a right to my emotions!*

J.C.: You need this, you need that. That's your whole attitude! Let's not talk about it anymore ... I'm not *against* you. But I don't act like that.

QUESTION: *A little while ago you said that the most important emotion was tranquility. But for a good portion of time, you composed works whose sonorous intensity inhibited that tranquility! And I believe that I am correct in saying that when your friends mentioned this to you, you consulted the* I Ching *and asked the oracle to answer this question: should I or shouldn't I continue to produce music that defies tranquility? Well, what I detect in your most recent works I heard yesterday is that your sense of tonal plurality and plurality of perspectives is incompatible with that excess of musical intensity. The decibels destroy that tranquility to which you profess allegiance, and which is necessary for an appreciation of what you set in motion.*

J.C.: Each person, I repeat, is free to experience his own emotions. But they are no more important than ordering chicken! That means that you can't dwell on them, you must learn how to detach yourself from them.

QUESTION: *You appeal to an exterior flux and want the ego to open up completely to whatever happens. But won't this possibly alienate the listener in a new way and in fact suppress, despite what you say about it, not only the plurality of performances, but even the possibility of there being a listener?*

J.C.: I am not sure that I quite understand the question.

QUESTION: *Sometimes, the excess of intensity that you obtain electronically cancels out the listener's ability to feel any emotion at all. It rules out the possibility of a plural existence. Isn't tranquility contradicted by the intensity of noises in your works?*

J.C.: No, it is increased by it!

QUESTION: *Intensity increases tranquility?*

J.C.: No, it increases discipline.

QUESTION: *Discipline is necessary?*

J.C.: Precisely.

QUESTION: *Yesterday evening, we listened to two pianists, the lecturer, the other instrumentalists, a drummer and a string bass player performing simultaneously. Each performer maintained a dynamic register which allowed the others to exist. I wanted to know exactly what your position is regarding the intensity of noises produceable with the aid of electronic methods.*

J.C.: To that I will answer that discipline is, before everything else, a discipline of the ego. The ego without discipline is closed, it tends to close in on its emotions. Discipline is what ruins all that closure. With it one can open up to the outside, as well as to the inside. Perhaps it becomes more difficult, in a situation of heightened amplitude, when one is surrounded by a music of stronger intensity. But it is more effective. One opens up even more.

QUESTION: *That is asceticism.*

J.C.: Certainly.

D.C.: *The more intensity there is, the more austerity you demand on the part of the listener.*

J.C.: I am giving him the chance to open himself up!

QUESTION: *But in the end there is an audible result. Does it ever happen that, despite your austerity, you are more or less happy with the achieved result? I am thinking of the two concerts yesterday. I have the feeling that the audible result of the first was interesting, but of the second one, less so. That probably is a personal opinion. But do you ever have an opinion like this or are you completely disinterested? Do you manage to abstract yourself?*

J.C.: Absolutely not! But since you mentioned the two concerts from yesterday, you have to remember that I wrote the first pieces you mentioned, the five superimposed works, around 1954 or 1955; I only just completed the *Song Books*, to which the second concert was devoted. Well, what I am about to say is perhaps not very original, but I find the *Song Books* more interesting.

QUESTION: *Why?*

J.C.: Because I know them better, since I just finished working on them, but also because I know them less. I remain perplexed before the *Song Books*! But I've already gotten to know the other works a little bit ... From the point of view of my personal situation, I find them less interesting.

QUESTION: *And if instead of talking about one work in relation to another we talked about one performance in relation to another? Isn't the problem different? There are probably times when you feel the performance succeeds on a sonorous level, while other performances might come off less successfully.*

J.C.: But my answer is still the same. I find that the sound, the sonorous level, is much more interesting in the *Song Books*. These are works that interest me in any case ...

QUESTION: *Could you be more specific?*

J.C.: I can imagine, for example, not having *Rozart Mix* played at the same time as the *Song Books,* I mean with the singers. I can imagine replacing it with my *Cartridge Music.* What I wonder is whether it would be more or less lively. And I don't know. While writing the *Song Books,* it occurred to me that it would be a mistake if I were to superimpose *Rozart Mix* or the percussion parts of *Atlas Eclipticalis* or even both of them on the *Song Books.* But when I heard the tapes that Davorin Jagodic and the students from Vincennes made, especially from the rehearsals when we were all together in the theater with the voices, then I was truly very happy ...

QUESTION: *Because of a specifically tonal success?*

J.C.: Yes. And I would like to point out that the superimposed pieces performed at the 6.30 concert could be considered even more as a work of art. And that doesn't interest us. *(Laughter.)* But at the present time to consider the *Song Books* as a work of art is nearly impossible. Who would dare? It resembles a brothel, doesn't it? *(Laughter.)* And even the subject seems absent: you can't find either Satie or Thoreau in it! Not even both of them!

QUESTION: *Very often the notation of your scores is ambiguous. Why?*

J.C.: I have decided that my task is to open up the personality; I also want to open up the work so that it may be interpreted in various ways.

QUESTION: *But aren't your 'indeterminate' works too 'open'? The public hardly notices the difference!*

J.C.: One day I said that writing music is not the same as performing it, nor as listening to it. They are three completely different things. What you hear, what comes from the writing, is absolutely different from the fact that I was able to write it. For there to be a connection, I would have to get up on stage and begin writing in front of you. That is what I did yesterday evening! But if you hear something other than what I write, I see no treason in it. There is simply a lack of rapport there where there once was – perhaps – a rapport ...

QUESTION: *However, even* your *music is written to be heard* ...

J.C.: I think that we should forget the relationship between writing and what is heard. I achieve it through a purposeless writing.

QUESTION: *Is there really a purposeless writing?*

J.C.: Indeed, there can be a purposeless writing, a pure writing! And also a pure performance, a pure listening. And each has nothing to do with any of the others ...

QUESTION: *To repeat the question I asked a moment ago: don't you ever feel betrayed by different performances of the same piece?*

J.C.: I am going to tell you a story. One day, around 1940, a musician, a pianist, phoned me to say that he was coming from South America, where he had played *The Perilous Night,* and he wanted me to hear it. He wanted to know what I thought about it, no matter what the cost. So, I went to his studio, and he banged out a *Perilous Night* that was perfectly horrible! At that moment, I would have preferred never to have written *The Perilous Night*! In the years that followed, when pianists came to me while my works were not yet published, I advised them especially not to play *The Perilous Night.* And then, by chance, in the course of a tour in the southern United States – it was at a university, I believe – another pianist[1] said to me: 'I play your *Perilous Night,* and I would like you to hear it.' I replied that I did not want to. He insisted. I ended up letting myself be convinced, and I followed him to his piano. I listened. It was marvelous.

QUESTION: *A little while ago you said that some people insist that your music is not music, and that in their understanding of the term, you don't practice politics. Can you expand on this point and tell us once and for all whether, yes or no, you practice politics?*

J.C.: Listen. Practicing politics consists in accepting and using the principle of government. On the contrary, anarchy is concerned only with the absence of government. And I believe that we would be able to live much better than at present if we were in a world which contained no nations – even united nations! And if instead this world contained a network of utilities ...

QUESTION: *What do you mean?*

J.C.: A network of all the things necessary for everyone's life! Such a network is the object of Buckminster Fuller's present research.

D.C.: *In the spirit of Buckminster Fuller, you recently gave – in the course*

---

[1] It was Richard Bunger, who has recently completed a very instructive book: *The Well-Prepared Piano.* (John Cage; footnote of 1972.)

of an interview broadcast on French radio — an example of utility which struck me. You talked about a magazine that we could eat after reading it. What good can such a project do us?

J.C.: First of all, here is what Buckminster Fuller says: we must put all the resources of the world into a fluid, fluctuating, mobile state so that nothing exists that we have to try to get rid of. That is the first point: no more pollution! Instead of allowing our atmosphere to be invaded by polluting substances, fatal to the very air we breathe, we must put them where they will do good. Right?

D.C.: Certainly, but where is the connection?

J.C.: Well, instead of throwing our old papers all around, and placing ourselves in the position of having to get rid of them, wouldn't it be better to make them edible? Couldn't we eat them?

D.C.: And you seriously think that we can eliminate pollution like that?

J.C.: It has become quite easy today to produce stuff we could write on — stuff we could eat afterwards! The inks could have new scents and flavors. You could go out for a newspaper and at the same time buy a pepper steak! We must find analogous solutions for everything that pollutes ...

D.C.: But you're still not dealing directly with the problem of politics.

J.C.: Yes, I am! Instead of trying to act against pollution, we behave more and more like *connoisseurs*. I mean that we remain rigidly closed, that we even close ourselves off more and more blindly to everything that doesn't seem good enough for us. We adopt exactly the same attitude towards politics — or race ... We tell ourselves, for example: it is better to be black than white, or the opposite! That is what I call giving in to emotions. But that leads nowhere. In music, we should be satisfied with opening our ears. Everything can musically enter an ear open to all sounds! Not only the music we consider beautiful but also the music that is life itself. Through music, life will take on more and more meaning. But you can well understand that in a certain sense music must be abandoned for it to be like that. Or at least *what we call* music! For politics, it is the same thing. And so I may indeed talk about 'non-politics', just as people talk about my 'non-music'. It's the same problem! If we could come to accept putting aside everything entitled 'music', all of life would become music!

QUESTION: *Would it be too indiscrete to ask you for some details on daily life at Stony Point?*

J.C.: I live in a little community at Stony Point, which is an hour and fifteen minutes from New York, in the mountains, near a forest. There are about fifteen individuals, with about fifteen children ... Now there are about eleven houses. Yes, perhaps there are a few more than fifteen adults, but there are indeed eleven houses. And the group of five friends who began this community was formed at Black Mountain College, in North Carolina. One of them inherited a lot of money ...

D.C.: That was Paul Williams?

J.C.: Yes, the one who gave his name to *Williams Mix*. As a philanthropist, he wanted to devote this money to a community, for the purchase of houses and land. And he insisted on a building plan free of all the rules of architecture common in the city. So the community was built; and now, over a period of thirty years, each of us repays what he owes in monthly installments. If one of us leaves the community and goes away, he doesn't have the right to take anything at all with him; he must leave everything. But, inversely, he may stay as long as he likes. And if a new follower wishes to join us, nothing is simpler. All he has to do is to buy a bit of adjacent land and have the money to build another house.[1] If I pay for thirty years, no one has to pay after me for the next thirty years, even if I die. My heirs won't have to do a thing, they won't have to pay for the land or the house. The taxes are a great inconvenience. But the principle that inspired us and that I believe is interesting is that we substitute the meaning of *utility* for that of *possession*.[2]

D.C.: Or that of property?

J.C.: That's right. Utility must, according to us, and in all areas, be substituted for property.

[1] This remark is not correct (adjacent land was not for sale). (John Cage; footnote of 1980.)
[2] I left the community since these words were spoken. It was not at all because of any infidelity to the meaning of utility, but because that meaning has, little by little, tended to disappear from the community. It is today becoming like a shanty-town: the roads are no longer maintained, the garbage is no longer collected. All that is probably linked to the tax burden on the people there! And then, I am getting old; in the winter I'm afraid of the ice. (John Cage; footnote of 1972.)

INTERVIEWS WITH JOHN CAGE

FOREWORD I

As a continuation of the preceding dialogue, John Cage agreed between Christmas and New Year's Day of 1970-1971 to answer additional questions touching upon his career and especially his ideas. For clarity's sake, I have edited and rearranged his answers, since the original tape was anything but clear!

I have therefore assumed the role of copy editor, and I accept full reponsibility for the imperfections of the definitive text, even if it was, twice, entirely corrected by John Cage. I must stress that it did not seem to me to be necessary to give precedence in the transcription of these conversations to a concern for form which would necessarily have disguised their informal character. So consequently, the reader is asked to excuse the repetitions connected with the strictly oral aspect of our interviews.

Daniel Charles

FOREWORD II

While rereading the pages that follow, I sometimes managed to remember our interviews, and thus, to hear myself talking. At other times, I no longer heard myself. This uncertainty is probably connected to the manner in which this work was composed. I shall speak more about this in the Postface at the end of the book. With the help of Daniel Charles' editing, it was natural that I should sometimes be surprised to discover myself anew. But I see no reason to refuse to be credited with certain ideas on the pretext that they were stated outside of these interviews. And this interplay by collage has allowed Daniel Charles to bring in new information and original insights into my thinking. Therefore, I didn't want to cut out anything. Whenever I came across in my rereading remarks that I could not remember having directly made in the course of our conversations themselves, I simply suggested that they be printed in brackets.

John Cage

FIRST INTERVIEW

The beginnings: Buhlig, Cowell, Schoenberg

On the importance of time

Fischinger and the question of noise

Distance with regard to Varèse

Concerning electro-acoustic music

Discussion on the idea of solfeggio

Experimental and anarchical music

Criticism of relationships

Indeterminacy and its precariousness

The world evolving

DANIEL CHARLES: *People don't think about you in quite the same way that they used to.*

JOHN CAGE: I would like to say right away how important it seems to me that things change. Now, although I am a part of this change, it wouldn't take much for everything to be able to change quite well without me.

D.C.: *Is that so certain?*

J.C.: I am convinced that I owe my relative fame, before anything else, to my age ...

D.C.: *Why?*

J.C.: Look at Thoreau – he died at forty-four. People knew about him, but so little. His work was only understood and appreciated later on. There are innumerable examples of posthumous celebrities. I have had the good luck to have lived up until the present ...

D.C.: *And to be younger than most of your contemporaries!*

J.C.: That's right. All around me are people born old, even very old ...

D.C.: *Your youth is synonymous with a prodigious power of invention ...*

J.C.: In any case, I value the faculty for inventing more than anything. My father was an inventor.

D.C.: *Schoenberg correctly recognized in you 'not a composer, but an inventor – of genius.' But how did you become a student of Schoenberg?*

J.C.: That's a rather long story. I must first tell you about Richard Buhlig. He was the first American pianist to perform Schoenberg. I left for Europe after college, and when I returned, I ended up in Los Angeles, right in the middle of the Great Depression and without a cent to my name. To earn a living, given my enthusiasm for modern painting and music, I decided to give lectures. I didn't want to become a professor, I just wanted to get by. So I went from door to door, offering a subscription to ten of my lectures for two and a half dollars ... I told all the housewives that I didn't know anything about modern painting or modern music, but that I was enthusiastic about both, and that each week I would study the subject of my coming lecture. I ended up having more than twenty or thirty people for my series of lectures. The week came when I was to speak about Schoenberg. I had learned, sometime earlier, that Richard Buhlig had been the first to play *Opus 11* – Schoenberg's first three piano pieces – and it suddenly occurred to me that he might be living in Los Angeles ... So I ran to the telephone book. His name was listed! I phoned him, and asked him if he would agree to play Schoenberg's pieces for me. He replied: 'Certainly not!' and hung up. Next, I wanted somehow to get him to illustrate my lecture by performing those pieces. So I decided to see him personally, so as to avoid having him abruptly end things by hanging up on me again. Well, I made the trip from Santa Monica to Los Angeles in a great hurry to go to see him ... But when I knocked on his door, there was no answer. I stayed in front of his house for twelve hours waiting! Finally, around midnight, he returned home, and when I explained to him that I had waited at his door for twelve hours, he agreed to see me. I asked him to play the Schoenberg pieces at the next lecture. He again answered, 'Certainly not!' So then I asked him to teach me composition. He replied that he did not teach composition, but piano, but that he would, nevertheless, agree to do his best. After several months of work with him, he told me he couldn't help me any more, and that I should send my compositions to Henry Cowell.

D.C.: And it was Cowell who introduced you to Schoenberg?

J.C.: Henry Cowell looked at my work, and told me that of all the living masters, the best one for me would be Schoenberg. Only I had to prepare myself to receive this instruction; I really didn't know enough, and I would have to work with Adolph Weiss, who was Schoenberg's first American pupil.

D.C.: Did you remain a student of Weiss for long?

J.C.: About a year. I studied harmony with him. At the same time, I attended Henry Cowell's courses at the New School for Social Research. The subjects were Modern Harmony, Musics of the World's Peoples, and Survey of Contemporary Music.

D.C.: In France, Henry Cowell is known, although not very well, as a musical pioneer or inventor.

J.C.: Yes, he was the first to play a piano with his fists, with his entire forearm. He was also the first to play inside the piano, using his hands directly on the strings! He also thought of putting various objects on the strings, like a darning egg! When you position it so you can slide it along a string, you get a glissando of harmonics. But you need fairly weighty objects for that. We are also indebted to Cowell for his important book on rhythm; unfortunately that book has remained unpublished. I, however, was able to read it ...

D.C.: And to make use of it?

J.C.: Certainly. At that time, though, the essential thing for me was that Cowell led me to Schoenberg. But I forgot to mention that Richard Buhlig taught me something significant and even more important: TIME. The absolutely fundamental character of time.

D.C.: How did he do that?

J.C.: It was the simplest thing in the world. For one of his lessons I arrived a half-hour early, because, in order to get around, I depended more on hitch-hiking than on any regular means of transportation! So, I arrive, I knock on his door, he opens it, and says to me, 'You are one half-hour early. Come back at the correct time.' Well, I had some books with me that I had to return to the library. I took advantage of this time to run this errand. I went to the library, turned in my books, and came back to his house. A half-hour late! When he opened the door for me that second time, he was furious. That afternoon, he gave me a two-hour session. He refused to look at my work, and gave me only a lecture on time; on the importance of time not only in music but also in the life of anyone who plans to give his life to music.

D.C.: You haven't forgotten that lesson.

J.C.: No, never! Since then, I have always considered time as the essential dimension of all music.

D.C.: Have you, since then, considered stepping back from or establishing a critical distance with regard to Schoenberg himself? Later, you came to maintain that dodecaphony is only a method and that Schoenberg did not structure his works according to the fundamental dimension of time.

J.C.: In reality, when I found myself face to face with Schoenberg I was the most docile of students. I worshipped him! To me, he seemed completely different from all other musicians, from all other men. Everything he said, I believed. And much of what he said was quite terrifying. I went to all his classes, at the University of Southern California, and, later, at the University of California at Los Angeles, and likewise at his home, where he gathered small groups of students. One day I heard him proclaim in front of a whole class: 'My goal, the goal of my teaching, is to make it impossible for you to write music.' Perhaps it was at that moment that I began – despite my fanatic devotion to him – to revolt. In any case, I remember at that precise moment swearing that I would devote my entire existence to writing music.

D.C.: Was that when you decided to break away from harmony?

J.C.: Not immediately. Of course, Schoenberg knew as well as I did that I had no feeling for harmony. But one day when I was working with him he spoke in praise of harmony. According to him, I would never be able to compose, because I would always find myself in front of a wall, harmony, through which I'd never be able to get. So, I replied to him that I would spend my life banging my head against that wall ...

D.C.: *Did Schoenberg convert you to dodecaphony? You did compose some twelve tone music.*

J.C.: What struck me all the more was his insistence on teaching tonality as structure, as a structural means. When you think about it, composing with twelve tones was only a 'method'. What I liked in that method was the equal importance accorded to each tone. But I found the obligation to continually submit to that theory to be exaggeratedly constraining. I began to look for ways to compose twelve tone music without the row, where the row would go unnoticed. Even before I studied with Schoenberg, I had already written pieces with several voices that relied on a gamut of twenty-five half tones. I particularly watched for non-repetition. I strove to maintain very great distances between the repetitions of each given pitch; I considered the octave of a note 'x' as a different note 'y', and not as the octave of that note 'x' ... It was upon seeing this music that Cowell sent me to study with Schoenberg. After I had studied with Schoenberg, I strongly felt the necessity of writing with twelve tones; but my principal concern was not to make the row noticeable, but to mask it, even though it was being used as the basis for the entire method. To accomplish that, I undertook the division of the twelve tones into little groups; each group was to remain static, that is, was not to vary.

D.C.: *The subdivision of the row into fragments is used by the dodeca-phonists and most serial musicians. But how did you connect your frag-ments?*

J.C.: I took those groups of tones, and at the end of each group, I arranged things so that I could begin any other of the remaining groups[1] from the following or preceding degree of the row. This could be done following either the form of the original or the inversion, or its retrograde or retrograde inversion. At the conclusion of each group, I had all these possibilities.

D.C.: *So were your sequences free of any harmonic restraint?*

J.C.: Entirely. I kept some works from that period – not because they have any sort of value, but to demonstrate my evolution; for the use of my biographers, if you will. And we noticed together that one of them, *Metamorphosis,* which we discussed at the Museum of Modern Art, was written with a method but without a structure. I only truly detached

[1]Or repeat the one just used. (John Cage: footnote of 1980.)

myself from Schoenberg's teachings on the structural character of tonality once I began to work with percussion. Only then did I begin to make structures. But structure then became rhythmic; it was no longer a tonal structure in Schoenberg's sense.

D.C.: But was rhythmic structure enough to make up for a lack of tonality? Aren't we dealing with two different dimensions which cannot be substituted for one another? Did you really never have the feeling of losing something by abandoning tonality?

J.C.: On the contrary! I never really worried about losing anything; rather I was concerned with the need to accomodate all possible noises within the body of a musical structure. Tonality was what was a loss. To my eyes it represented a waste. A closed door!

D.C.: How did you get the idea of constructing your works according to duration?

J.C.: I came to this notion of musical time – or, if you prefer, phraseology – through a consideration of the nature of sound, which to me seemed to include four dimensions: pitch, amplitude, timbre, and duration.

D.C.: The four parameters of sound according to the serialists ... but the authenticity of their distinction was quickly questioned.

J.C.: Perhaps, but at the time, that was not the case. I realized that a structure based on rhythm or time, on duration, could be just as hospitable to noises as to so-called musical sounds.

D.C.: From a student of Schoenberg, you turned into a disciple of Varèse ...

J.C.: But, remember, I never worked with Varèse. I was happy to just enjoy his music. Particularly *Ionization,* which I heard at the Hollywood Bowl during the Thirties – in 1935, I believe.

D.C.: Your percussion work during those years when you conducted percussion orchestras was not then directly guided by Varèse's example?

J.C.: To tell the truth, it didn't happen that way. One day I was introduced to Oscar Fischinger who made abstract films quite precisely articulated on pieces of traditional music. He constructed his films on Brahms' *Hungarian Dances* and other pieces of the same genre. He said, however, he would have liked some new music written for his films. When I was introduced to him, he began to talk with me about the spirit which is inside each of the objects of this world. So, he told me, all we need to do to liberate that spirit is to brush past the object, and to draw forth its sound. That's the idea which led me to percussion. In all the many years which followed up to the war, I never stopped touching things, making them sound and resound, to discover what sounds they could produce. Wherever I went, I always listened to objects. So I gathered together a group of friends, and we began to play some pieces I had written without instrumental indications, simply to explore instrumental possibilities not yet catalogued, the infinite number of sound sources from a trash heap or a junk yard, a living room or a kitchen ... We tried all the furniture we could think of.

D.C.: *But without selecting the noises of that 'furniture music' according to some aesthetic criterion?*

J.C.: No. All noises interested me. I must admit that at that time I really didn't have a cent. Perhaps, if I had been a bit better off, I would have used slightly more conventional instruments ... Maybe there is a connection between poverty and music! That connection existed, in any case, between 1935 and 1937, when I wasn't always able to rent a tympani, a tam-tam, a very simple gong, or some woodblocks. If our orchestra made little use of these conventional instruments, it was because of our impecunious situation ... Later, I got a little money. In Seattle, I solicited contributions from some of the rich people of the town and obtained two hundred dollars to begin my collection. I then bought all sorts of instruments. I managed to amass a collection of around three hundred! And the habit stuck. I have never stopped trying to get objects or unconventional instruments to do everything they are capable of doing.

D.C.: *That brought you into harmony with Varèse.*

J.C.: What I appreciate about Varèse is obviously his freedom in choosing timbre. He, along with Henry Cowell, has very greatly contributed to getting us used to the idea of a limitless tonal universe. No matter how refined Schoenberg's timbres may be, they hardly ever get away from the number twelve ... While with Varèse, whatever his 'organizational' notions may have been, you feel that everything is possible. Nevertheless, there is still in Varèse a prejudice towards controling sounds or noises. He tries to bend sounds to his will, to his imagination. And that is what very quickly bothered us. We knew that he wouldn't let sounds be entirely free. What we were looking for was in a way more humble: sounds, quite simply. Sounds, pure and simple.

D.C.: *Without the least musical* a priori?

J.C.: To us any sound seemed capable of becoming musical by the simple fact that it was incorporated into a musical piece. That's not what Schoenberg taught, and not exactly what Varèse was pursuing.

D.C.: *When Fischinger taught you to listen to the soul, or to the spirit of things, didn't that bring to mind certain oriental doctrines on the genesis of sound?*

J.C.: With Fischinger, everything was situated at a level which you could simply label 'spiritualist'. It wasn't until after the war, ten years after my meeting with Fischinger, (which took place in 1935 or 1936) that I became seriously interested in Oriental thought and in the myths you mentioned.

D.C.: *But weren't there Javanese or Balinese or even African influences in your writing for percussion? Were you acquainted with any music from the oral tradition?*

J.C.: As I mentioned, I attended some of Henry Cowell's classes in New York where I heard some music of that type. If there were any influences, I was not conscious of them; anyway, at that time I had not seriously studied the theories of Indian or Indonesian music.

D.C.: *You were only interested in sonority?*

J.C.: All through the pre-war years, yes. But in sonority in connection with a rhythmic structure. What I wanted was a situation open to all sorts of sonorities. And it appeared clear to me that this situation had to do with time.

D.C.: *At the Museum of Modern Art, you mentioned your desire to get out of the Schoenbergian circle of repetition-variation ...*

J.C.: In all of my pieces coming between 1935 and 1940, I had Schoenberg's lessons in mind; since he had taught me that a variation was in fact a repetition, I hardly saw the usefulness of variation, and I accumulated repetitions. All of my early works for percussion, and also my compositions for piano, contain systematically repeated groups of sounds or durations.

D.C.: *It was only after the war that, in France at least, we gained access to the universe of noises which you had been contemplating since 1935. Your 1937 text on the future of music now appears to have been an advance warning ...*[1] *In it, you use the adjective 'experimental' — well before Schaeffer made the term popular — to qualify this music of noises. You advocated establishing 'centers of experimental music' in which composers would find the electro-acoustic equipment needed for their work.*

J.C.: That's true. A few years later – it must have been between 1941 and 1942 – I spent a few months, even a year perhaps, trying to found a 'center of experimental music'. I then possessed enough information on electro-acoustic technology to think seriously about developing a music which would not pass up any of these new possibilities of sound produc-

[1]'The Future of Music: Credo,' in *Silence: Lectures and Writings by John Cage*. Middletown, Conn.: Wesleyan University 1961 and Marion Boyars Ltd, London, 1973. Pp. 3-7.

tion. At that time, people didn't think about using tape recorders, but 'film phonographs'. With the help of this particular kind of camera, we thought we could save certain sounds, building libraries of them and composing on the basis of these catalogued elements. Magnetic tape eventually made this possible. At first, we thought that this result could be obtained with films. Next, people considered wires. Of course, all this did not really become 'operational' until after the war, with the development of magnetic recording tape.

D.C.: Throughout that 1937 text, you suggested replacing the word 'music' with the expression 'organization of sound'.

J.C.: Yes. The label 'music' seemed so restricted to what could be done with instruments invented or perfected in the eighteenth and nineteenth centuries that even the inventors of electrical musical equipment couldn't figure out anything else to do but to imitate those 'musical' instruments. Moreover, it is a very nearly universal phenomenon. Instead of immediately assuming a definitive form, all technological inventions start by copying preceding inventions and go on doing this for several years. Cars were carts before becoming cars. Likewise, electric instruments were first used to reproduce traditional sounds which, however, were worn-out sonorities.

D.C.: Do you acknowledge the idea of a 'concrete solfeggio'?

J.C.: What can that possibly mean?

D.C.: Schaeffer's doctrine, in the 1950's, set up a classification of noises according to a certain number of taxinomic criteria that could serve as the basis for a reading or deciphering of the most diverse tonal expanses. According to Schaeffer, this would facilitate composing in a less 'surrealistic' and more organic way.

J.C.: I'm afraid that such an *attempt at organization* is a regression to the very process of copying from the classics that we just discussed. The idea of a *solfeggio of noises* includes the word 'solfeggio', doesn't it? And what could be more worn-out than that notion?

D.C.: Then solfeggio, according to you, is nothing more than a compromising inheritance from the eighteenth and nineteenth centuries?

J.C.: That's about right. You see, what always made me ill at ease with Schaeffer's work from the very beginning was his concern for relationships – in particular the relationships between sounds. He could have taken advantage of various machines, but he never used them for anything more than to demonstrate the relationships between noises and tonality. That was always his problem. For example, the phonogene, he was convinced, had to run at twelve speeds; how could he not end up with anything but a twelve tone system? Even though he insisted that that was what he didn't want to do! It's the same problem with solfeggio. It's a mental tool, not a machine, but the result runs the risk of being the same thing. We inevitably fall back into sounds, in the 'musical' sense of the term: noises which can go only with certain noises and not with others. Yet, what I wanted to accomplish was exactly the opposite: not the repetition of a situation to which we are accustomed and which can remain what it is without our feeling obliged to intervene, but an entirely new situation, in which any sound or noise at all can go with any other.

D.C.: *What you call an 'experimental' situation.*

J.C.: Yes, one in which nothing is selected in advance, in which there are no obligations or prohibitions, in which nothing is even predictable.

D.C.: *A situation of anarchy?*

J.C.: Certainly! Thoreau described it quite clearly [when he replaced Jefferson's maxim 'That government is best which governs least' with 'That government is best which does not govern at all!]

D.C.: *Then you would place Schaeffer on the side of government?*

J.C.: I think that he and I do not agree with each other on the difference between the number two and the number one. [I have always sought to grasp the plurality of the figure one, while for Schaeffer, plurality only begins with the figure two.]

D.C.: *Do you mean that with the number two, we remain at the stage of the relationship between objects?*

J.C.: For clarity's sake, let's go back to the example of 'experimental' music. Formerly, people imagined that music first existed in people's minds – and in particular, in the composer's mind. It was written and was supposed to be heard *before* it became audible. On the contrary, I believe that *nothing* is heard *before*. Solfeggio is precisely the discipline which allows a sound to be heard even *before* it has been emitted ... Except, with that discipline, we become deaf. We put ourselves in the position of accepting certain sounds but not others. To practice solfeggio is to decide *a priori* that we find the sounds of our environment to be poor. That is why there cannot be a 'concrete solfeggio!' All solfeggio is, of necessity, by definition, 'abstract' ... And dualistic! For the practitioner of solfeggio, any environmental sound is mutilated; it lacks tonality. Now you can see why I do not have the slightest interest in solfeggio. I have never put in my head any idea about perfecting sounds, nor any commitment to bettering the sonorous race. I simply keep my ears open.

D.C.: *Allow me to quote you: 'Happy new ears!'*

J.C.: That's right! I keep my mind alive and alert, or at least I try to. As a result, everything dissonant, I hear as consonant. [I hear not only the number two, but also the plurality of the number one.]

D.C.: *Nonetheless there is a difference ...*

J.C.: Of course there's a difference! But it's not one that must be approached in terms of value. What I try to approach is the sound in itself, as it is.

D.C.: *Not as you would like it to be.*

J.C.: Not as it's 'supposed' to be. And I think that works better for sounds which *are not* 'music', in the eighteenth and nineteenth century sense, than for sounds which *are* music.

D.C.: *You are a perfectly 'concrete' musician!*

J.C.: If it's all right with Schaeffer, yes! What makes sounds 'abstract' is, instead of listening to them for themselves, being content with listening to their relationships. It would be just as valid, as I once said, to express musical ideas with lights ...

D.C.: *Certain composers dream of doing that, some do it ...*

J.C.: Or with apples!

D.C.: *Doesn't your hostility with regard to the notion of relationships come from a certain type of American philosophy? I am thinking of William James' criticism of relationships. However, James did not maintain that criticism to the end. He ended up recognizing that relationships were themselves 'wholes', 'ones'. For him, relationships* also *existed in experience.*

J.C.: I know perfectly well that things interpenetrate. But I think they interpenetrate more richly and with more complexity when I myself do not establish any connection. That is when they meet and form the number one. But, at the same time, they form no obstruction. They are themselves. They are. And since each one is itself, there is a plurality in the number one.

D.C.: *But how can you abstain from all relational activity? Isn't perception itself a positioning in relation to something else?*

J.C.: I can accept the relationship between a diversity of elements, as we do when we look at the stars, discover a group of stars and baptize it 'The Big Bear'. Then I make an object out of it. I am no longer dealing with the entity itself, seen as having elements or separate parts, I have before me a fixed object which I may cause to vary precisely because I know in advance that I will find it identical to itself. From this point of view, I am practicing what Schoenberg said: variation is a form, an extreme case of repetition. But you can also see how it is possible for me to get out of this circle of variation and repetition. By returning to reality, to that particular entity, to that constellation which is not yet completely a constellation. It is not yet an object! I can quite easily perceive the thing that from one perspective forms a single object as a group of different and distinct things. What makes the constellation into an object is the relationship I impose on its components. But I can refrain from positing that relationship, I can consider the stars as separate yet close, *nearly* united in a single constellation. Then I simply have a group of stars.

D.C.: I am beginning to understand your choice, for the orchestral work Atlas Eclipticalis, *of astronomical maps, borrowed from the Wesleyan University Library, which dictated the topography itself of your score.*

J.C.: You're talking about a topography. You're making an object out of what's nothing but a network of chance operations.

D.C.: But I have to! If I want to escape precise cause-effect relationships, I have to change the measuring means. I have to deal with clouds, with trends or laws of statistical distribution.

J.C.: Yes, from the physicist's point of view. But the chance of contemporary physics, tables of random numbers, corresponds to an *equal* distribution of events. The chance to which I resort, that of chance operations, is different. It presupposes an *unequal* distribution of elements. That is the contribution of the Chinese *Book of Changes*, the *I Ching*, or the astronomical maps I used for *Atlas Eclipticalis*. I never achieve the physical object that interests the statistician.

D.C.: Or the composer Xenakis! But nonetheless I can obtain it ...

J.C.: Yes, if I *want* it. But I must *want* it. In indeterminate work, such as I conceive it, there is *a priori* no such logic.

D.C.: Logic is born in he who listens ...

J.C.: And who decides to deal with an object. Any one of my indeterminate pieces, if recorded, becomes an object at the moment when you listen to it knowing that you can listen to it again. You listen again and the object surges forth. There is repetition; it sounds the same each time. You can learn what you are listening to by listening to it again. You are free to infuse it with all the logic you care to.

D.C.: At that moment, there is no difference between a determinate and an indeterminate work?

J.C.: No, with the exception that, in the case of the indeterminate work, I'm not the one who put the logic into the score.

D.C.: Ultimately, this indeterminacy is a quite fragile, precarious reality ...

J.C.: Yes, even in my pieces you can find a logic! But it requires will, even good will. The problem was very clearly formulated by Duchamp. He says, more or less, that one must strain to reach the impossibility of remembering, even when experience goes from an object to its double. In contemporary civilization where everything is standardized and where everything is repeated, the whole point is to forget in the space between an object and its duplication. If we didn't have this power of forgetfulness, if art today didn't help us to forget, we would be submerged, drowned under those avalanches of rigorously identical objects.

D.C.: *But doesn't an Andy Warhol get us used to repetitions?*

J.C.: No, in fact he makes us lose that habit. Each repetition must authorize an entirely new experience. Of course, we don't always manage it, but we are on the way.

D.C.: *Then art as you define it is a discipline of adaptation to the real as it is. It doesn't propose to change the world, it accepts it as it presents itself. By dint of breaking our habits, it habituates us more effectively.*

J.C.: I don't think so. There is one term of the problem which you are not taking into account: precisely, the world. The real. You say: the real, the world as it is. But it is not, it becomes! It moves, it changes! It doesn't wait for us to change ... It is more mobile than you can imagine. You are getting closer to this reality when you say as it "presents itself"; that means that it is not there, existing as an object. The world, the real is not an object. It is a process.

D.C.: *There can be no custom or habit in a world in the process of becoming ... Is that your idea?*

J.C.: Yes, it is an idea of changing, like all my music, which could be defined as a *Music of Changes.* And I found that title in the *Book of Changes,* the *I Ching.*

D.C.: *I cannot help but believe that* logos, *logic, has only the slightest hold on this world as you define it.*

J.C.: It's simply that I am not a philosopher ... at least, not a Greek one! Before, we wished for logical experiences; nothing was more important to us than stability. Today, we admit instability alongside stability. What we hope for is the experience of that which is. But 'what is' is not necessarily the stable, the immutable. We do know quite clearly, in any case, that it is we who bring logic into the picture. It is not laid out before us waiting for us to discover it. 'What is' does not depend on us, we depend on it. And we have to draw nearer to it. And unfortunately for logic, everything we understand under that rubric 'logic' represents such a simplification with regard to the event and what really happens, that we must learn to keep away from it. The function of art at the present time is to preserve us from all the logical minimizations that we are at each instant tempted to apply to the flux of events. To draw us nearer to the process which is the world we live in.

SECOND INTERVIEW

Virgil Thomson

On immobility and mobility

While going nowhere

Art as life

Against philosophies of life

Stasis and absence of goals

Pupils

Universities

McLuhan: opening onto that which is

The will to disorder

On the opportunity for non-intention

Interpenetration and non-obstruction

The question of Nothing

Fuller and the number three

On chance

Suzuki and *Chuang-tze*

About the *I Ching*; Taoism and modern science

Debate on noise and the non-act

Responsibility toward everything that is

Importance of utilities

Abundance and disrespect

Liberty: live and let live

D.C.: Among the contemporary composers you have known, I notice the name Virgil Thomson, to whom you devoted a work. How did that happen?

J.C.: When I went to New York for the first time, I had the chance to meet him one day when I was preparing a percussion concert for the Museum of Modern Art. He was a member of the music committee of that museum. We got along very well; I enjoyed his conversation. He wrote an article on my music, and that text was the origin of the interest which was just then beginning to be connected with what I was doing. And later, in particular, he had a hand in getting me a Guggenheim Fellowship and an award from the National Institute of Arts and Letters. Shortly thereafter, he asked me to write a book on his works, and I agreed to do so. I felt that the activity that I would have to devote to such a study would be useful to me. So I decided to examine each of his compositions in detail and chronologically. I wanted as much as possible to repeat the work he had already done.

D.C.: Did this task require much time?

J.C.: It took me ten years! With some interruptions, it's true. In reality, Thomson was so prolific that each time I thought I was catching up with him, he continued on his course and advanced another step. And then, when I had finished the first chapters, he asked me to read them to him. Unfortunately, he was not in agreement with the result. He set out to look for someone else for the job, but he couldn't find anyone to his satisfaction and after several years came back to ask me to finish it. So I replied that I would accept only if he himself agreed not to demand to see the result before everything was finished. Thus passed ten years.

D.C.: Then, you had a falling-out with each other?

J.C.: In the first chapter, I began by dealing with both the life and the work of Virgil Thomson. In fact, I figured that there was no way in this case to separate one from the other. That was what had not pleased him … While I was getting back to work, he gave the task of writing his biography to Kathleen Hoover without telling me a thing about it. Once I completed my text, the difficulty arose: he had to find a reader to edit my work – to filter out everything that had to do with his life, and only leave in print whatever dealt with the works themselves and their analyses. I did not get along with the first person Thomson had picked out for this task of rereading and editing,[1] the importance of which I still did not suspect! He then suggested taking this task into his own hands.[2] I explained that this would not do. The problem lay in his style; it was famous and would be immediately recognized! We managed to reach an agreement on a third reader. And everything went fine until the proof sheets came. This was the first time I saw to my great surprise the *Life of Virgil Thomson* by Kathleen O'Donnell Hoover! What's more, I realized that the final 'editor' of my text had been Virgil Thomson himself! I found this objectionable and completely contrary to our understanding. Such that ... I always greatly enjoyed his conversation, but we see each other very seldom.

D.C.: He, though, has continued to write about you. He has even at times criticized you.

J.C.: His criticism consists in maintaining that, in his eyes, my work lacks necessity. According to him, my early work or the first period of my work was interesting. But since my music no longer attempts to go anywhere, according to him, it no longer presents any interest. And he wonders why I continue to write it.

D.C.: Do you agree with this objection?

J.C.: My intention was precisely to stop my music from going anywhere! I sought to let sounds go wherever they would go, and to let them be whatever they are. That led me to a continuity, but one that no longer tries to reach a *climax*. A continuity that doesn't go up or down!

D.C.: You started with rhythmic structures, which were supposed to organize your music temporally. But in order for this temporal dimension to be felt, and even for there to be any time in general, don't you have to go somewhere?

J.C.: Not at all. You can very easily stay put ...

D.C.: Remain immobile?

J.C.: Yes, quite easily.

D.C.: Would you care to explain this theory of time? How do you reconcile it with the idea of becoming, of the world as process?

J.C.: [A Zen monk came out of his house with one of his disciples, and saw a flock of wild geese fly past. 'What is that?' he asked. 'They *were* wild geese.' The master violently twisted his disciple's nose. 'You think

[1]Kathleen O'Donnell Hoover. (John Cage; footnote of 1980.)
[2]He would correct my work anonymously without taking credit on the title page. (John Cage; footnote of 1980.)

they have passed, but they have always been here.' Then the disciple was enlightened.]

D.C.: A French writer close to Taoism, Jean Grenier, explained in his book Daily Life *how a Hindu monk from the 'Ramakrishna sect' observed the most perfect silence before an assemblage gathered for a lecture, and did so for an entire hour. 'It cannot be said that this action abolished the feeling of time, it was dominated by one of its components, which was the stable, while the other component, the unstable, was its harmonic.' Would you accept this dichotomy for speaking of time? Can it be applied to your music?*

J.C.: [It seems to me that it is more applicable to La Monte Young than to me. The stable and the unstable cannot, for me, present themselves as the fundamental and the harmonic, if that implies a hierarchy.]

D.C.: Is the act of leaving the world of hierarchy what you call 'life as art'?

J.C.: No. It is art as life.

D.C.: Would you care to expand on that?

J.C.: If I want 'life as art,' I risk falling into aestheticism, because I would appear to be trying to impose something, a certain idea of life. It appears to me that music – such as I envision it, at least – imposes nothing. It can effectively change our manner of seeing, making us view everything around us as art. But that is not the goal. Sounds have no goal! They are, and that's all. They live. Music is this life of sounds, this participation of sounds in life, which may become – but not voluntarily – a participation of life in sounds. In itself, music does not obligate us to anything.

D.C.: If, through your music, you achieve a certain continuity, then, it is not at all intentional?

J.C.: I simply notice what happens. I used to talk about a 'continuity of discontinuity.' I wanted to avoid the melodic aspect, because as soon as there is melody there is a will and desire to bend sounds to that will. However, I do not refuse melody. I refuse it even less when it produces itself. But it must not begin through imposition. I do not want to force sounds to follow me.

D.C.: So, about time itself, you would say that it cannot *be represented?*

J.C.: You mustn't become hypnotized by intellectual categories, continuous-discontinuous, stable-unstable, etc., which supposedly make it possible to think time.

D.C.: That could be considered a vitalist profession of faith.

J.C.: Nothing eludes philosophies of life more than life does! No, I am not on the verge of joining such philosophies. An inanimate being has as much life as a living being. A sound is alive. Philosophers of life don't say that, do they?

D.C.: *At the time of our interview at the Museum of Modern Art, I mentioned the objection which Leonard Meyer addressed to you and which is similar to Virgil Thomson's: he accused you of extolling a static music, a music of* stasis, *therefore, of letting musical time escape. You avoided giving him a direct answer, or perhaps I misunderstood you?*

J.C.: In fact, I accept that accusation. And I do not consider it an accusation. Life indeed includes this *stasis*. But I am not extolling anything. And I don't let anything escape. If by 'musical time' you mean only a fixed, determined music that has a before and an after, in short, a music made of finite temporal objects, then I would indeed concede that my music is not like that at all. But perhaps 'musical time' is something else ...

D.C.: *And when one of your colleagues, Morton Feldman, asserts that your music is not identical to life inasmuch as it assembles together only a part of life's tonalities ...*

J.C.: I would also say that it doesn't let anything escape. Or rather, that it escapes from the idea that it would let anything at all escape.

D.C.: *Aren't you avoiding the objection?*

J.C.: But everything is possible! My music lays down no restrictions! It simply happens that the life we lead is partial, and many sounds are difficult to gather into the concert halls we now use. I try to avoid this obligation of selecting what is suitable for a concert, an audience, a place, etc. I enlarge the conditions of the performance of my music to the maximum. I go to circuses, clearings, art galleries, rooftops ... My music is surely partial, but I'm not the one who aims at this partial side. If there is something I'm aiming at, it is the absence of any goal; what is partial always corresponds to a goal.

D.C.: *That must make the fact of being a student of John Cage rather frightening! How have you been able to have students and give them instruction without a goal?*

J.C.: It happens that a lot of people have come to study with me. But for each one I have tried to discover who he was and what he could do. As a result, most often, I am the one who is the student.

D.C.: *Is that also true in a university setting? I have the impression, nonetheless, that some of your students learned a great deal around you ...*

J.C.: At any rate, they taught me – at least those at the New School for Social Research – that I preferred not to teach.

D.C.: *However, you haven't really given up all pedagogical activity?*

J.C.: I have tried, as much as possible, to avoid universities.

D.C.: *Why?*

J.C.: They are too close to government, both here in France where nothing is done without permission from the authorities, and in America where the authorities are individuals. But it ends up as the same thing, doesn't it?

D.C.: *But wouldn't that change if someone like you agreed to appear more often?*

J.C.: Recently, at the University of California at Davis, I gave a course which had as its premise the hypothesis that we didn't know what we were going to study and that we wouldn't divide ourselves into students and non-students: all of us, including myself, were students.

D.C.: *And what happened?*

J.C.: We subjected the university library to chance operations and in the group – there were about a hundred of us – each person had two chance operations to determine the works he would have to read. Next, still by chance operations, we divided up into flexible groups. Each group had to meet and exchange information on what had been read. It was a technique fulfilling McLuhan's wish. He considers that our work must henceforth consist in brushing information against information.

D.C.: *Brushing?*

J.C.: Yes, like a suit of clothes.

D.C.: *If there is information in a circuit, there must come a time when no one can teach anything to anyone anymore. Once the library has been exhausted (supposing that occurs – we can do that, can't we?) what happens?*

J.C.: I believe that information never stops appearing.

D.C.: *In the sense that there are always many new books?*

J.C.: Not just that. If I am in a forest where there are no fir trees, my information differs from what it would be in a fir tree forest. Everything depends on the circumstances and our intentions.

D.C.: *So you are asking that people relax their attention.*

J.C.: Information can be found anywhere. We can be in the presence of information without receiving it.

D.C.: Then we should open ourselves up to all the information we don't receive.

J.C.: It's a little like noise compared to musical sounds: the more we discover that the noises of the outside world are musical, the more music there is.

D.C.: And do you think that this ideal opening-up to whatever comes can be transposed into all domains and that it is suitable for all university studies?

J.C.: Certainly.

D.C.: But aren't all the 'assemblages, environments, and happenings,' to borrow the title of a famous book – written by one of your pupils, Allan Kaprow – aren't they all in the end somewhat contrary to your ideal of opening up to everything that exists? For these are indeed oriented activities. The absence of a goal can become a goal, even for you. It could prove to be just as constraining as the situation we had in the beginning, the one where everything was subjected to a goal. Didn't you yourself recognize this at one of those happenings when you were told what you had to do, like go from one room to another?

J.C.: My answer is like the one I gave you a little while ago when we were discussing Feldman. We are not free. We live in a partitioned society. We certainly must take those partitionings into consideration. But why repeat them? Why should happenings duplicate the most constraining aspects of daily life? We always seem to believe that, in art, we must install order everywhere. And what if art incited disorder?

D.C.: Wanting disorder is still wanting.

J.C.: The question is not *not to want*, but to be frée with regard to one's own will. In a university, in my music, in my everyday life, I happen to use chance operations. But I do not exclusively, solely use chance operations! Recognizing chance's place does not mean sacrificing everything to it.

D.C.: Your teaching – if you accept that term – then, could be defined as a pedagogy of non-intention? A detachment with respect to will?

J.C.: A progressive detachment, yes, and one which would not fall back into any attachment. A detachment that would not repeat anything.

D.C.: That places us in the Orient ...

J.C.: Or only, as I already told you, very close to Fischinger. Each sound has its own spirit, its own life. And we cannot pretend to repeat that life. It can never become the example of a life, an example for another life. What is true for sounds, applies equally to men. And that is exactly why men are not sounds, nor are sounds men. Musicians spend their time forgetting that. My pedagogy is that we must not forget that any more.

D.C.: *You defined your great work of 1958,* The Concert For Piano and Orchestra, *as a 'collection of extreme difficulties.' You were then finding inspiration in the Orient ...*

J.C.: Of course.

D.C.: *I emphasize this point only because people could have thought that you, like Fischinger, were dipping into a sort of pantheism.*

J.C.: Before my encounter with Oriental thought, which occurred around 1945, I no longer recognized the need to speak of God with regard to this idea of the life of each thing. But I like to think that each thing has not only its own life but also its center, and that this center is always the very center of the Universe. Well, that is one of the principal themes which I have retained from my study of Zen.

D.C.: *Must the idea of life be dissociated from the idea of center?*

J.C.: What Suzuki taught me is that we really never stop establishing a means of measurement outside the life of things, and that next we strive to resituate each thing within the framework of that measure. We attempt to posit relationships between things by using this framework. So, we lose things, we forget them, or we disfigure them. Zen teaches us that we are in reality in a situation of decentering in relation to this framework. In this situation each thing is at the center. Therefore, there is a plurality of centers, a multiplicity of centers. And they are all interpenetrating and, as Zen would add, non-obstructing. Living for a thing is to be at the center. That entails interpenetration and non-obstruction.

D.C.: *How can there not be any contradiction between those last two terms? For two sounds not to mask or screen out each other, they must be separated. How can they interpenetrate?*

J.C.: You say that they must be separated. Well, just don't put anything in between.

D.C.: *How?*

J.C.: There must be nothing between the things which you have separated so they wouldn't obstruct each other. Well, that *nothing* is what permits all things to exist.

D.C.: *To interpenetrate, that is?*

J.C.: That they interpenetrate means there is nothing between them. Thus nothing separates them ...

D.C.: You say nothing. *Let me raise a question of translation. Do you prefer* nothing *to be translated as* 'rien', 'nothing', *or as* 'le rien', 'nothingness'? *Do we have the right to say that the* nothing *which you have in mind is* 'the Nothing'; *Nothingness, Silence? Or, according to the opposite hypothesis, we would have to translate the title* Lecture on Nothing *as* Discours sur rien. *Which should we choose?*

J.C.: The first one, it seems to me.

D.C.: That would be the 'Western' solution. As with Eckhart — whom you often quote — Nothingness 'exists' and is the Deity *or the* ground *of* God. *In this sense, there is no place for absolute Nothingness, for pure Nothingness. In Zen isn't the void on the contrary a* nothing, *written without a capital* 'n'? *Isn't that where certain Japanese philosophers get the basis for differentiating Zen (or Oriental philosophies in general) from Western thought?*

J.C.: And what did my French translator do?

D.C.: He hesitates, sometimes opting for the capital letter sometimes for the small letter. Sometimes for the West, sometimes for the East!

J.C.: I wonder which should be chosen. But it's difficult because it's all wrapped up in intellectual categories. Naturally, saying 'Nothingness' is not going far enough either, because it still implies that Nothingness is a being. That's not very satisfactory.

D.C.: Then we must also reject that solution which only a moment ago you said we should accept?

J.C.: If you oppose Something and Nothing, you still remain within the game of intellectual categories. What I meant when speaking of the *nothing in between* is that the Nothingness in question is ... neither Being nor Nothingness.

D.C.: It is outside of the relationship between Being and Nothingness?

J.C.: That's right. Each time we establish a relationship, each time we connect two terms, we forget that we have to go back to zero before reaching the next term. The same goes for Being and Nothingness! We talk about and try to think through these notions – like sounds in music – and we forget what really happens. We forget that we must always return to zero in order to pass from one word to the next.

D.C.: You once spoke of an 'alternating current' ... Wouldn't Nothingness be discontinuity?

J.C.: It is the impossibility of stopping with a relative Nothing, with the relationship. The relationship comes afterward.

D.C.: Through the power of language, then, you are returning to an 'absolute' nothing?

J.C.: Yes, and I can thus stick with my first label: 'Nothingness.' On the condition that we don't let ourselves get carried away with words, we can accept it.

D.C.: Do your ideas on this come from Suzuki?

J.C.: Yes, and also from a wonderful book, *Neti, Neti*,[1] which taught me that, in the domain of created things, there is something which is, so to speak, nothing; and moreover, a nothing which has *nothing* in it. That's what the *nothing in between* is. More recently, I found the same idea in Buckminster Fuller. He describes the world to us as an ensemble of spheres between which there is a void, a necessary space. We have a tendency to forget that space. We leap across it to establish our relationships and connections. We believe that we can slip as in a continuity from one sound to the next, from one thought to the next. In reality, we fall down and we don't even realize it! We live, but living means crossing through the world of *relationships* or representations. Yet, we never see ourselves in the act of crossing that world! And we never do anything but that!

D.C.: Everything is quite simple then?

J.C.: I would say the opposite. It is our manner of thinking that is so simple, while our experience is always and in every case extremely complex. When we think, we continually return to those opposed pairs, sound and silence, Being and Nothingness. We do this to simplify experience which is far beyond that simplicity. Ultracomplicated and not at all reducible to the number two.

D.C.: Aren't we going to end up back at the number one, with a sort of monism?

J.C.: Buckminster Fuller insists on the number three,[2] and believes that there is hardly any useful thought which can advance without always taking at least three things into consideration at a time. And, as far as I'm concerned, the best way to escape the number two is to use chance operations. Because that lets an enormous amount of things enter into a single complex event. And thus we avoid that simplification characteristic of our way of thinking.

D.C.: Nevertheless, I wonder how you cannot be shocked by the mechanical, automatic character of chance operations. Isn't picking sounds by lot

[1] Mrs L.C. Beckett (New York: Ark Press, 1955)
[2] Or is it five? (John Cage; footnote of 1980.)

an easy way out of the problem? Whatever the role of chance may be in daily life, don't we have to admit that chance often oversimplifies things?

J.C.: But how can we explain the fact that we are present here, that we are in the present, but not in that present which would, for example, include fir trees in a forest? We owe this complexity to chance ... Our life is intensely complex, with layers of chance superimposed at every moment. Chance allows this and excludes that.

D.C.: It forces us to think presence and absence together?

J.C.: At least to reject exclusions, radical alternatives between opposites.

D.C.: The other day I was listening to Father Houang, who stated that there are three types of thought. Western thought, which endlessly poses dualities, but never resolves them; Chinese, which is the thought of wisdom and which reveals in each term of the duality the complement of the other; and Indian thought, which asserts that the two terms of the duality are one and the same thing. As for you, I believe you are more Chinese than Indian ...

J.C.: Yes, or at least, that is what I have become ...

D.C.: How did this happen?

J.C.: It was after 1945, between 1946 and 1947 I suppose, that I began to become seriously interested in the Orient. After studying Oriental thought as a whole, I took Suzuki's courses for three years, up until 1951. He taught at Columbia and I liked his lectures very much. Quite often he suggested that we read *Chuang-tze*. So at that time I read and reread *Chuang-tze*. And I deeply admired the writing, the thought. *Chuang-tze* is full of humor ... One of the characters, Chaos, is more loved than feared. Suzuki did not appreciate the *I Ching* as much; he seemed to consider it a very important book, but not one to be entirely accepted. I believe that, of all the books he mentioned to us, *Chuang-tze* was the one he preferred. I have worked a lot with *Chuang-tze*.

D.C.: But you don't reject anything in the I Ching?

J.C.: I do accept, I have always accepted everything the *I Ching* has revealed to me.

D.C.: Why?

J.C.: I never thought of not accepting it! That is precisely the first thing the *I Ching* teaches us: acceptance. It essentially advances this lesson: if we want to use chance operations, then we must accept the results. We have no right to use it if we are determined to criticize the results and to seek a better answer. In fact, the *I Ching* promises a completely sad lot to anyone who insists on getting a good answer. If I am unhappy after a chance operation, if the result does not satisfy me, by accepting it I at least have the chance to modify myself, to change myself. But if I insist on changing the *I Ching*, then it changes rather than I, and I have gained nothing, accomplished nothing!

D.C.: Didn't you say one day that the property of all poetry was neither to obtain nor to accomplish anything?

J.C.: Well, let's not talk about changes in terms of accomplishment ... But you can see that the *I Ching* orients us toward flexibility rather than toward inflexibility.

D.C.: The I Ching *bore out your idea of the changing of everything that is.*

J.C.: Our inflexible attitude towards change must cease. My own experience proved to me that all I need to do is to listen to the sounds around me. They change. I always and everywhere listen to the sounds surrounding me, but if I were to feel that one of them didn't please me or wasn't suitable for me – if I would have preferred that it didn't exist or hadn't happened – then you could immediately see why such a notion of preference is in a way illegitimate, since in fact the sound did occur.

D.C.: Is time the fact of appearing on the scene?

J.C.: Appearing, changing, and then disappearing: it is the accumulation of all that. And it is the fact of thinking this coming and going, this presence and absence, together.

D.C.: At Saint-Paul-de-Vence, at the time of the Museum Event *with Merce Cunningham, you replied to a few listeners who had criticized you for making noises of too great an intensity that these noises had come and disappeared despite you. You didn't actually want them yourself. The audience should imitate you in that acceptance not only of time, but of everything time brings and carries away with it.*

J.C.: That's right, people have often pointed that out to me. At the Museum of Modern Art, I replied that the louder the sound, the greater the chance it gave us to discipline ourselves.

D.C.: If you yourself as a composer cannot and do not want to intervene in the development of sounds and things, can there ever exist a technology that would permit us to act on the world? Deep inside yourself, you maintain a fatalism and indeed even an indifference to whatever happens. But isn't that attitude inhuman? How can Taoism be reconciled with modern science?

J.C.: That is a very serious question. I don't know if my answer will be completely satisfactory. First of all, I recognize that there exist aspects of our life which make it necessary to act on that life. But there are also times when it can be just as important, precisely in view of acting on life, for us not to try to influence it, but to become as open as possible to what passes and to what appears. In the case of sound, whether the sound be loud or soft, flat or sharp, or whatever you like, that doesn't constitute a sufficient motive for not opening ourselves up to what it is, as for any sound which may possibly occur. We must leave sounds alone.

D.C.: And is there a criterion which allows us to distinguish what we must leave alone from what we must change?

J.C.: As far as sounds are concerned, I can say that I have not yet heard a sound that was really unbearable.

D.C.: But noise is one of the sharpest or, if you prefer, gravest problems of our present environment!

J.C.: Many people consider some sounds dangerous. I have not yet heard any, despite my wanderings. I know that the government of the United States tried to construct machines designed to deafen people in case of riots or demonstrations, machines capable of producing sounds which would render those exposed to them definitively deaf. But, even with all that technology, they didn't come up with any useful results from their point of view. No really effective equipment has been perfected in that field. Also, they have more or less abandoned this idea of a police or military use of sounds.

D.C.: But you cannot deny allergies to noise. Nor acquired deafness.

J.C.: I don't deny them. I'm simply stating that, at the present time, noises cannot be mastered in a governmental or police manner. That doesn't mean that there is no place for fighting against noise pollution. But that also doesn't imply the negative aesthetic criterion which the refusal of noises as such would be. Indeed, on the contrary, I believe I am able to draw from my own experience the idea that our aesthetic attitude should become more and more open to whatever may happen. And if I were to try to answer you more completely, I would say that the notion of a change of existence in general, for the better rather than for the worse, and – this seems to be a different point of view – for the majority of people rather than for an élite, doesn't seem to me to be ultimately incompatible with an opening-up of possible aesthetic responses.

D.C.: Chuang-tze insists that non-action doesn't mean complete inaction, an idea that appears earlier in Lao-tze. Taoist quietism is consequently not at all comparable to the quietism of the Molinists or the Christian mystics.

J.C.: That's right, the role of action must be recognized within non-action. All you need is to be intelligent ... to know how to distinguish those aspects of existence in which there is, in an obvious way, good and evil, and to go in the direction of the good.

D.C.: Would you go so far as to give complete primary importance to this good, that is, to a concern for everyone's responsibility to others?

J.C.: Then it would be not only toward others, but also in relation to any being, living or not. Or as the Buddhists put it: for all beings, sentient and non-sentient.

D.C.: It seems to me that one of Koichi Tsujimura's phrases could help us out here. He defines the 'holy fool' of Zen as 'a man capable, in every simple and daily thing, of seeing the One and letting it act. Such a capacity is gentleness, gratitude, and mercy toward each thing, not only toward men, but toward everything that exists.'

J.C.: That text goes along with what I tried to say in the preface of my book *A Year From Monday*. Between your availability to experience whatever happens (what I called aesthetic openness a moment ago) and the desire to change the world (an active responsibility for the littlest things) there is no break or reversal. From *Silence* to *A Year From Monday*, I was dealing with the same problem. But it's not a question of Christian morality.

D.C.: Let's say, still following Tsujimura, that we're dealing with impersonal mercy, not charity or personal love.

J.C.: Still I must insist on this idea of responsibility for what is simplest. Water – what could be simpler? – could be provided to us not as chlorinated water but as mountain water, water from a stream or mountain spring. Because there and only there is water what it really is.

D.C.: Then utilities must be treated with the greatest deference?

J.C.: Take food, drink, transportation, communication lines, electricity, etc. For all of these, you can discover a good and an evil, a perfectly defined good and a perfectly defined evil. And we must strive for the good – which is, in itself, susceptible to change – with the aid of our technology. Buckminster Fuller demonstrated this. Men are going to become more and more numerous, but the amount of natural resources will not increase. Only technology can allow us to obtain more goods without having to work more. Only technology will procure enough resources for the increasing numbers of people who will be born.

D.C.: Can sounds be considered utilities?

J.C.: Apparently the attitude towards sounds is different since we can fully appreciate sounds only if we refrain from applying criteria of good and evil to them. If water ceases to be drinkable and if the air becomes unbreathable, how could we get even the slightest joy from a sound? We ought to reach the point of behaving towards utilities in the same way we behave towards sounds – that is, applying the criterion of good and evil only where it should be applied.

D.C.: In short, music as you conceive it is in its existence a function of the technology which you say will modify our approach to utilities.

J.C.: Certainly. In a more or less brief amount of time, we should have access to every television broadcast, every art reproduction, film, or desired book, thanks to video. And music will find itself developing in and through that abundance made available to us by the media.

D.C.: There will be no more concert halls?

J.C.: Even if they no longer seemed to fill a need, why would we do away with them? Abundance proceeds by accumulation, not by selection or elimination. Why shouldn't we have useless theaters for unnecessary concerts, to which we would still go?

D.C.: Perhaps that is what is hardest to grasp for anyone who accuses you of wanting to sack and destroy everything like those musicians clouded by their own egos. You have an entirely different conception of music in general and of your own music ...

J.C.: I don't see why *my* music, even granting that I may have some sort of property right over it, should replace existing music or dominate music to come! Sounds have always existed, they will continue to emerge after my death. They have always coexisted with different kinds of oral, written, or electronic music. All I am doing is directing attention to the sounds of the environment. The music world shouldn't disappear just because I am trying to restore dignity to these sounds. I hope that in the future Beethoven will continue to be celebrated!

D.C.: But in a slightly different way than he used to be. In 1970, works like Ludwig Van *by Mauricio Kagel or* Opus 1970 *by Stockhausen, works which would have been unthinkable without you, without the example set by* Variations IV, *were already the topic of conversation. In large measure it is thanks to your activities that it is becoming easier to* use *Beethoven – like a 'utility'.*

J.C.: We celebrate Beethoven with less gravity than we did twenty or fifty years ago. And that's not a bad thing ... why should a celebration have to be sad?

D.C.: Yesterday Pierre Belfond asked you if you would ever agree to conduct one of Beethoven's symphonies – the Ninth for example. Could you repeat your answer?

J.C.: I told him that I would agree if I could use enough musicians to conduct, in one single concert, all nine symphonies superimposed![1]

D.C.: And, of course, you weren't kidding?

J.C.: In any case, it seems difficult for me to really believe any more in a music which is not flexible. That doesn't mean that fixed, determined music should cease to exist. What should hardly ever exist any more is blind piety with regard to whatever is not flexible. All the seriousness which the period of 'great music' lavished on the construction of inflexible edifices we can now safely transfer to other tasks. Like the improvement of utilities, among others. Likewise, all the importance we accorded to quarrels between composers – and here I am thinking of the entire beginning of the twentieth century, almost up the the present, when we were forever wondering who invented what and on what date – seems really anachronistic to me. We have better things to do! But that's all because at the time of fixed, determined music, the simplest score required a signature and served as an introduction to the world of so and so, to the poetic universe of so and so. It was an external sign of wealth, a sign of prestige. However, there's no reason to liquidate this past of inflexibility. We don't have to deprive ourselves of a single pleasure – especially not useless pleasures ... not even the tonal archaeology still so important to some of our contemporaries. These things must be able to coexist and accumulate. Everyone deserves to have his own music, the music he freely chooses – whether or not he is a composer! And each person must be able to live in a way that suits him.

D.C.: Such an ideal is much more individualist than social ...

J.C.: We need a society in which every man may live in a manner freely determined by him himself. I am not the first person to say so – I am only repeating Buckminster Fuller.

D.C.: The liberty which you envision would, then, be integral and universal?

J.C.: Yes.

D.C.: But doesn't the welfare of others come before that liberty? Mustn't each individual first think of others?

J.C.: The best – and only – way to let someone be what he is, and to think of him, thus to think of the other, is to let him think himself in his own terms. As that's a difficult thing to do, and as it's impossible to get yourself to think of the other in his own terms, all we can do is to leave space around each person. To be as careful as possible not to form any

[1]Hal Freedman, working at the Yale Electronic Music Studio (1974-75) superimposed all parts of Wagner's Ring Cycle in *Ring Précis* and in *Précis 2* all of Bartok's String Quartets. I recently heard both of Freedman's works and found them extremely beautiful. (John Cage; footnote of 1980.)

ideas about what each person should or should not do. To strive to appreciate, as much as possible, everything he does do — even down to his slightest actions.

D.C.: We must keep ourselves from imposing some idea of what is good.

J.C.: That's exactly it. Impose nothing. Live and let live. Permit each person, as well as each sound, to be the center of creation.

THIRD INTERVIEW

The aesthetic thought of India and the theory of emotions
Access to impersonality
Accepting
Homage to Coomaraswamy
Meister Eckhart
About Alan Watts on the correct usage of the Far East
In praise of Buckminster Fuller
The Marxist objection
Discussion: the meaning of anarchy
The example of Thoreau
Criticism of prisons
The need for a poetic life: Norman O. Brown
Attitudes toward technique
Indeterminacy applied to language: *Thoreau Mix*
Homage to Duchamp
About lettrism
'A poetry of infinite possibilities'
From *Silence* to *A Year from Monday*
The mosaic form or chance in letters
Significance of Joyce
Vocal music: Cathy Berberian and the *Song Books*
Non linearity

D.C.: In your Eastern itinerary, first there was India, then the Far East.

J.C.: Yes, you could conclude an evolution of that kind from my works. The early ones could have been considered expressive. It sometimes seemed to me that I managed to 'say' something in them. When I discovered India, what I was saying started to change. And when I discovered China and Japan, I changed the *very fact of saying anything*: I said nothing anymore. Silence: since everything already communicates, why wish to communicate?

D.C.: Tell me about India.

J.C.: Thanks to India I said or expressed a certain number of things connected with the seasons: creation, preservation, destruction, quiescence. I was especially convinced of the truth of the Hindu theory of art. I tried to make my works correspond to that theory. It teaches us that for there to be *rasa,* that is, aesthetic emotion on the part of the listener, the work must evoke one of the permanent modes of emotion [: *bhava* – the mode to which all other emotions must be subordinated.] There can also be a combination of two permanent modes.

D.C.: What are the permanent modes?

J.C.: [According to Hindu theory, there are eight involuntary emotions: the *attvabhava.* There are also thirty-three transitory modes of emotion, which derive from pleasure and suffering. But all that is nothing compared to the nine permanent emotions. They are permanent, that is, they lead to the true *rasa;* they are that without which there is no *rasa.*] They are the heroic, the erotic, the wondrous, the tranquil, sorrow, the odious, the furious, the terrible, and – I don't know how to say the ninth one correctly ... possibly – the mirthful. Tranquility lies between the four 'white' modes and the four 'black' modes; it is their normal propensity. That is why it is important to express it before the others, without even worrying about expressing the others. It is the most important emotion.

D.C.: And why didn't you hold to these great modes of Indian aesthetics? Did dissatisfaction motivate you at all?

J.C.: My ballet, *The Seasons,* and the *Sonatas and Interludes* for the prepared piano were fully expressive works, as well as my *String Quartet.* In 1950, I composed *Sixteen Dances* for Merce Cunningham and I was wondering how to achieve a clear graphic view of the rhythmic structures I wanted to use. I arrived at the idea of using charts, diagrams. And while notating the sounds and aggregates of sounds on those diagrams, I realized that by thus inscribing them, they were sufficient in themselves. Instead of transferring what I wanted onto the diagrams, I could just as well begin by directly drawing the combined movements of the sounds, without having to decide on a particular movement beforhand. The decision could be made by itself, without me, *just as well as* with me. My tastes seemed secondary to me.

D.C.: *Did you immediately feel the need to see this idea through to its logical conclusion?*

J.C.: No, not immediately. The *Concerto for Prepared Piano and Chamber Orchestra* is an example of the lack of resolution I felt at that time, around 1950 to 1951, between letting the aggregates of sounds emerge by themselves, by the technique of direct inscription onto the diagrams. And continuing to experiment with my own personal tastes. These are the two poles of that *Concerto.* I talked about that at the Museum of Modern Art.

D.C.: *You said that everything is completed in the third movement, by the abandonment of personal taste. The conflict is resolved, then.*

J.C.: Yes, at that moment I had decided to accept rather than seek to control. The pianist, who, in the second movement, followed the orchestra as a disciple follows his master, in a sort of antiphony, then comes to join the latter in his impersonality. At the same time I grant more and more space to silences. Which may signify that I ceased being a composer. The silences speak for me, they demonstrate quite well that *I* am no longer there.

D.C.: *They are no longer expressive silences?*

J.C.: No. They say nothing. Or, if you prefer, they are beginning to speak *Nothingness*!

D.C.: *But your earlier works were filled with silence ...*

J.C.: Expressive silences.

D.C.: *This penchant for silence struck me in the* Sonatas *and* Interludes ...

J.C.: Which date from a period when I was a reader of Coomaraswamy — that is, when I dreamed of the Orient, not so much of the Far East.

D.C.: Are you indebted to Coomaraswamy for your Hindu culture?

J.C.: He was the one, in the first place, who convinced me of our naiveté with regard to the Orient. At the time – it was at the end of the war, or just afterwards – people still said that the East and the West were absolutely foreign, separate entities. And that a Westerner did not have the right to profess an Eastern philosophy. It was thanks to Coomaraswamy that I began to suspect that this was not true, and that Eastern thought was no less admissible for a Westerner than is European thought.

D.C.: Despite linguistic barriers and differences in mentality?

J.C.: Do you honestly think that none exist within Europe, or between Europe and America?

D.C.: So you adhered to Coomaraswamy's theses on the correspondence of Indian aesthetics to Occidental theories of art at the end of the Middle Ages, as he develops them in The Transformation of Nature in Art?

J.C.: Not exactly. I read the *Dance of Shiva* which is simply about India, [but also, you must admit, about Nietzsche and 'the intellectual fraternity of the human species'.]

D.C.: The Transformation of Nature in Art *deals not only with Hindu theories on art, but also with what the author considers to be the greatest aesthetics of the West: Meister Eckhart's. What do you think of such a comparison?*

J.C.: In the past, when I was reading Meister Eckhart, I discovered ideas which from my point of view were completely analogous to those my Oriental readings afforded me. I even wonder whether these ideas came to Meister Eckhart from the Orient, through the intermediary of Arabic philosophies.

D.C.: In any case, it is remarkable that Suzuki continually referred to Meister Eckhart to authenticate the message of Zen for his Western readers or listeners.

J.C.: Yes, he frequently spoke of him, and often quotes him in his writings.

D.C.: So you were not taken out of your element by following Suzuki to Columbia University? In your eyes, does Eckhart find his place more naturally amongst the Zen masters than amongst Indian mystics?

J.C.: That is indeed the impression I had when reading him. [When he talks about the *Gottheit,* the Deity, or even the *Grund,* the Basis, it sounds like Zen; that becomes clear when you examine him in detail.]

D.C.: You yourself quote Meister Eckhart rather frequently. Grund returns like a litany at the end of each paragraph in your lecture on indeterminacy.

J.C.: [I wanted to keep the German word because my lecture was given in Germany ...]

D.C.: *It was better to speak German to Germans? Your argument is typically Zen!*

J.C.: [My entire lecture is an illustration with musical examples borrowed from the works of Bach, other contemporary composers and myself, of a speech] Suzuki gave on the nature of the mind and the function of the ego, which either closes itself off from its experience, whether that comes from within or from the outside, or suppresses itself as ego and becomes open to all possibilities, whether internal or external. What Suzuki said about this seemed, and still seems, to me directly applicable to music.

D.C.: *But your originality lies in not limiting yourself to that application. 'Oriental influences' are usually noticeable only at the tonal or formal levels in the works of composers who nonetheless do not at all alter their vision of the world. When Messiaen uses the* tala, *he is no less a Catholic musician. On the other hand, you seek first of all to renovate your mental equipment.*

J.C.: Let's say instead that I strive toward the non-mental.

D.C.: *Yet, one is tempted to wonder how it happened that Zen – which in the past, and particularly in the realm of painting, gave rise to so many minutely elaborated works, and which took for granted the subservience of the artist to the finished object which he was about to bring into existence – how then Zen was able to lead you to works which could no longer really be called works, which can't really be called anything anymore.*

J.C.: But Zen itself has changed! It is not possible today to repeat what Zen produced yesterday.

D.C.: *Then you are not really a Zenist?*

J.C.: If you mean a Buddhist monk, no!

D.C.: *But your music is the Buddha?*

J.C.: [No more than any other!]

D.C.: *Then where should we situate it? Where do you situate yourself in all this change?*

J.C.: We are at a stage of change with which many elements – and events – are collaborating. There are many voices. Mine is only one of them. If what I say only has a small effect, it is not of the slightest importance. For there are so many other voices speaking that the effect will come. Anyway, things are really changing.

D.C.: Then I would like to know your opinion on certain ideas that Alan Watts developed in the past which seem to me to go against what you are attempting. In Beat Zen, Square Zen, and Zen, *he refers to artists who use Zen to justify 'arbitrary gratuitousness'. He mentions in particular musicians who compose silent music, and he qualifies this practice as beat Zen. Don't you feel like one of his targets?*

J.C.: I do indeed know that Watts had me in mind when he wrote that, but he hadn't yet read my books. After reading them, he changed his mind! His point of view concerning music was that city noises shouldn't be excerpted and transplanted into a concert hall. Separation of sounds from their environment was in his opinion deadly. Well, I never claimed otherwise! And my deepest wish is that people finally listen to sounds in their own habitat. In their natural space. Granted he didn't like my silent music; he considered it only 'modern art' – a provocation. But he read my book *Silence,* and his opinion toward me changed entirely. Today we are in full agreement, I think.

D.C.: Then I suppose you share his opinions on the harm done to Zen during its Westernization, on the square Zen mentality (intellectual snobism) and the beat attitude (rash hippy curiosity)?

J.C.: [Yes, Alan Watts is undisputably erudite, but he has gone beyond his erudition, although what he writes is very readable. And he is not a hippie. He defines himself as a 'bohemian'. I think, as he does, that Zen is on the 'bohemians'' side, not necessarily on the hippies' or even the Sinologists' side.] Now, we must add that Alan Watts has never had any particular taste for the arts. But he has for thought. And for cooking. He is an extraordinary cook!

D.C.: In an interview he gave a while ago,[1] he did clearly express his opinions on taste: 'Ultimately', he said, 'we are never anything but what we eat ... As for myself, I know what I want. If you are interested, right now I'd like a veal pâté.'

J.C.: He is absolutely right! He speaks exactly like Thoreau, for whom there wasn't even the slightest separation between mind and body. Thoreau remarked that his thoughts were better when he was well than when he was sick.

D.C.: And you find in Watts that same sense of respect for utilities which you have.

[1]*L'Express,* No. 1000; September 7, 1970.

J.C.: He also said that private property would crumble away thanks to technology. He has ideas very close to my own on abundance and accumulation. He deals with the problems of quantity, as does Buckminster Fuller; that is, we will have quality *in excess, to a superfluous degree,* once we have learned to obtain quantity.

D.C.: *Is it because of Fuller's influence that he talks like that?*

J.C.: If you are asking whether someone can have an influence on someone else, well, I believe that Fuller's books are, in any case, the most important ones around today. But the question about the influence of Fuller himself remains secondary! The world, in all the ways it relates to utilities, is in such a state of disorder that our most urgent goal must be to resolve its physical problems. Or even, as Fuller says, to change the environment. In my books, in my lectures, I have often dealt with other subjects. For the past several years, I have started talking about utilities. Watts, too. But beyond whether or not Fuller has had any influence, what is important is that the first great change will take place in and through the achievement of what Buckminster Fuller has been saying.

D.C.: *Then you do indeed consider his thought more decisive than any other?*

J.C.: It is an absolutely elementary and fundamental thought for the survival of the human race. I see no other possibility. If I were to hear another solution mentioned, I would be very interested, but I have not found a single one.[1]

D.C.: *Could you describe the main points of Buckminster Fuller's solution?*

J.C.: It consists of examining our relationship with the technical world and in seeing to it that this relationship is regenerative. All we have done is to disorganize the utilities. We subject them to our concerns for production and property, while what should have been done is to universalize the benefits of technology. We should reach a stage where machines free us from work. To do so, we must rethink our models of order and disorder on a world-wide scale. We must let technology act, let it be. That is only possible if we think in terms of the whole, whereas until now our thoughts have been partial, political, or economic. All that

[1] I have become more and more interested in the ideas of Mao Zedong. The Maoist model managed to free a quarter of humanity: that gives cause for thought. Today, without hesitation, I would say that, for the moment, Maoism is our greatest reason for optimism. We must welcome its lessons with great attentiveness. Certainly, it is an eminently Chinese movement which we would not be able to import as it is; and we must avoid using it in a scholastic way. I am however convinced that, henceforth, if we were to manage to combine it with Thoreau's anarchism and Fuller's apoliticism we would obtain something which would provide a *real* solution to our problems. (John Cage: footnote of 1972.)

should count now is the universalization of thought. You see, it is not a solution, it is a program!

D.C.: A Marxist would raise the objection that this program is utopian, if not dangerous. For, he would tell you, the most striking aspect of the current social situation, the economic struggle, goes unmentioned. Don't you think that this so generous vision of things overlooks daily necessity, and that it lacks a theory of the relationships of production?

J.C.: But it is work, the fact of working, which is the oppression. Changing economic systems will not change the fact of work. It's asking for a surplus of work. What we should seek is something altogether different, the suppression of work.

D.C.: What do you think of the Marxist analyses that have sometimes been proposed for some of your works? The German critic Heinz-Klaus Metzger believed your insertion of a dancer, Merce Cunningham, into the traditional role of orchestra conductor (Concert for Piano and Orchestra) *anticipated revolution. But doesn't the revolution seek to kill the orchestra conductor who directs the world — that is, capitalism?*

J.C.: Unfortunately for that analysis, I believe that the role of orchestra conductor in my 1958 *Concert* is not a caricature. Not of a conductor or a leader, but of a utility! Consider an orchestra; if each musician had a watch and if all these watches could be synchronized there would be no need for an orchestra conductor. But the musicians don't have a watch, and it's better to have at least one person around who has one – that is, a conductor who could *be* one! All that supposes a measured time, regularly tapped out: the tempo of a work. So, I added to my *Concert* the requirement that it had to go at different speeds. If you only have one precise chronometer, a regular time-piece, you will never obtain but one single speed. But with a dancer scanning an irregular tempo, no one has to feel bound by clock time. And with a small advance in technology, we could easily create a mechanical clock with a variety of speeds. Or we could even produce, as Wittgenstein projected, a ruler which would not be straight. Then we could definitively get rid of *measure*.[1] My solution, in the *Concert for Piano and Orchestra,* is not yet technological; it is hand-made.

D.C.: Do you mean that you reject all political interpretations of your activities?

J.C.: He who says politics says government, and I have often asserted that if there is indeed one useless thing it is government! Fuller even put

[1]Currently I enjoy the use of a *Gerber Variable Scale* both in the composition of graphic works and in *Thirty Pieces for Five Orchestras.* This scale enables me to divide any length into sixty-four parts. (John Cage: footnote of 1981)

it better than I. He says that if we were to take all the politicians, government chiefs, ministers, and other bureaucrats, and if we were to shoot them off to the moon, everything would probably go along just as well, if not better, at least no worse, than when we keep them with us the way we do. While if we were to send to the moon the technicians in charge of the utilities, we would suffer very quickly. So we have no need for government. No more than for politics! In this morning's *Le Figaro*, someone from the government said that an entity like the State exists because of our need to defend the weak from being controlled by the strong. What does this formula really mean? That the State's mission is to protect the weak, who have become rich, from the strong, who are poor? Don't you think that this is the real meaning of that statement?

D.C.: *Probably. But if you say that, aren't you participating in politics?*

J.C.: Not at all. I am only noting how things really are. If I were practicing politics, I would be trying to impose a government that according to me was better. But there is no better government.

D.C.: *Doesn't what you are saying separate you from all Marxism?*

J.C.: When I say that there is no better government, it doesn't mean that the present government is good. It implies that any government in whatever form is to be rejected. It is the *fact of governing* which must be suppressed. That is what we must fight for. And this struggle must go on in all areas. Most important is the area of technology. Thoreau says nothing else. You know, technology is not foreign to Thoreau.

D.C.: *Can Thoreau really lead us to a contemporary change in political or social order?*

J.C.: There are the Danes, Gandhi, and Martin Luther King. That makes at least three cases of deep change in the lives of entire peoples. All three are due to Thoreau. [In Denmark, during the war, the Nazis ordered all Jews to wear the yellow star. The resistance movement managed to get Thoreau's *Essay on Civil Disobedience* distributed everywhere. So, first the King, then all the Danes began to wear the yellow star. Enraged, the Nazis locked the King in his palace and said he was sick. Then, all the Danes started sending him flowers, and all those who could went to the palace with their flowers. The Nazis had to give in and free the King.] It was from Thoreau that Gandhi and Martin Luther King found the energy which allowed them to practice passive resistance and non-violence and to convince those around them to do the same. Both of them said so quite clearly. The Indians and Blacks owe an immense debt to Thoreau. And I think that we must not minimize the role of non-violence.

D.C.: *I wonder if these three examples will suffice to convince those who, today, insist on making a primarily political reading of your music and your actions.*

J.C.: If they make it primarily political, it is because they cling to the idea of government. Well, if you look closely, in detail, at what a government is, you cannot avoid a feeling of disgust. In 1967, I went to a trial. It was in Cincinnati and I was invited by a psychoanalyst. They made all sorts of very poor blacks appear there. Every night they caught them on the streets of Cincinnati, and they brought them before the Court to be condemned to a certain period of imprisonment or placed in a rehabilitation program. Well, do you know what they had done? They had committed a real crime: playing poker, even though it's against the law! That's all they did. And all the rich people in Cincinnati could very well have played poker the same evening. No one ever bothers them. I think everyone, rich and poor, plays poker in the evening in Cincinnati ...

D.C.: *You're talking about one injustice, but does this example permit us to extrapolate an opposition to all politics and all governments on a universal level?*

J.C.: I believe that organization, which is bound up with the very idea of governing, and which is a general phenomenon, incites all the particular cases of that kind; they would not exist without it. Consider bureaucracy, which is common to all so-called developed countries. We are all its victims at every moment of our existence. Even I, who remain outside a lot of things, I notice it too. The other day, in Paris, I received a payment notice from O.R.T.F., and I went to their big round building. I entered the first office, and they looked at the pay order; a second office, and they looked at it. Only in the third office ... only then did they give me a little money. You mean three bureaucrats have to look at it so no one will be at fault? What waste! And it's a daily problem!

D.C.: *You have a very broad definition of government – you not only include politics, but bureaucracy as well.*

J.C.: Yes, all forms of organization, and everyone who wants those forms, that organization. I hold a great deal against this system of organization, that is, [the separation ot things which should not be separated.] We categorize everyone. We send the old here, the young there. We ship adolescents off to war. We send everyone to prison every day: the children to school, the parents to the office or the factory, the musicians to concert halls in the evening. And we separate the rich from the poor. What is a government? That which maintains these divisions. In other words, our body is divided against itself. Just about everywhere anybody has tried to organize, that is *to articulate that body,* it doesn't work; we are not dealing with a healthy organism.

D.C.: To hear you speak, politics would not at all be the struggle against oppression and for liberty, the struggle against the evils of society, but the origin of those evils?

J.C.: Politics consists of affirming and wanting domination. Norman O. Brown has admirably grasped that the present problem is not political. The problem is to put an end to politics. That is also my opinion.

D.C.: So, in the polemic which opposed Herbert Marcuse to Norman O. Brown on this subject, you would place yourself on Brown's side?

J.C.: Without even the slightest hesitation. I consider *Love's Body* a great book. Norman O. Brown completely rejects politics, Marcuse fights for it.

D.C.: In Life Against Death, *Brown maintains the need to break down the opposition between the life instinct and death instinct. You apply to society what Brown said of the body.*

J.C.: Brown particularly and compellingly demonstrates in *Love's Body* that to bring our body to its fullness we must open ourselves to *imagination*. Brown's notion of true life is poetic. And he has seen quite well that politics on the other hand consists in suppressing life, at least wherever it is poetic.

D.C.: And do you picture this poetic life as following Thoreau's example?

J.C.: Yes, to the extent that Thoreau envisioned anarchy without police. It's not a new idea. But it seems to me that it can be achieved or is achievable only through technology. Thoreau shows us that we have very little direct contact with government, generally utterly formal matters which can be quickly forgotten or broken. What Thoreau insists on is the looseness of these ties, these chains. We wouldn't be able to survive if they were tighter.

D.C.: Nevertheless, when Thoreau refused to pay his taxes they really did put him in prison ...

J.C.: Yes, but for only one night. His aunt paid his bail; what's more, he was furious about being released so quickly. This episode, like Thoreau's entire life, demonstrates that you can free yourself ... We have trouble imagining it but the organization only holds together because we support it.

D.C.: You were saying there was technology in Thoreau. He, however, is famous for his hatred of 'civilization'. He was indignant over the idea that the water from his pond could supply the town of Concord.

J.C.: But his life at Walden was, technologically, extremely fruitful. He was the first to have the idea of making a pencil,[1] rather than inserting a piece of lead between two little pieces of wood. But he only wanted to produce two or three. His idea was that we possess technical objects in the wrong way. For example, we use trains, we travel. And what did we have to do for this? We just paid for a ticket. We don't even know what a railroad is. A legitimate use of technical objects is to mold them to our purposes. Or to get close enough to them to understand their possibilities. Thoreau could quite easily tolerate the existence of railroads, and even very close to where he lived. But he knew how to rig his boat and make sails for it. He worked constantly and brilliantly at all forms of manual labor. Technology was not, in his time, around the middle of the nineteenth century, what it has become. But we aren't following Thoreau's example. We could do much more – we could study technical objects closely, live with them, not be prisoners of our technological surroundings. Abolish that prison, too!

D.C.: *If I may now transpose everything you just said to the area of* language, *it seems to me that Thoreau is no less fascinating when he writes, when he frees words. Isn't he concerned with opening up words? And haven't you taken up this concern in turn? Aren't your lectures, for example, musical works in the manner of the different chapters of* Walden?

J.C.: They are when sounds are words. But I must say that I have not yet carried language to the point to which I have taken musical sounds. I have not made noise with it. I hope to make something other than language from it.

D.C.: *How do you expect to accomplish that?*

J.C.: It is that aspect, the *impossibility of language*, that interests me at present. I am now working on that problem in a text taken straight from the *Song Books*, which deals directly with letters, syllables, etc., mixing them in such a way that you could call it a *Thoreau Mix*. It is my most recent work.[2]

D.C.: *In the* Song Books *you had already invented an entire language: false French.*

J.C.: What I am working on now goes in the same direction. I approach language in different ways so as to reach a discourse which *appears* to make sense. One day, I gave *Thoreau Mix* in the form of a lecture. It lasted forty minutes. Well, the result has no meaning, or only a very little. But while I was practicing for that lecture, I discovered that I

[1] As we know it, that is, with lead down the center of a piece of wood. (John Cage: footnote of 1980.)
[2] I have since made *Music of Thoreau* from it; it's the work I entitled *Mureau*, which I myself performed in concert. (John Cage: footnote of 1972.)

could improvise, but only along the same lines! And yet, I didn't know if I would be able to do it before an audience. When I improvised by myself, I used all the resources of my voice and all the elements of language without falling back upon known words or a syntax. I found this experience thrilling. As for my text, I noticed on two occasions, while giving my lecture in Virginia and Philadelphia, that a lot of people in the audience were suddenly extremely happy. They suddenly felt liberated, yes, almost immediately delivered from all those constraints of language that we consider fixed once and for all and that we imagine to be impossible to eliminate.

D.C.: You also liberate typography. Through chance.

J.C.: To verify the appearance or impossibility of a meaning? Yes, there's the 'multiple' that I made with a designer, Calvin Sumsion. It was in 1969 and was called *Not Wanting to Say Anything about Marcel*. It's a tribute to Marcel Duchamp. But I didn't want to say anything about Duchamp, as the title indicates. So I subjected a dictionary to the *I Ching*; I picked words, then letters from those words, and finally, their arrangement in space by chance operations. I distributed these words, according to a typography likewise based on chance, on sheets of plexiglass. I put the eight sheets of plexiglass parallel to each other on a wooden base. Thus the letters appear in depth, they are superimposed and combined as we look at them. There are four bases, each holding eight sheets.[1] The whole thing comes from chance, including the colors. It is an object that has no meaning and which cannot be said to refer to a text. And yet, it seems to me that Duchamp would have been, as he used to say, 'amused' by that object.

D.C.: If I understand you, these words are a continuation of your strictly speaking literary texts: for example, those which were the result of chance operations in Silence *or* A Year from Monday.

J.C.: As soon as you surpass the level of the word, everything changes; my essays in the books you mention, didn't deal with the question of the impossibility or possibility of *meaning*. They took for granted that meaning exists.

D.C.: Would you compare your way of presenting *the problem of the appearance of meaning to the way the* lettristes *envision their own activity? They take a randomly attained sample number of letters or elements of language. They assemble those letters and progress from letters to pseudo-words, and from pseudo-words to pseudo-sentences to constitute the apparent homologue of a language. But this language is not a language.*

[1]Actually, there are eight 'plexigrams' and two lithographs in this work. (John Cage: footnote of 1980.)

J.C.: I don't pretend to end up with a language either.

D.C.: But the lettristes don't consider the non-language they achieve to be poetry. Or music.

J.C.: How can they avoid music?

D.C.: They distinguish lettrism, which specifies no voice pitch, from music, which is based on pitch and instrumentation.

J.C.: That seems quite puzzling to me. Music as I envision it can indeed be separated from instruments and the notion of pitch.

D.C.: And as far as I know, they very rarely allude to your activities. They must take you for a belated disciple of Russolo ...

J.C.: At any rate, my musical works, strictly speaking, have managed to arouse either indignation or sympathy – nothing compared to my books. You can't imagine how many people were touched by Silence! I received many letters, sometimes extremely lucid, always interesting. Next to that, the reactions to my music are predictable ...

D.C.: Since you alluded to Silence, how did you compose that book? Certainly you must have chosen your own texts to make them go together.

J.C.: I am not at all responsible for that choice. It is simply a result. I gave the people at Wesleyan University everything, absolutely everything I had written. The choice was made outside of my presence and my responsibility. So was the order of the pieces.

D.C.: Then that book doesn't belong to you?

J.C.: Yes, there is one idea that came from me. The idea of distributing stories here and there! And I also take credit for a few general suggestions concerning the order of the book as a whole. As for the rest, I think that my editor at Wesleyan did a fine job.[1]

D.C.: Where did the title come from?

J.C.: Me. The book was put together before a title had been found for it. And it appeared to me, when I went through my work, or what was to become my work, that the experience I had had in the sound-proof room at Harvard was a turning point. I had honestly and naïvely thought that some actual silence existed. So I had not really thought about the question of silence. I had not really put silence to the test. I had never looked into its impossibility. So when I went into that sound-proof room, I really expected to hear nothing. With no idea of what nothing could sound like. The instant I heard myself producing two sounds, my blood

[1]The late J.R. de la Torre Bueno, 'Bill' Bueno. (John Cage: footnote of 1980.)

circulating and my nervous system in operation, I was stupefied. For me, that was the turning point.

D.C.: Then, apparently, you stopped composing. Just as Duchamp, apparently, stopped painting after Le Grand Verre.

J.C.: Yes, he pretended to stop. At the same time that he kept on going. Do you know his posthumous work?

D.C.: La Mariée nue? *I read Yve-Alain Bois' text.*[1]

J.C.: It's all Duchamp. He spent twenty years, ten more than for *Le Grand Verre*, collecting all the objects for this extraordinary collage. He constructed a wall of bricks he had sent from Spain. He himself modeled in plaster covered by a stretched pigskin the body of a woman which you can see through two holes in the old door ... And all that while pretending to do nothing!

D.C.: Critics are perpetually linking you with Duchamp. Yet, the differences between you are significant. Not only have you not in fact stopped composing, you have never tried to persuade anyone of your silence. Yet, you have composed while denying that you are a composer. In a way, you are at once very close to Duchamp and anti-Duchamp. Your use of silence is not the same as his.

J.C.: I must confess that the contradiction, composing and not composing, has haunted me for a long time. Do you know the story of my relationship with psychoanalysis? It's short. It must have been around 1945. I was disturbed. Some friends advised me to see an analyst. All the psychoanalyst was able to tell me was that thanks to him I was going to be able to produce more music, tons of music! I never went back.

D.C.: Then, does 'silence' as you understand it now represent the style of life you desire and which is probably best characterized by Jean Grenier's expression 'an inchoative creation'?

J.C.: It's the poetic life.

D.C.: Why do you insist on that word poetry?

J.C.: There is poetry as soon as we realize that we possess nothing.

D.C.: But if the book entitled Silence *translates your thinking accurately, it should have remained without a sequel. Or, at least, any sequel should have also been called* Silence.

J.C.: But I don't possess silence.

D.C.: Well, where did the title of your second book, A Year from Monday, *come from?*

[1]In the periodical *VH 101*, No.3; Autumn 1970, p.63ff. The exact title of Duchamp's work is *Étant donné: 1° La chute d'eau, 2° Le gaz d'éclairage.*

J.C.: From a plan a group of friends and I made to meet each other again in Mexico 'a year from next Monday'. We were together on a Saturday. And we were never able to fulfil that plan. It's a form of silence ...

D.C.: *Is your second book very different from the first one?*

J.C.: It deals in particular with change. Consequently, it touches on plans. Or at least, it englobes something in the future – keeping the future in sight. Frankly, when I thought of the title, I wasn't being pessimistic, contrary to what you might be led to think from what I'm saying. The very fact that our plan failed, the fact that we were unable to meet does not mean that anything failed. The plan wasn't a failure.

D.C.: *In that work, you owe many of your texts to chance. The proportion is higher than in* Silence. *And it also differs from* Silence *in its typography; it's much more varied.*

J.C.: It's a way of presenting my ideas, which, partly under McLuhan's influence, have dealt more and more with the media.

D.C.: *People have sometimes objected to the 'mosaic' nature of* Gutenburg Galaxy. *Why should a book reflect the innovations of its content with its form?*

J.C.: Perhaps because the difference critics think they have to find between form and content doesn't exist.

D.C.: *Isn't there a contradiction in asserting throughout a work that the very notion of an opus or a book is outdated, while devoting many pages to demonstrating that outdatedness?*

J.C.: The *Gutenberg Galaxy* is made up of borrowings and collages: McLuhan applies what I call silence to all areas of knowledge, that is, he lets them speak. The death of the book is not the end of language: it continues. Just as in my case, silence has invaded everything, and there is still music. There is even more and more of it, once all psychoanalysis has been pushed aside! Thanks to silence, noise – not just a selection of certain noises, but the multiplicity of all noises that exist or may occur – makes a definitive entrance into my music. Typographic changes, like the 'mosaic' form, are noises which erupt in the book! At one and the same time, the book is condemned to nonexistence and the book comes into being. It can welcome everything.

D.C.: *Without a doubt, the book is no longer that linear tool in which we have learned to take pride.*

J.C.: That is because it can receive anything. And it will work even better when it breaks all restrictive conventions, all forms of organization, all the norms, including typography.

D.C.: And Joyce is the origin of all that.

J.C.: Certainly. I would say, however, that my work is much less dense than Joyce's. Joyce compresses what he says extraordinarily. And that goes for my music as well. Feldman is right to find it too restrictive. What I have done musically doesn't come from as broad a comprehension of possibilities as what Joyce did in literature.

D.C.: Weren't you tempted to put one of Joyce's texts directly to music?

J.C.: Yes, of course. You know my melody for voice and closed piano, *The Wonderful Widow of Eighteen Springs*. And one of these days I hope to finish the composition of the *Ten Thunderclaps*, also from Joyce.[1] In the *Song Books*, too, I have a text which comes from him.

D.C.: The Song Books *then reflect more than just Satie and Thoreau?*

J.C.: No. Each of the ninety pieces can either relate or not relate to the subject, which is 'We connect Satie and Thoreau.' When the song doesn't relate to the subject, it can relate to Joyce or someone else. And as it happens, for one of the songs I used Joyce.

D.C.: Then, far from being entirely subject to chance, the elaboration of this work appeals to a concerted reflection?

J.C.: I simply, and very quickly, looked for some authors different from Satie and Thoreau. And the first one I found was Joyce. You know, I had to compose the *Song Books* very quickly! In three days I just about conceived the entire work.

D.C.: You managed to imagine all that complexity of adapted, copied, and mixed texts in three days? And also the gestural, scenic and tonal effects?

J.C.: I really had to hurry. I only had a very small amount of time.

D.C.: Looking at the enormous score you ended up with, I would never have suspected such speed. I was especially aware of the difficulty of what you were asking the singers to do.

J.C.: On the subject of vocal technique: in a few days, we are going to perform the *Song Books* again, but only as a duet, Cathy Berberian and I, with David Tudor's and maybe Gordon Mumma's electronic accompaniment. I had a long conversation with Cathy Berberian on this subject. And she explained to me that she would have preferred, at the time of the Music Weeks of Paris, to sing without all the sonorities of *Rozart Mix* and *Concert for Piano and Orchestra*.

---

[1] In 1979, with John Fullemann, sound consultant, at IRCAM in Paris, I made *Roaratorio, An Irish Circus on Finnegans Wake*. (John Cage: footnote of 1980.)

D.C.: And what were her reasons?

J.C.: She wanted to perform the work for an audience listening more attentively to her. But you can guess that what interests me is to go beyond a situation like that. So I explained to Cathy that I personally preferred a concert that actually developed through indeterminacy. So that no one knew when it began or when it ended. And I told her that that's what I expected for the new performance of the *Song Books* – an indeterminacy of the temporal limits of the work. And also a performance where the audience would not be seated in rows of theater seats.

D.C.: What does she think about all that?

J.C.: Well, first of all she insists on the fact that the audience must be seated and remain where they are, without leaving their seats. It just so happens that in New York, the hall allows for freedom of movement. But she pointed out that if the people move around, they'll probably also climb up on the stage as they did in Paris and that then she would not be able to go on with her work.

D.C.: But in Paris, that ultimate eruption of the audience onto the stage was justified.

J.C.: I myself explained to Cathy Berberian that I very much liked a situation in which art disappears and becomes little by little immersed in what we call life. So here is what we will do. We shall each perform in a different way. I shall proceed in an 'open' way. And she will perform as she wishes, in a 'closed' way. When the audience is entering the hall, I shall already be playing; she will appear on the stage at the announced time, and will leave it when the end requires, that is, at a certain time. I myself shall continue. We shall both be on stage, however, for any other arrangement bothers her.

D.C.: Each of you will be in the center in his own way.

J.C.: When she understood that our viewpoints on the subject were different, she asked me: 'Do you want me to change?' And I replied: 'Certainly not, I like you as you are.' It would be marvelous to demonstrate that two people whose viewpoints are radically distinct can work together. That's how I am now preparing for the next performance. Whether it will work or not, I cannot predict. I don't know what is going to happen.

D.C.: It is the ultimate 'experimental' situation.

J.C.: Yes, no one can foretell what will happen. I don't know myself. This is an explosive situation. Art goes in all directions, and you cannot even discern what the directions are as long as you haven't taken them yourself.

D.C.: So, your conception of the Song Books *doesn't have to be imposed. It has no more value than Cathy's. It's true that it has no less value either.*

J.C.: On that subject, I also discovered, while thinking about this work again, that in a way, everything I have composed since 1952 was written for David Tudor. He was always in my mind when I was composing. And in the *Song Books*, I changed the singers into David Tudor! Certainly they were not David Tudor. So, what I had in mind while composing this work, or rather the state of mind in which I conceived this score, didn't come about at all. I don't mean to say by that that I didn't like what happened. But what happened is not what I had foreseen.

D.C.: And that doesn't matter to you or to the work?

J.C.: Not in the least! You can always foretell what will happen in linear art. And be sure of it. It's as if you're following its tracks. You eventually catch up with it, and then you make it your own thing. While uncloseted art can only escape. Then, I place myself in a situation where I am unable to evaluate. When I make a judgement, I have the impression that I am becoming narrow-minded. That's why I prefer abundance, non-linearity.

D.C.: But how easily can you tolerate someone contradicting you? Do you really accept juxtaposing Cathy Berberian's point of view with your own? Is there ultimately a difference between the 'open' and the 'closed'?

J.C.: All I know is that it's hard for me to extract myself from my own opinions. When I say I 'prefer' abundance, that still seems to be a value. Perhaps I am still a victim of language? At any rate, I try to go from one activity to another without remembering too much about the first one. I try not to be inhibited: blocked by a value, and slave to a judgement. Of course, I rarely manage to do this. However, that is what poetic life is! It is salvation. But it is also the leap that makes you fall back to the starting point.[1]

[1]The preceding pages retrace my state of mind in the beginning of 1971, as the concert I was to give with Cathy Berberian approached. Well, fifteen days before the date of this concert, I received a telegram from Cathy. It informed me of her illness – she would be in no condition in March to perform with me in New York. At first I thought of looking for another singer, then I realized that there wasn't enough time left for a stranger to work on the *Song Books* to prepare a lively interpretation of them. That's when I decided to present, all by myself, a performance of *Mureau* – I would sing the first part of my *Thoreau Mix*, accompanying myself with three recordings, of the second, third and fourth parts, also sung by me.

When I began my European tour from May to July, 1972, with David Tudor, I continued singing. We presented *Mureau* and the *Mesostics re Merce Cunningham*, superimposing them on Tudor's electronic works, *Rainforest* and *Untitled*. I show the audience how I am, how I sing. I give them my voice. (John Cage: footnote of 1972.)

FOURTH INTERVIEW

David Tudor: interpreter and composer

Touring with David Tudor

Abolishing the composer's ego

Writing *Variation II*

On notation, conceived as a means of liberating time

The performer's revolt

The meaning of space: superimposed works and non-linearity

A criticism of recordings: *Variation IV*

About *Cartridge Music*

From object to process

Live electronic music: the problems of conception and performance

D.C.: Since 1952, your work has fallen under the sign of David Tudor. How did you meet him?

J.C.: While I was here in France in 1949, I became interested in the music of Pierre Boulez, and I brought the *Second Sonata* back to the United States with me. I had the first copy published in Paris, and later, Boulez gave me his original manuscript. So I passed on the copy I had to William Masselos who was at the time the best pianist I knew, and suggested that he play the *Sonata*. And I showed the manuscript to Morton Feldman, whom I had just met. He told me that the first pianist to play the work could only be David Tudor. And he introduced me to him. David immediately set to work on this music. And not just the music: he learned French in order to read Artaud, Char, and Mallarmé in the original, that is, to live as much as possible in the very atmosphere of the Boulez of the *Second Sonata*. The music closest to Boulez that Tudor had played until then was Stefan Wolpe's *Battle Piece*. It's a horribly difficult and very fascinating score. Like the *Second Sonata*, it at first reduces you to a nearly total absence of comprehension. The difference is that it contains more passion than the *Sonata*. The effect of the two works is to make you tremble, at least when you hear them for the first time. But the *Battle Piece* not only makes you tremble, it also overwhelms you with its power. Though Boulez is usually more gentle, he becomes even gentler with *Structures* and, later, with the second *Structures* and *Le Marteau sans maître*. So I discovered that David Tudor was not only really learning the *Second Sonata* and succeeding in getting through it, but also that he had undertaken very complete and diversified studies, for example, reading *The Theater and Its Double* – and all for nothing! He was not even thinking of playing that *Sonata* in public. In fact, Masselos was supposed to give the first performance at a concert sponsored by the League of Composers, as I had advised them to include the *Second Sonata* in their program ... When I realized all that, I said to myself that I must go see what Masselos was doing. And when I spoke with Masselos I discovered that he had not yet found a way to work on the *Sonata*. In fact, it wouldn't bother him at all if David Tudor played it instead of him. So the plans were changed and it was announced that the first performance would be by David Tudor. And that is what happened. Naturally, he gave a brilliant performance.

D.C.: In David Tudor you had discovered not only the ideal interpreter of Boulez, but also of your own works.

J.C.: Yes, that 'premiere' of the *Second Sonata* was the initial link between us. I was then in correspondence with Boulez, and Tudor and I deciphered and translated the letters he wrote to me. It was an extraordinary period. We worked together with Morton Feldman and Christian Wolff. Earle Brown joined us a little later. I was then writing the *Music of Changes* and Feldman was writing his first graphic pieces. We composed everything thinking it would be performed by David. We knew that he would be capable of executing everything we entrusted to him, and that his playing would be absolutely faithful to what each piece required.

D.C.: That reminds me of Bussotti's Five Piano Pieces for David Tudor. *Bussotti explains in the preface that the phrase 'for David Tudor' in the title must be taken as an instrumental indication. Later, David Tudor turned to composition ...*

J.C.: Of course, he is composing today, but he wasn't then. When he was younger, he tried composing, but didn't like to show the results to anyone; they somewhat resembled some of Messiaen's pieces,[1] and he didn't consider them successful. So rather than composition, he devoted himself to the piano. He started by being an exceptional organist. By the age of thirteen I truly believe he had played everything written for the organ! When we began to work together, he had performed everything ever written for the piano. He was devoting himself to the most recent piano music.

D.C.: Even then he was never satisfied with being just a performer?

J.C.: No. When I started writing *Williams Mix*, the quantity of work I had to do was so immense that David learned all my composition techniques and composed at the same time as I, along with me. His assistance helped me a lot. And afterward, he and then also Earle Brown and I did all the work of splicing the tapes; we also mixed and edited the tapes with the help of Louis and Bebe Barron.

D.C.: That explains his understanding of your work — he was able to follow its progression in detail.

J.C.: You know that he also taught some extraordinary courses in Darmstadt in 1958.

D.C.: You were then performing as a duo?

J.C.: Yes. Since 1943, I tried to give at least one concert a year, and sometimes two, in New York. When I got to know Tudor, I quite natur-

[1]Not Messiaen, but Leo Ornstein. (John Cage: footnote of 1980.)

ally became his manager. I knew more people then he did, and I was older – which made it easier for me to write to universities, for example, and to organize tours. That is how we both got to travel across the United States. Then there was London in 1954, with a European tour: Cologne, Paris, Brussels, Stockholm, Zurich, Milan, and, of course, Donaueschingen. It was the first time David had been to Europe. Since then, we have returned there together. We have also gone separately.

D.C.: Why is that tour still famous?

J.C.: I don't think they took us that seriously in Europe.

D.C.: Yet it was after having heard you and David Tudor in Cologne that Karlheinz Stockhausen immersed himself in 'open' music – in the European sense of the term – with his Klavierstuck XI, *whose structure depends on the performer's choices.*

J.C.: Yes, perhaps he was impressed by what we were doing.

D.C.: Did your tours meet with different reactions in the United States?

J.C.: I think that everyone who attended the dance performance with Merce Cunningham in October, 1955, in the Clarkstown High School auditorium in New City remembers it. The evening was organized by a rather extraordinary person, a film maker and polemicist, Emile de Antonio, who was then the director of the Rockland Art Foundation, an art center. Quite a few people had insisted on coming from New York, despite the bad weather, for that day there were real tempests, floods! Roads were washed out ... But there was also a whole group of the audience disconcerted by our program who wanted to leave the hall. Unfortunately, the more they wanted to leave, the worse the storm became. They were forced to remain for the entire session ... It was also Emile de Antonio who helped organize the retrospective concert commemorating my twenty-five years of activity as a composer, in May, 1958, at the Town Hall in New York. My painter friends had decided to give me that concert, and it was thanks to them, thanks to the generosity of Jasper Johns and Robert Rauschenberg, that this concert took place. It was recorded thanks to George Avakian.

D.C.: Was this when you really began to become famous?

J.C.: Yes. Until then many people were only sporadically interested in my activities. In 1952, I used to give small private concerts in my apartment on Monroe Street. Sometimes, *Harper's Bazaar* or *Vogue* sent models to be photographed in the 'Bozza Mansion.' 'Bozza' was my landlord's name. Afterward, everything changed. Everyone started writing to me, phoning, etc.

D.C.: 1958 is decidedly a pivotal year in your career. At the Town Hall concert you premiered Concert for Piano and Orchestra, *your most strik-*

ing work of the entire 'indeterminacy' period. And it was also in 1958 that you and David Tudor made your second major European tour.

J.C.: Yes, at the last minute I had been asked to teach a course in Darmstadt. In fact, I was replacing Boulez who had declined at the last minute. Tudor taught there, too. And we covered almost all of Europe.

D.C.: Those who had heard David Tudor and you in Darmstadt and elsewhere seem either to have been won over to 'open' works, or to have broadened their instrumental and ... theoretical ... palette into indeterminacy. That brought about a rather profound upheaval in the musical mores of Europe!

J.C.: I have often been told that. But I think David Tudor had a lot to do with this movement of ideas. Even more than I.

D.C.: What new ideas did he contribute on the level of performance?

J.C.: The most remarkable thing was his ability to play by making sounds of opposing intensities succeed one another. He knew how to produce a sound of any amplitude at all after a very loud sound. He had a prodigious sense of the qualities of each sound. And he clarified everything he touched. For him, the difficult passages seemed to be a way of distinguishing each sound, rather than confusing them. In reality, whatever the undertaking, he almost immediately becomes a virtuoso.

D.C.: Has he authorized other recordings besides the ones we know here, for example the Sonatina for Flute and Piano *by Boulez? Has he recorded any less recent music?*

J.C.: He never would have agreed to do so.

D.C.: Later on he devoted himself entirely to a completely different form of performance or composition: live electronic music.

J.C.: Yes, he is presently working with circuits controlling video and audio effects, with feed-back between the two.

D.C.: Which forces him to redefine entirely the very profession of composer?

J.C.: His compositions consist of circuits which he can activate in various ways.[1] He is not the only one to have so completely separated himself

[1] I mentioned above that at the time of our 1972 tour I had on several occasions (London, Basel, Pamplona, etc.) sung the most recent of my works, *Mureau* and the *Mesostics*, while David Tudor performed two of his, *Rainforest* and *Untitled*. *Rainforest* dates from 1968; David defines it as an 'assemblage of electronic transducers which modify any input signal as a function of the distinct resonant characteristics of various physical objects.' As for *Untitled*, it is not *a* work, but a series of works dedicated to Toshi Ichiyanagi. The author treats the electronic components in it 'as though they were natural objects.' He picks out a certain number of them, avoids the intrusion of any input signals, and produces an interplay of unpredictable interrelations between components. 'Outputs' may be video or audio, even audio-visual. (John Cage: footnote of 1972.)

from traditional modes of creation. Max Neuhaus, for example, who was formerly an extraordinary percussionist, now uses nothing but circuits.

D.C.: The most recent tour of Merce Cunningham's Dance Company in the spring and summer of 1970 included a few performances of this live electronic music, sometimes presented under your name, sometimes under David Tudor's name, and sometimes Gordon Mumma's. Do you in fact all work on it together without distinctions or hierarchy?

J.C.: You must be referring to the accompaniment for *Signals*, which Mumma, Tudor, and I play independently but at the same time.

D.C.: Is there an over-all plan?

J.C.: No, none at all. We each maintain the freedom to form our own plans independent of the plans of the other two. We each have enough confidence in the other two to know that it will work. And I find these performances very interesting.

D.C.: They have no title?

J.C.: For a title we use the months and the weeks. It will be 'the second week of April' or 'the third week of March.' And on the program we change the order of the composers.

D.C.: In a sense, then, you are no longer the 'music director' of the Merce Cunningham Dance Company?

J.C.: No, and I'm delighted with that. Everything works much better than it used to.

D.C.: It's true that many works signed John Cage served as the basis for performances that differ in every respect according to who performs it. So for you the performer becomes the composer.

J.C.: Yes, and the audience can become the performer.

D.C.: What does the composer become?

J.C.: He becomes a member of the audience. He starts to listen.

D.C.: Sounds exist before the composer, and they even lead him; but the composer is none other than the performer, who is none other than the audience. Henceforth it is impossibe to distinguish among various roles.

J.C.: They interpenetrate.

D.C.: That means that music is a perfectly global — and englobing — phenomenon.

J.C.: Yes, it implies that we are all *in* the sounds, surrounded by them.

D.C.: The work David Tudor is doing with you now challenges the distinctions and hierarchies upon which traditional music is based. But specifically, if we take the case of Variations II, *how does he perform this work so as to convert it into one of his own?*

J.C.: David Tudor is so secretive that it is very difficult, even for me, to know exactly what he is doing at any given moment. All I know about his work is that he puts together circuits with audio and video effects, and that he produces feed-back between them. The audio is inseparable from the video, but when the circuits are turned on, they can produce as 'output' either visual or audible effects. But there is also another side to David Tudor: he loves puzzles. My *Variations II* is a kind of puzzle. Give it to a more conventional musician and he wouldn't know what to do with it. In principle, *Variations II* is nothing but a series of transparencies. Some of these transparencies have only a point on them, others a line. On none of them is there more than a single point or a single line. The idea was that these lines and points could be superimposed in any way at all, preferably by mixing them up without any plan at all. After that, you drop perpendiculars from the points to all the lines, and then by using any means of measurement, arrive at a precise idea as to each parameter of each sound.

D.C.: In a score like Variations II, *my impression is that all parameters are equal — I mean that they are equally measurable.*

J.C.: Yes, we know that we can easily measure time — with a chronometer, for example. We can relatively easily measure pitch; and, with the help of electronics, we can obtain very fine differences of frequency. If we really wanted to, we could even measure intensity with the help of a decimal system. But we cannot measure timbre. Also keeping in mind this question of a moving approach to parameters, when David Tudor began work on *Variations II*, he decided to begin with what was unknown — to start with the unknown rather than to force the unknown to become the known. His point of view was that we must use the unknown to make the known unknown. And not the other way around. That comes from his genius for solving puzzles. And I strongly doubt that anyone else ever had the idea of going about it that way. I must admit that it is an idea that would never have occurred to me. Consequently, when he considered this question of measuring tones, and when he realized that he didn't know how to proceed, he said to himself: all that I can affirm about this structure of timbre is that it is either simple or complex. And so, just like all the other things I know how to measure more exactly, I shall say that all I know about them is that they are either simple or complex. So, using my transparencies, he obtained directives concerning the simplicity or complexity of each musical event, and I believe he let them establish their own time. In other words, for each sound, he responded to the information supplied by the transparencies and their combinations, requiring, for example, a complex overtone structure, simple frequencies, and a complex amplitude for a given sound. Once he had found these characteristics, I think he sought a time duration which would respond to the whole of these characteristics, that is, which would let this whole find its own time. I believe this is the case, but I'm not sure about it, as far as duration is concerned.

D.C.: In Languages of Art, *Nelson Goodman comments on one of the figures of the* Solo for Piano *from your* Concert for Piano and Orchestra,[1] *a figure similar to those in* Variations II, *which seems to me to go in the same direction; he notes that in the performance or recreation of your scores, there are absolutely no indications governing time. Goodman demonstrates that there can be no authentic performance of something written like* Variations II. *There can be no performances according to the schema in question, but there can be performances following this schema. They come* after: *perhaps you have broken the links of intelligibility, of causality, or of property between the written text and the instrumental or electronic acts which it elicits from the performer.* But you have not broken time. *On the contrary, you make it surge forth in all its purity. You free it from the bonds which can screen it out. The way in which David Tudor reduces the known to the unknown, that is, the causal to the indeterminate, is in no way paradoxical; it prolongs what you are trying to do yourself. That he leaves time completely free is completely natural. We cannot see how he could do anything else.*

J.C.: Yes, time is inevitably beyond measure. It can't ever again be clock time. Another way of saying it is to affirm that writing is one thing, performing another, and listening a third; and that there is no reason for these three operations to be linked. If I write by imposing a particular measurement of time, the listener will not be confronted with time itself, but with the way the performer understands what he has read. And the performer will not have read time, but one measurement of time. That is what happens in conventional music.

D.C.: In your music, measurement itself forms itself. It doesn't have to precede what comes forth. It emerges with time. Not before ...

J.C.: [You could never impose a previously determined measurement.]

D.C.: The 'experimental' character of your undertaking lies strictly in the free functioning of time.

J.C.: Yes, 'experimental' – meaning what happens *before* one has *had the time* to measure it.

D.C.: And this is how you free the performer. For example, the students in the Department of Music at Vincennes who prepared and performed

[1]London: Oxford University Press, 1969. Cf. figure BB of the score, p.53; and p.188 *et passim.*

Rozart Mix *with Davorin Jagodic at the* Song Books *concert were free not to be David Tudor. They were no more Tudor than Simone Rist and Cathy Berberian were in the performance of the* Song Books. *But that didn't matter.*

J.C.: No. They gave a very beautiful performance of it I think.

D.C.: In what sense was it a beautiful performance?

J.C.: In that they performed with great care to make sure that each sound was really itself.

D.C.: Great care, that is with devotion to each sound? Immeasureable devotion?

J.C.: [Exactly]

D.C.: Yet, they ultimately acted in a way which David Tudor would have never chosen. We already talked about this at the Museum of Modern Art; they urged the audience to move around by holding up that sign behind your back. Do you still consider that intervention, that interruption of the entire process which you had begun, as a simple student reaction?

J.C.: Yes, it's a facet of what I would call youthful energy.

D.C.: But in order to enter into your work, and this is according to your own views, didn't the audience need to be forced? *The plan you were suggesting seems to defy most concert lovers' habits. It had to be emphasized, exaggerated, for these habits to give way. Is that what the performers of* Rozart Mix *felt?*

J.C.: Yes, they were moving in the direction of the work, and in the spirit of the work, rather than opposing it. Except, they lived too close to a society linked to the police: they became volunteer policemen.

D.C.: The feeling of the Rozart Mix *performers was that, given the situation, they had to* order *everyone to be* disorderly.

J.C.: Perhaps, too, we aren't sufficiently considering the physical nature of the situation. You said so yourself. The *Song Books* present the same problem as *Musicircus*: no one in the auditorium of the Théâtre de la Ville could get up or move around, no more than anybody could really circulate in Jean Richard's circus.

D.C.: When you began planning Musicircus *in June and July, 1970, you insisted on the need for providing everyone with a maximum amount of space. But none of the organizers thought the turn-out would be so large.*

J.C.:And these works require more and more space ... an undivided space which truly allows artists and audience complete freedom of movement. Space must be just as free as time. Sound sources need an extremely wide spatial dispersion, especially if amplified sounds are involved along with ordinary unamplified sounds.

D.C.: But the United States can provide you with all the space you want.

J.C.: In fact, I did greatly appreciate the very large hall at the University of Illinois for the creation of *HPSCHD*. It would have been difficult to find the equivalent in Europe.

D.C.: Do you think that it's only a question of ecology?

J.C.:It's possible that at the present time America is preparing a music worthy of the Fuller dome of the future! In the immense geodesic domes that Fuller as architect foresees covering large cities, the acoustic situations will be very different from those to which we are accustomed, and which have been forced on us by the necessarily small scale of our urban concert halls. But in a Fuller dome, you have a hard time making yourself heard. So, the old idea of art as *communication* will be thrown out the window; but there won't even be windows any more.

D.C.:That reminds me of that kind of Earth Art *which consists in covering miles of the Australian coast with wrapping paper . . . But even in these gigantic domes, wouldn't you still feel imprisoned? Some of Charles Ives' works could be played not only on a mountain, but also echoed from one mountain to another . . .*

J.C.:But there are also recent works by Christian Wolff which may be played in the fields or in the woods, and which use instruments that are characteristic of such situations.

D.C.:What do you think about that?

J.C.: Well, I find all that splendid, of course!

D.C.: All of this is consistent with your insistence on the necessity of freeing time, as towards the end of your lecture on Indeterminacy. *When you call for the superimposition or simultaneous performance of different works, it intensifies the feeling of space.*

J.C.:Yes, then there is the confluence of several musics, as with Ives' notion of different orchestras meeting at a cross-roads. Wandering around an orchestra which was playing in the square of a New England village, Ives was dumbfounded by the effect of spatial change on what he heard. I performed a similar experiment in Seville when I was seventeen. I found myself at an intersection and I felt a sudden joy upon realizing that I could hear different musics at the same time. In the lecture you were quoting, I also spoke of the need for separating the performers from each other as much as possible, in order to avoid ending up with a single work, as a result of not enough space between musicians. Crowded together, they can only play one thing at a time, which ultimately means that even in the most complex polyphony they play the same thing.

D.C.:What gave you the idea of superimposing Rozart Mix, Concert, *and the* Song Books *specially for the Paris Music Weeks concert?*

J.C.: Well, I believe that at the time of the conversations we had in Paris in June, 1970, everything revolved around the *Concert for Piano and Orchestra.* First of all we were going to perform that; only later did we begin to wonder if other works could go along with it.

D.C.: Was that the only reason?

J.C.: It seems to me that that was the first reason; I thought of *Rozart Mix* because I felt the need for a continuum capable of perpetuating itself for any length of time at all. And I wanted something which could begin before the audience entered, and continue until everyone had gone to get rid of the experience of a beginning and an end. It also seemed to me to be practical, because tape recorders are a little like pianos – they're everywhere. If I had thought of a piece of the sort that David Tudor is presently preparing, everything would have been different. And very difficult, technically speaking. But putting together these two pieces, *Concert* and *Rozart Mix,* seemed quite feasible to me. In any case, in the concert which we are going to give in New York, we will play the *Song Books* without *Concert* and without *Rozart Mix.* And that will provide a rather strange situation, because most of the solos in the *Song Books* consist of simple lines without any accompaniment at all. So environmental sounds will have a chance to penetrate into the music. They will make the *Mix.*[1]

D.C.: Thus, on the one hand the works invade space, they invest it, and, on the other hand, space in return enters 'into' the works, it infiltrates the body of the works themselves.

J.C.: And indeed, a space arises out of the fact that the works are superimposed and accumulate *their own* spaces. There is no single space, finally – there are several spaces and these spaces tend to multiply among themselves.

D.C.: But doesn't this proliferation of spaces, this impression of plurality, of polyphonic liberation, which arises merely from a reading of your Concert for Piano, *run the risk of disappearing when you return to the monody of a solitary performance of the* Song Books?

J.C.: I hope not. I mentioned that alongside the 'closed' space of Cathy Berberian would be my 'open' space. That already makes two spaces.

---

[1]The last three sentences should be read in the past conditional tense. As I have explained earlier, what I had foreseen did not take place. (John Cage: footnote of 1972.)

And then, the surroundings exist and will make their contribution. By combining the spaces of different works, the environment can spontaneously give us anything that we could have produced artificially. [There is always an ecology, and that ecology is alive.] And the works, no matter how numerous they may be, can always melt into it. Whence its multiplicity.

D.C.: On this point, let me bring up the recording of Variations IV. *I know that you don't like records, but this one seems significant to me. On the surface, it's a guessing game, almost a quiz. It seems the listener is called on to sharpen his memory; he is asked if he recognizes Schumann, or Tchaikovsky, or such and such a tango. And since all that is going on at once, it gives the impression of a limitless sound assemblage. But this ecology becomes subject to the limitations of a recording.*

J.C.: The record you're talking about is of a performance of *Variations IV* which is itself a variation of *Variations IV*. The original piece dealt with space and space alone. And it didn't have anything to do with the sounds which happen in that space. Most of the sounds in the recording were in reality located outside[1] of the space in which the system belonging to these *Variations IV* was set up. When you listened to the original work, it appears quite tranquil! Then, why is the recording so unfaithful here? Because the performance should have moved from one area of its space to another, travelling according to the programs of action which the performers had prepared themselves, using the transparencies which made it possible to create a map. A faithful recording would reflect these movements from one spot to another.[2] Consequently, it would include the projection of silences. And very few sounds would then be caught in the space of the performance itself. What strikes me in that recording is that it contains, so to speak, no silence at all.

D.C.: But you have taught us that this silence you are demanding doesn't exist anywhere or at any time!

J.C.: What I mean by that is that the conditions of the work's spatiality itself were not respected during the recording process, nor could they have been. What should have been recorded, and I really regret that it wasn't possible, is the fundamental characteristic of *Variations IV*: sounds coming from a distance, with a very small number of sounds coming from the spot where the audience was located and with clear distinctions of intensity. Sounds from the audience should have seemed overly intense compared to those coming from greater distances. On the record, everything is alike, everything is equidistant.

D.C.: How did these distortions happen despite your intentions?

[1]Not outside, inside. (John Cage: footnote of 1980.)
[2]Mostly around, rarely within, the auditorium. (John Cage: footnote of 1980.)

J.C.: Well, we happened to choose this piece as accompaniment for one of Merce Cunningham's dances. And in the course of one of our tours, we had to play in a theater in Little Rock, Arkansas. It was a beautiful modern theater which included a splendid control studio. We were able to use this control studio to send sounds both into the auditorium and into the hallways around the auditorium. Well, that day, David Tudor hurt his knee, so that it was difficult for him to move about. The result was that he remained seated in the control room while I moved about in the space. And he was delighted at being able to project all the sounds into the hall at once, no matter how far away they came from. Now you can better understand from this experiment in Little Rock the way the recording was made. We were in a little art gallery in Los Angeles, and both of us, David and I, had a separate control table. All of the different sounds, which initially were completely distinct because of their dissimilar spatial origin, were now at the control centers together, in the form of recordings at their own particular level. But there was no way for us to simulate the distance between the different points in space where each sound source originated.

D.C.: *So then, thanks to David Tudor, one of your objectives, the interpenetration of sound sources, was nonetheless fulfilled?*

J.C.: Not at all! All we achieved on that record was a typically Schoenbergian variation, with certain things changed and others not.

D.C.: *You mean that you regressed to an object, to a stable opposition between what it is and what it isn't?*

J.C.: The recording lacks any feeling of depth, of the spatial diversification clearly indicated in the score.

D.C.: *Still, the result is appealing from a strictly audible point of view.*

J.C.: Of course. I think if you listen to the record only as a variation of *Variations IV*, it's not so bad. Moreover, that recording has become famous. It fascinates religious groups ... At the Montreal Exposition, they broadcast it night and day, continually, in a pavilion devoted to religion in general! It's the ideal ecumenical music!

D.C.: *In spite of everything, you remain quite rigorous. Would you be just as critical of Max Neuhaus' version of* Fontana Mix: Fontana Mix-Feed?

J.C.: As far as I know, what Max did is much closer to the original score than our variation on *Variations IV*.

D.C.: *And at the Museum of Modern Art, you justified recording* Cartridge Music, *the superimposition of four versions of that work, by the idea that the record still allows the production of an auditory whole which would be impossible to construct otherwise.*

J.C.: Exactly. There, there is a true fidelity to the score, because it calls for all those sounds which two instrumentalists could never feed into a tape recorder at one time. In this case, the recording gains from the particular facilities offered by a recording studio. Previously in the course of our tours, we performed *Cartridge Music* directly by super-imposing the four 'voices' of the recording onto the live version.

D.C.: *Then your superimpositions don't relate to a single principle, not the stratifications of the same work nor the accumulation of different works?*

J.C.: No, there is no constant. Most of the time, it depends on what happens to be around. I rely on human resources and available techniques.

D.C.: *For example, when you superimposed* Winter Music *on your great orchestral piece* Atlas Eclipticalis, *you at first felt that there would be no particular correspondence between these works. Had you thought of a complementarity of timbres? Or were you still obeying a structural rationale as when Pierre Marietan and his group played five scores together at the Music Weeks performance?*

J.C.: When I wrote *Winter Music*, David Tudor and I played it as a duet without electronics. I don't remember now if *Atlas Eclipticalis* includes any specific mention of *Winter Music*. It's possible ... Yes, I believe that's the case. So from the outset I had envisioned the possibility of combining those works. But you see, once I had suggested that each of these scores could on occasion go with another, people were delighted; and they're still delighted with putting any piece at all with any other piece. And recently, a young Czech composer who is working in Buffalo, Peter Kotik, became interested in performing the *Song Books*; he wanted to know if any music at all could go with it. Before I even had time to answer him, he added: 'I'm not talking about your music, but other people's.' So, I said yes. For, of course, that goes perfectly in the direction of the circus. That also means that I have abandoned any pretense of structure. Or any illusion concerning the correspondences that you brought up, and which could only exist within a 'measurabilist' – measuring – conception of time ... or structure.

D.C.: *Christian Wolff wrote in a text on you that even when your works are extremely 'pared-down,' that is, as 'open' as possible, they are still works. They subsist, even if only as pure* transparencies.

J.C.: That's certainly true. I imagine myself to be composing processes, and I end up with objects. Actually, if my works are superimposed, if they are, then 'furnished' or filled by each other, they nonetheless maintain their individuality – at least for me.

D.C.: That's not all that Christian Wolff is trying to say. He suggests that you remain a creator, whatever you introduce into your works. You admit chance, but you are the one who establishes what chance lets into the audible universe. You certainly don't let it be what it is. In your own way, you tame it.

J.C.: But what is even more interesting is that the music I composed in the past, and which I never pretended was anything more than an object or a collection of objects, can henceforth quite easily be integrated into processes.

D.C.: Like a contagious quality spreading from process-works to object-works.

J.C.: Yes, henceforth we listen to object-works differently. We listen to Beethoven in a new way. It is strange that this can happen. Long ago, that would have horrified me.

D.C.: Have you ever noticed the reverse movement – the objectification of processes?

J.C.: I can tell you about an experience I had in New York last Spring. It was during a four piano concert at the Whitney Museum. The program had been prepared by Morton Feldman, and included music by Christian Wolff, Earle Brown, and me. The musicians, who were excellent, were all composers, I believe, and not just pianists. So I went to the concert; obviously you couldn't help being ecstatic over music so well prepared and presented. Well, excluding my still very keen interest in Christian Wolff's music, I found the entire evening nearly unbearable. Was it because of me? Anyway, this series of pieces, one after the other, to which we had to pay attention simply because of the program, bored me so deeply that I promised myself then and there never again to go to a concert. And to think that a few years ago I had found that music in particular so exciting to create and to hear! And now it ressembled church music ...

D.C.: But you once mentioned that some scores like Winter Music *became melodies as soon as you played them and despite long silences. They were compressed into objects in spite of your intentions.*

J.C.: That is correct; moreover, I owe that observation to Christian Wolff.

D.C.: And you said that you were no less aware of the reciprocal development. How does an object-work become a process-work?

J.C.: Let me tell you about another experience. In Palermo, where not very long ago they played that same *Winter Music* in conditions just as exceptional as at the Whitney Museum but with the assistance of Paul

Ketoff and his electronic equipment – which had not been the case for the Whitney Museum concert – suddenly the work came alive again. In other words, contrary to what Virgil Thomson asserts in a recent article, I think that thanks to and through electronics, we are leaving the church and have dived into life.

D.C.: Yes, but there are all kinds of electronics. Most of the electronic works produced in studios are certainly nothing more than objects; the same goes for much computer music. On the other hand, live electronic music has its own fascination. Perhaps an explanation for this phenomenon lies in the fact that live electronic sounds are manipulated in front of an audience and that they cause a certain balance of cause and effect to appear between the instrumentalist and the resulting sound. What would bother us in ordinary electronic music would be the tape. The dehumanization! What do you think!

J.C.: I think that live sounds really have a different quality and that they reach greater extremes of softness and loudness. They have a presence, and this presence is intact, while conventional electronic sounds, those from studios of 'experimental' music, are necessarily compressed. By their very nature, they can only give you a little more difficult form of Muzak!

D.C.: What do you consider Muzak!

J.C.: Music for factory workers, or for chickens to force them to lay eggs. The miscellaneous music played throughout the day by most radio stations.

D.C.: Your own use of live electronic music has no connection with what is technically defined as high fidelity. Everything changes when you move beyond that ...

J.C.: Yes, you are free to accept whatever happens without worrying, as you forego pursuing control in the world of sounds. You're no longer mortally vexed by a little distortion.

D.C.: And indeed, distortions are welcome, if I can judge by David Tudor's or Max Neuhaus' use of feed-back.

J.C.: Today, live electronic music lets sounds be surprises. If you mix live instrumental sounds with taped electronic sounds, as I have sometimes done, you can lose this idea of surprise.

D.C.: Unless you complicate the system, as in Rozart Mix?

J.C.: But then you must work very closely with the distribution of sounds. You cannot sit with your arms crossed and let them string along if there is just one tape. You have to put a lot of them into operation, and then introduce changes into what's happening. [This is the minimum cost of escaping linearity.] What counts is that the sound be transformed and restored simultaneously, but in an unrecognizable manner! It is reborn. It is perpetual rebirth or reincarnation. It is life. Time is with the sounds, in each one of them. And that goes on and on.

FIFTH INTERVIEW

HPSCHD: A collaboration with Lejaren Hiller

The difficulties of programming

Mozart computerized

Cheap Imitation

Concerning the *Concert for Piano and Orchestra*: a bringing
  together of differences

The circus situation

Concerning Xenakis

Openness

Contingency

Conversation and communication

On La Monte Young and Feldman: music-objects

The riddle of process

Musicalization of language

About Terry Riley

In praise of Christian Wolff

On conceptual art

The impossibility of eliminating experience

The paradox of *Vexations*

In reference to Wittgenstein

D.C.: Does 'live electronic music' have any future in your opinion, and if so, what is it?

J.C.: We are full of contradictions. Even though I talk about the need for electronic sounds, I still have worked last year and this year on a 'normal' orchestral work.[1]

D.C.: HPSCHD used both harpsichords and tape recorders. Don't you see a contradiction in that?

J.C.: So many things can go together! But the important thing about *HPSCHD* is the use of the computer.

D.C.: Did that work require a lot of programming?

J.C.: When I received Lejaren Hiller's invitation to go to the University of Illinois to work with computers, I accepted immediately. I would not have sought to use a computer left to my own devices, but when I was offered the use of one, I wondered what I would actually be able to get out of it. But at the same time, I had a strong desire to do something with it. Hiller asked me to plan to finish two works during my year's stay at the University of Illinois. Then I conceived the framework of *HPSCHD*, involving fifty-two tapes and all the divisions of the octave from five to fifty-six tones. I chose these because they were fairly easy to produce with a computer, whereas it would have been difficult to obtain them without a computer. As for the seven solos, I hadn't thought about that at first.[2] They presupposed a division of the octave into twelve half-tones and lent themselves to a live performance. That is what was done.

D.C.: And what was the second score to be?

J.C.: The *Ten Thunderclaps* from *Finnegans Wake* – the transformation of a live orchestra and chorus into a genuine hurricane.

D.C.: The work was not completed?

[1]The orchestration of *Cheap Imitation*, completed in 1972. (John Cage: footnote of 1972.)
[2]Since the work was supposed to fulfill a commission by Antoinette Vischer, I had planned only one solo for harpsichord. It was Hiller who thought of the seven solos, and the decision to add the other six came only as the result of a discussion with him. (John Cage: footnote of 1972.)

J.C.: I am still thinking about it, and it will come. All the details of organizing *HPSCHD* took so much time that not one, but two years had to be devoted to it. We spent the first year programming the computer. At first, I was supposed to have an assistant who would program according to my instructions. But that assistant never came, and it was finally Lejaren Hiller himself who volunteered to do the programming. As he is a composer, I suggested that the work be signed by both of us. And he accepted.

D.C.: *Then* HPSCHD *is your collaboration?*

J.C.: I have always been very fond of working in a team. It is a way of working which conforms to chance's way of necessarily liquidating the habits of the ego. The more egos you have, the better chance you have of eliminating the ego altogether. We worked together in perfect harmony.

D.C.: *But it still took you a year to finish programming ...*

J.C.: And even at the end of a year we hadn't achieved as much as we hoped. Clearly, the music we are capable of imagining by far surpasses everything that we can program. If we had to produce exactly what we planned, we could well have devoted the second year to it as well! What is difficult is synchronizing simultaneous events.

D.C.: *Why?*

J.C.: We had studied the computer music programs set up by Max Matthews at Bell Telephone, and we realized that the sound of a harpsichord included a very brief attack, followed by a decay which was itself characterized by a curve. Thus, we tried to program a coincidence between this decay and a secondary attack of lesser intensity, followed by a weaker, second decay, itself complicated by its own curve. We recognized that it would be difficult to produce the second curve. In the most extreme cases, we could ignore it. But we couldn't ignore the curve following the first attack. So we began to program the synchronization of the two attacks all over again. This was equivalent to plucking the strings, letting them decay and, during this decay, to attack them again. Well, we found it impossible to get the computer to consistently coordinate the two acts. Not only would we have had to devote a considerable amount of time to it, but it would have been very expensive. And we had already spent a lot. So we decided to forego the second attack. We had to be happy with the simple curve of the first decay. We inscribed it into one of the *I Ching* charts and had the *I Ching* itself programmed. But the curve would only fit into a part of the chart, and when the *I Ching* gave other numbers in other parts of that chart, we had to ignore them. On the other hand, any number appearing at the bottom of the diagram would have an effect on the variations. We could thus end up with very different versions of the same attack. It was interesting. That gave us the idea of devising ornaments that would improve the connected sounds. We did everything possible to program them, but it was wasted effort. These preliminary programs combined with the programs controlling sound production on actual tapes surpassed the capacities of the computer. There, again, we had to abandon our plans. All in all, we could only integrate a very few chance operations – much less than you would believe. On the other hand, we achieved a higher level of complexity than had ever been reached. I doubt that anyone had ever heard the result of 52 different divisions of the octave simultaneously.

D.C.: And in what way was Mozart a guide for all that?

J.C.: Do you know Mozart's *Instructions for Composing Waltzes With the Help of Two Dice*? One of the harpsichord solos in *HPSCHD* is a computer rendition of the waltz Mozart had in mind. We finished it and then revised it by replacing the measures Mozart had written with others from his *Sonatas for Piano*; they served as substitutes for the waltz. We had two-handed music – we separated the hands, making a different computer program for each one. The right hand made use of certain *Sonatas,* the left of others. Little by little, the *Waltz* disappeared, replaced by more and more of the *Sonatas.* Next, we extended this principle to the entire history of music, from the time of Mozart to that of Hiller and myself. We chose composers according to the 'place' each occupies in musical history by working with more or less equal historical intervals. They are, respectively: Mozart, Beethoven, Schumann, and Chopin, Gottschalk, Busoni, Schoenberg, Hiller, and Cage. We did it for both hands together, and for the hands in opposition to one another.

D.C.: To what extent have you been converted to the computer? Is it now indispensable to the elaboration of your works?

J.C.: I use it only when it is at my disposal. Previously, I didn't use as many numbers as I do now. In fact, only since my work on *HPSCHD* have I begun to use the *I Ching* on a very large scale. I no longer toss coins myself – the *I Ching* has been 'computerized.' I can now picture working on a large number of hexagrams at once. In the past I sometimes did need numbers, but my projects were a little less ambitious. When I needed to toss coins for the composition of *Atlas Eclipticalis*, I had to rely on the good will of the dancers of the Merce Cunningham Company, and I paid them for their work. That is no longer necessary with the computer.

D.C.: What do you think about using a computer to synthesize sounds?

J.C.: You mean to construct sounds? That's Matthew's position. Hiller also had this idea, of using elaborate programs to have the computer invent new sounds that otherwise would be impossible to produce. They are already working on that at the University of Illinois. The attack can be that of one kind of sound, then, as it continues, it can take on the nature of a completely different one. Sound synthesis has become possible today.

D.C.: Weren't you tempted to use that kind of experiment for your most recent works, like Cheap Imitation, *which you are presently orchestrating?*

J.C.: No, I didn't think about it, perhaps because that composition is directly inspired by Satie. I like Satie's *Socrate* so much that it probably keeps me in a more conventional framework of music.

D.C.: Then is Cheap Imitation *an exception in your production; will it be a 'classical' work?*

J.C.: Certainly not! It might contain some rather strange sounds ... They might even be not too far from the sounds that we hope to get from the computer. I have been listing the instruments capable of playing each piano phrase in *Cheap Imitation* with no problem. Once each phrase had its list of instruments, I ask the *I Ching* how many of them should play. While there may be fourteen that can play, the *I Ching* may tell me to use six. I again consult the *I Ching*: among the fourteen instruments I started out with, which six are going to play? How many notes, and which notes of the phrase will they play? In what way? Should they hold each note until the next, shorten it, or give it its own length? Etc.

D.C.: What kind of audible results do you think this will produce?

J.C.: The work will be strange in that it will have to move from a rich sonority to a very thin sonority. With the feeling of a perpetually shifting timbre. It will not be like a contralto's melody which has consistency and homogeneity; it will be as though that melody were going wrong. It will be something that I will take great pleasure in hearing!

D.C.: The computer, you said, neutralized chance in HPSCHD. *Will chance truly be responsible for* Cheap Imitation?

J.C.: I left only one element 'free': the register in which the sound appears. I didn't control the choice of registers by chance operations.

D.C.: Did you choose them as a function of timbre?

J.C.: No, for the work was first written for the piano; but I chose the piano before even having decided exactly what the work would be. I went through many trial runs with the *I Ching* to determine the way in which I would compose it. For the first page, let's say I have several ways. Then, I choose one with which to continue. It's like discovering a computer program; but once I find a program, I let it operate.

D.C.: *That reminds me of the* Solo for Piano *in your* Concert for Piano and Orchestra; *you use eighty-four of these 'ways of composing,' which result in a large number of different systems of notation. In the* Solo, *didn't you introduce a system into these notations, a relationship between one system and another?*

J.C.: I asked myself whether I should repeat a way of composing which I had already used, whether I should vary what I had done, or finally, whether I should innovate. I assigned a letter to each possibility. A second letter served when there was a varied repetition of a type of composition already elaborated. Different letters represented variations and innovations. Only repetitions kept the same letters. And they were nothing but repetitions of composing means, not repetitions of the music itself.

D.C.: *Then it was not a matter of true repetitions.*

J.C.: No, Schoenberg would have called them variations.

D.C.: *You didn't* control *the choice of registers in* Cheap Imitation *by means of chance operations. Does chance imply for you determinacy as well as indeterminacy? Is it a means of control?*

J.C.: Yes, and I believe that we must not leave everything to chance.

D.C.: *Then would the notations in the* Solo *of* Concert *indicate a rejection of chance?*

J.C.: A rejection of determinacy through chance. I used the same principle in the *Song Books* to discover whether particular solos would or would not relate to the 'subject' of the work, whether I should already have followed certain manners of composing or not, whether the next segment should be variation or innovation. A certain family relationship exists between the *Song Books* and the *Solo* from *Concert for Piano and Orchestra*.

D.C.: *Although that music is still indeterminate, is it less subject to chance than your earlier works composed according to imperfections in the paper — works which were a rigorous outgrowth of chance?*

J.C.: Imperfections in the paper? They are comparable to my use of templates.

D.C.: *How would that term be translated in French? Would it be 'model' or 'module' or 'tracing'?*

J.C.: You could also say 'pattern' or 'diagram'. If I take a sheet of paper and make a few holes in it, it becomes a template. I can place it over another sheet of paper and draw through the holes. That is how I composed my *Music for Carillon No. 1*. I used pieces of folded paper with holes, and the latter led me to the pitches.

D.C.: Does your use of a template lead to a result much different from that obtained by the use of charts? We already talked about those charts, those diagrams, with regard to your Concerto for Prepared Piano and Chamber Orchestra. *Has there been any development in your handling of chance?*

J.C.: If you use a template, you can use it over again as many times as you want, even on the basis of chance operations. That ability to make use of something over and over again is reminiscent of the repetition of motifs. But composing by using charts, as in *Music of Changes*, cannot easily allow such variation or modification. Later, when I wrote *Music for Carillon No.4*, I used astronomical maps, as I had already done in *Atlas Eclipticalis*. So, you can say that the stars became templates for me. But I used chance operations to avoid repositioning the page at the same point. Thus, the template could no longer serve as a basis for repetition. There is indeed a progression in these ways of working. They go from the possibility of repetition to the improbability of any repetition.

D.C.: But aren't you delimiting a Stockhausen sort of continuum?

J.C.: [Possibly, if I used all those eventualities at once, in one single work. But I have always used them one after the other.]

D.C.: Is it possible to draw a parallel between this evolution, from repetition to non-repetition, and the progressive abandonment of all expressivity in your music? Do you have the impression that there is still tranquility, heroism, anger, etc. in your recent works? Or have those emotions completely and definitively disappeared?

J.C.: It seems to me that those emotions are no longer found in my works, but in the people who listen to them. They have changed places. When I listen, I can feel an emotion.

D.C.: Even though you know that the work no longer provides a pretext for that feeling?

J.C.: In my more recent music, my intention was to avoid forcing anyone to feel in any particular way any more. Feelings are within each of us, not in exterior things. Or indeed, if there are still some elements which could be called 'expressive', as in the *Song Books*, they should be set in a circus situation. The expression of an emotion may well resemble an object; but if it arises in a circus situation, it is no longer capable of changing the nature of the process.

D.C.: What do you consider a 'circus situation'?

J.C.: The process opens up to include things which have no emotive properties, but also to reinclude objects charged with significance and intention. These objects are carried along in the process, they no longer dominate it and turn it into an object. For example, in the *Song Books*, there is a refrain, the refrain of an anarchist chant which repeats the words of Thoreau: 'The best form of government is no government at all.' Well, we will have that kind of government, that is, no government at all, when we are ready to accept it. Hearing it, it's practically a popular tune, as popular as a slogan or a flag. But it can enter into this enlarged situation, without determining the nature of the situation.

D.C.: If I understand you correctly, the Song Books, *among other objects, conveys its own argument — which is that objects can no longer exist. Then finally there will be no emotion?*

J.C.: Let's imagine a street with a lot of people. We can presume that each individual feels some emotional stress. But the situation as a whole can be seen or experienced outside of a consideration of each individual.

D.C.: If I compare your position to Xenakis', for example, I see that you begin much the same as he. Xenakis uses probability formulae to describe and to make *his music* describe, *in the graphic sense of the term, the movement of a crowd, or the tapping of hail on a window pane. But he controls these movements by collecting them into a rule which controls the direction of the general, statistical tendency. You, yourself, do not attempt to control or orient these movements.*

J.C.: What I hope for is the ability of seeing anything whatsoever arise. No matter what, that is, everything, and not such and such a thing in particular. The problem is that something occurs. But the law governing that something is *not yet* there. Now, if there were a tendency that controlled the appearance of one particular thing as opposed to some other thing, then that tendency — as a statistical tendency — would not itself be immobile. It would not be a law. It would be in a state of mutation which would prohibit describing it as a law. If you are in that state of mutation, you are situated in change and immersed in process. While, if you are dealing with a statistic, then you return to the world of objects, and the presence of emotions as linked to those objects can again come to constrain us.

D.C.: Indeterminacy, as you conceive it then could not be opposed *to what the physicists mean by that word. Your music is not* opposed *to Xenakis' music. It is situated* before *it; it describes its* condition of possibility.

J.C.: Yes, the opening up of everything that is possible and to everything that is possible is, I believe, what I am seeking.

D.C.: Contingency *rather than* chance.

J.C.: Chance, as I use it, is not something that I must control, nor that must control me. It is not the chance of the physicist. But that does not mean the physicist's chance shouldn't exist.

D.C.: And then, it is a kind of chance that leaves me alone or makes me free. Free, among other things, to feel — almost to choose — my own emotions. I understand better now what you were saying about stress, *and about the change in scale your music brings, when it turns toward indeterminacy. In a 'circus situation,' each person becomes responsible for his own emotions. Until then, he was only the witness, but the emotions are those of each subject, of each individual. That is less serious than if we were dealing with the emotions of a crowd.*

J.C.: Say it in a positive way. Two people have different feelings and that is what allows them to converse.

D.C.: Non-repetition — it is difference that makes dialogue possible.

J.C.: Yes. And, sometimes, when I speak, I give the impression that I am against feelings. But what I am against is the imposition of feelings.

D.C.: So in your ideal society, people would be near each other, but not communicating ...

J.C.: They would not communicate, but they would talk, they would carry on dialogues. I much prefer this notion of dialogue, of *conversation*, to the notion of communication. Communication presupposes that one has something, an object, to be communicated. The conversation I'm thinking about would not be a conversation which would concentrate on objects. Communicating is always imposing something: a discourse on objects, a truth, a feeling. While in conversation, nothing imposes itself.

D.C.: But if nothing imposes itself, we could say anything at all ...

J.C.: It is that 'anything at all' which allows access to what I call the *openness*. To the process. To the circus situation. In that situation, objects surge forth. But the fact that it is conversation, not communication, means that we are deterred from talking *about* them. What is said is not this or that object. It is the circus situation! It is the process.

D.C.: And according to you, we are *in that situation or process. What you aspire to you basically already have.*

J.C.: We never possess anything but objects. Here we're not talking about possessing anything whatsoever. But it's true that we are in process. Only, we have forgotten it.

D.C.: Must the call back to that situation necessarily take the shape of anarchy, of a dissolution of all principles and government?

J.C.: Principles and governments are what favor forgetfulness. They are in themselves forgetfulness. They distract us from what is.

D.C.: During an earlier interview, speaking about logic, you said that it must be forgotten.

J.C.: Logic, organization, government should all be forgotten inasmuch as they begin themselves by making us forget the essential!

D.C.: And it is not only your music, it is your life itself which you intend to devote to the essential, and to its remembrance. Or indeed, to the forgetfulness of what makes us forgetful.

J.C.: That is why I try to make my music resemble my life. May it be free and without goal! That is, without object.

D.C.: The young musicians who say they are inspired by your example – I am thinking about La Monte Young – don't seem to me to have followed that example to its end. Doesn't La Monte Young's music represent a return to harmony? That doesn't seem to belie the fascination that you otherwise hold for him. How is that possible? And what do you think about it?

J.C.: The extreme care that La Monte Young takes for microtonal relations and the attention he demands of his listeners differs, in fact, in every respect from the attitude that I have when I make music. My wish is to leave the attention of the faculties free; his is to concentrate them.

D.C.: Isn't that a conventional point of view in comparison with yours?

J.C.: You could also consider his music constructive, because he hopes to create tranquility in the listeners by means of that concentration of attention. I, on the other hand, presuppose that that tranquility exists. And that we have, so to speak, left school. That we are busy living, and that our elementary education has already taken place. Therefore, I don't construct anything.

D.C.: Didn't you make a similar sort of remark about Feldman a few years ago when you said that his music doesn't change, it *continues? Feldman, too, wants to make his composition a pedagogical exercise in tranquility.*

J.C.: And in the erotic. For me, Feldman's music is not only tranquil, it is extremely erotic. With La Monte Young, I feel no particular emotion other than tranquility.

D.C.: In both cases, La Monte Young and Feldman, a particular feeling is imposed on the listener. These are music-objects ...[1]

[1]Earlier this year I heard a String Quartet by Morton Feldman that was a single movement lasting an hour and a half. It was beautiful *because* it wasn't beautiful. Through length it became not an object. Nevertheless it would have given the same impression if instead of captive the audience had been in a different architectural situation permitting at any point in time or space exit and entrance, that is, at home. (John Cage: footnote of 1980.)

J.C.: But when I listen to La Monte Young, I conduct the experience in my way rather than in his. It's just that, in his music, you are free to discover a veritable world of possibilities and events. You can settle down within a single sound. At that moment, listening reverts to placing a particular object under a microscope so that the object becomes an entire universe, simply because it is enlarged to that extent. It ceases to be an object.

D.C.: *Is it possible to refashion* all *musical objects, or rather,* all *music-objects in this way?*

J.C.: Certainly. You must, however, place yourself in a state of process, a circus situation. That means a change of attitude in relation to conventional listening.

D.C.: *You have to change your attitude in order to move towards change?*

J.C.: Or to avoid getting stuck with what that music imposes on us: continuity. When I say that Feldman's music continues rather than changes, that doesn't diminish our appreciation of it. I escape what it imposes.

D.C.: *In order for you to appreciate it, you have to choose to listen to it in a sort of wrong sense.*

J.C.: Perhaps I'm not listening to it as Feldman thought I would. But that's not misunderstanding his work. I haven't *missed* any *understanding* of that music.

D.C.: *So wouldn't the work be missing an understanding of itself?*

J.C.: You could say that about all music-objects. They bend sounds to what composers want. But for the sounds to obey, they have to already exist. They do exist. I am interested in the fact that they are there, rather than in the will of the composer. A 'correct understanding' doesn't interest me. With a music-process, there is no 'correct understanding' anywhere. And consequently, no all-pervasive 'misunderstanding' either. So, music-objects, in themselves, are a 'misunderstanding.' But sounds don't worry about whether they make sense or whether they're heading in the right direction. They don't need that direction or misdirection to be themselves. They *are*, and that's enough for them. And for me, too.

D.C.: *Marcuse says somewhere about Heidegger that the question of being has always* already *been answered ... You use sounds. They* are.

J.C.: But we're not talking about possession or property. A sound possesses nothing, no more than I possess it. A sound doesn't *have* its being, it can't be sure of existing in the following second. What's strange is that it came to be there, this very second. And that it goes away. The riddle is the process.

D.C.: But there's nothing more to say about it ... We are always led back to this: there is nothing to say.

J.C.: That is, to silence — to the world of sounds. If I had something to say, I would say it with words.

D.C.: So music, then, seems to you to be the best way of making explicit this process of gaining access to being, this movement of 'openness' which we can't name without distorting it?

J.C.: Perhaps that's because I wasn't sufficiently inclined towards the world of language! But I have told you about some of my recent attempts in that realm. I don't know if I'll succeed.

D.C.: You propose to musicate language; you want language to be heard as music.

J.C.: I hope to let words exist, as I have tried to let sounds exist.

D.C.: To musicate language, is that to de-objectify it, to return it to a circus situation, to process?

J.C.: We would not have language if we were not in process. But I don't believe normal language can *provide* us with that process. That's why I insist on the necessity of not letting ourselves be dragged along by language. Words impose feelings on us if we consider them as objects, that is, if we don't let them, too, be what they are: processes.

D.C.: Sometimes you use the word 'process' in the singular, sometimes in the plural. That reminds me of Terry Riley. Perhaps he ends up with a music-object, but isn't the object he constructs the opposite of La Monte Young's? Instead of a single object viewed under a microscope, isn't his rather a myriad of little objects viewed through a telescope?

J.C.: Yes, if one listens to him in my way and not in his. But if you conform to what he believes to be the direction of his research, you perceive that his music encompasses a large number of relationships; and rather than coming freely, these relationships are chosen by him. They contribute to giving his music the appearance of a *raga*. You feel that there are many sounds which could occur that would constitute an interruption of this music.

D.C.: Do you consider this music as different from your own as La Monte Young's?

J.C.: It requires certain sounds rather than others. That is why I would say that it belongs to the same school as La Monte Young's. It teaches us the same lesson: the need for tranquility.

D.C.: What would you say, in comparison, about Christian Wolff's music?

J.C.: Well, I have already explained that it's a music I love, because it includes so many silences, and that each sound in it is so much the center of its own existence! I don't think that Christian Wolff's music opposes its environment. While in the case of Young and Riley, events occur which are very unique and have no resemblance to life around us. I already mentioned that some of Christian Wolff's most recent works were written to be played outdoors in an open space. That makes even more obvious the fact that they destroy barriers, that for them there are no walls that can hold up. You can't tell any more whether a given sound is part of the music or whether it, quite simply, happened.[1]

D.C.: *The work becomes the way itself in which we live in our environment?*

J.C.: Yes, and we could say the same for non-musical works: assemblages, or certain paintings.

D.C.: *What is your relationship to conceptual artists?*

J.C.: I don't know them well enough to talk about them. I'm not even up-to-date on their activities or their work.

D.C.: *I only mention them because they refer to you, as well as to Duchamp. You are one of the authors they quote ... For example, you're in the catalogue* Conceptual Art and Conceptual Aspects *edited by Donald Karshan from the 1970 New York Cultural Center Show in which they went back to Joseph Kosuth's text-manifesto.*

J.C.: And what do they quote from me?

D.C.: *The story about an Eskimo lady going on a trip who, not knowing English, repeats what she hears to the ticket clerk — that is, the destination of the preceding traveler ...*

J.C.: And she ends up learning a little English, and asks the ticket clerk: 'If you were going on a trip, where would you go?' And she gets a ticket for a little town in Ohio that the employee mentions to her — and that is where she goes to settle down for good. I don't see that there is too much logic in that story.

D.C.: *But it demonstrates rather well an indifference to goals, to teleology, which is one of your ideas. And it seems to me to be readily applicable to the realm of conceptual art — indifference, by hypothesis, to the result — to the very fact of whether or not there is an object to witness what has been made.*

[1]One of Christian Wolff's very recent pieces, *Burdocks*, is similarly based on silence. But the sounds that do occur are rather often supposed to be attached to each other in little rhythmic and/or melodic groups, which appear quite clearly as 'musical' in the sense of musical conventions of the past ... That creates a feeling of 'humanity' that is effective ... but not overwhelming. (John Cage: footnote of 1972.)

J.C.: Yes, nothing remains but the idea ...

D.C.: Or the concept. You might situate this conceptual art within a broader category, like the one Richard Kostelanetz analyzes under the name 'Inferential Art.' Your silent piece, 4' 33", inspired several nice pages from Kostelanetz with which you are quite familiar, since they are included in his book John Cage.[1]

J.C.: But what really pleases me in that silent piece is that it can be played any time, but it only comes alive when you play it. And each time you do, it is an experience of being very, very much alive.

D.C.: Your own non-conceptual interpretation would seem atrociously 'empirical' to the logicians of conceptual art ...

J.C.: Obviously, if under the title 'work of art' I am dealing with nothing but an idea – not an experience at all – then I lose the experience. Even when I tell myself that I could have had this and that experience, if I didn't experience it, it is lost for me! But I don't think you have to then deprive yourself of experiences. When I gave the first performance of the 840 repetitions of Satie's *Vexations* in New York with several other pianists, there was the usual amount of publicity before the concert, and many people were aware of what was going to happen. Most of them didn't want to come, because they thought they knew what would happen. And even those of us who were playing thought we were headed for something repetitive. We others, the pianists, *indeed had* to know what was going on. But this is what happened. In the middle of those eighteen hours of performance, our lives changed. We were dumb-founded, because something was happening which we had not considered and which we were a thousand miles away from being able to foresee. So, if I apply this observation to conceptual art, it seems to me that the difficulty with this type of art, if I understand it correctly, is that it obliges us to imagine that we know something *before* that something has happened. That is difficult, since the experience itself is always different from what you thought about it. And it seems to me that the experiences each person can have, that everyone is capable of appreciating, are precisely those experiences that contribute to changing us and, particularly, to changing our preconceptions.

D.C.: I read in a text by Peter Yates that he lent you the works of Wittgenstein, and that you felt at home in that philosophy.

J.C.: That's right. But I didn't understand everything. I retained this sentence: 'Something's meaning is how you use it.'

D.C.: That formula reappears, quoted by Joseph Kosuth, in the programmatic text I mentioned a moment ago.

[1]*John Cage,* Edited by Richard Kostelanetz. New York: R.K. Editions, 1974. Pp. 105-109.

J.C.: Not knowing conceptual art, I am unaware of what Kosuth draws from his reading of Wittgenstein.

D.C.: *But what is your reading?*

J.C.: That there are uses, forms of life, ways of treating music, language, etc. And that [everything we use is legitimate, since we use it. That is a situation of fact. There is no 'meaning' beyond this situation of fact. *Everything* is possible. Even conceptual art ...]

D.C.: *Nonetheless, in your eyes, we have to leave this world of discourse in which the conceptual artists are enclosed.*

J.C.: Yes, and understand that *use* rather refers to *experience*.

D.C.: *The logical discourse of the conceptual artists seems illegitimate to you in that it drops experience. But would you say that* all *discourse is in that situation, and that we should distrust language in general?*

J.C.: On the contrary! I can quite easily experience a particular discourse. I can *use* it. But a discourse is not all alone. There are others, and there is also I who am reading it. And I am not a category. Take the example of *Vexations* and the people who didn't come to the concert because they thought they knew beforehand what was going to happen. Well, during those eighteen hours they did other things. They slept, or ate, or worked ... They had other experiences. Well, I don't see how conceptual art differs from that attitude which consists in refusing certain experiences in the name of a certain discourse. That can only mean that you close yourself into a discourse, *in order* not to go to the concert, or *in order* not to paint in a classical or modern manner, etc. But the condition which allows you to minimize certain experiences, to refuse them, to suppress them, is precisely that you can have other experiences. Teleologies only come later. To get there, to neutralize certain experiences in favor of others, you must in fact concentrate and focus your attention on what you want to attain and possess. I, on the contrary, attempt to deconcentrate attention, to distract it. From the point of view of the one who believes himself imprisoned in his discourse, the environment and the reality which is only perceived in a relaxation of attention all flee his grasp, discourse has no hold on it, etc. For me, nothing flees. Nor is anything *present* any more without moving. Things come and go. [They are no more absent than present.] If they were more this or that they would be reduced to objects. Once again we are dealing with processes rather than with objects, and there would be no objects if there were no process of the whole, the process which each object is as well.

SIXTH INTERVIEW

Relationships with painters: Rauschenberg and Mark Tobey
Calligraphy
Developing techniques of writing
Notations: the aquarium
Collaborating with Merce Cunningham
Space: co-presence and simultaneity
The first happening at Black Mountin
Artaud and theatricalizing music
Different kinds of happenings
Kaprow and Higgins
Nam June Paik
Reunion and the idea of play
33 1/3
The audience as participant; *Newport Mix, Rozart Mix, Variations V*
Jazz and free jazz
Concerning the *Museum Event* at Saint-Paul-de-Vence
Canfield
In praise of rock

D.C.: In the last interview, you distanced yourself from conceptual art.[1] *This time, I would like to talk with you about those painters who are close to your ideas and who work in the same direction as you do. For example, Rauschenberg.*

J.C.: It was marvelous when I first met Rauschenberg. Almost immediately, I had the feeling that it was hardly necessary for us to talk, we had so many points in common. To each of the works he showed me, I responded on the spot. No communication between us — we were born accomplices!

D.C.: I remember a particular evening at Baux de Provence. The Merce Cunningham Company was performing during the Dance Festival. You were there with David Tudor. And they used a Rauschenberg set which was the biggest surprise of all. That set consisted entirely of automobiles that moved about — not too fast, of course — among the dancers.

J.C.: I liked the idea of introducing cars into a mountain landscape. They had a lot of trouble making it work in Baux; if you recall, the access road to the theater, or to what served as a theater for that festival — the edge of the crag at Baux — is hardly even a path. In any case, it's a route cars don't often hazard.

D.C.: So a set with only two or three automobiles moving around may be amusing or perilous. Is it sufficient, though?

J.C.: Of course not. When I said I felt in absolute harmony with Rauschenberg, I should have added that it was at the beginning in particular. That was when I met him at Black Mountain. He was then doing monochrome paintings, all in black. Next came his white paintings which used no figuration — simply canvases. Later, as when he was doing automobiles on the Baux crag, he began to put together a few works using specific objects, which he chose. And he systematically and repeatedly showed them. A little like variations, in the sense of Schoen-

[1]Actually I feel very close to conceptual art because of friendship with three extraordinary artists, Tom Marioni, Founder and Director of the Museum of Conceptual Art in San Francisco, and with Bill Anastasi and Dove Bradshaw with whom I play chess. (John Cage: footnote of 1980.)

berg, made for everyone to see. The idea of using cars must have come from theatrical influences. Even when Rauschenberg produced happenings, his theatrical ideas seemed much simpler than his painting ideas. When he painted, he could make you believe in a universe of infinite possibilities. You had the impression that anything at all could happen on the surface. In the theater, you left hungry, as he seemed to have had one rather unique idea and to have stuck to it.

D.C.: And what do you think of the light shows he thought up for other Merce Cunningham ballets?

J.C.: Lights refer back to that idea of a very vast universe, of a multiplication of possibilities. You never caught yourself paying attention to a single effect, and you yourself didn't need to continue concentrating to follow what he wanted to do.

D.C.: Have any other painters felt your need for the diffusion and dispersal of attention?

J.C.: Yes, Mark Tobey.

D.C.: Because of his Zen influences?

J.C.: No, he wasn't a Buddhist. He was interested in another Eastern religion the name of which I have forgotten, but which started in Persia.

D.C.: Yes, his inspiration came from the Book of Certitude *by Baha U'llah, a nineteenth century Persian prophet. But Tobey also was introduced to calligraphy by a Chinese friend, and he spent a while in a Zen monastery in Kyoto; according to Tobey himself, that altered his conception of nature.*

J.C.: Quite honestly, I have been around Tobey for only a short time, in Seattle, where he was living then. But in that small amount of time, we saw each other often – enough for me to be impressed by some of his attitudes. One day we were taking a walk together, from the Cornish School to the Japanese restaurant where we were going to dine together – which meant we crossed through most of the city. Well, we couldn't really walk. He would continually stop to notice something surprising everywhere – on the side of a shack or in an open space. That walk was a revelation for me. It was the first time that someone else had given me a lesson in looking without prejudice, someone who didn't compare what he was seeing with something before, who was sensitive to the finest nuances of light. Tobey would stop on the sidewalks, sidewalks which we normally didn't notice when we were walking, and his gaze would immediately turn them into a work of art. He was attentive to the slightest detail. For him, everything was alive. He had an extraordinary sense of the presence of things. His work was unbelievably diverse. He is often compared to Picasso. He was our own, an American Picasso! Then, of course, there are a lot of his works which don't interest me. But I believe I was fascinated by those I liked more than by any other paintings. Since then, perhaps I have never again quite had the same feeling.[1] The ones I prefer of them all are his *White Writings*.[2] These are white paintings from the Thirties which give the impression that each brushstroke bears a specific quality of white. In my opinion, they surpass Pollock's canvases. Pollock's colors seem to come out of buckets, and if you have five colors, that's all you get. While with Tobey, you can't count them all. Tobey is nature!

D.C.: Weren't you yourself a painter?

J.C.: In my early days, I did both music and painting. I decided to devote myself to music because the opinions of those who counted for me were more in favor of my music than painting.

D.C.: But, it seems to me that in the care you bring to the writing, I would almost say the calligraphy, of your scores there is a very elaborate technique. Am I mistaken?

J.C.: [You know, I simply invented a kind of circus for my own use. If you take the *Solo for Piano* from *Concert*, you will discover a lot of fantasy, a lot of rather chiseled details in it ...]

D.C.: In particular, an aquatic imagery of various algae and corals ...

J.C.: But it in no way tried to pass itself off as a visual rendering. Everything came from a musical demand – or rather from a notational necessity. Because that graphic work, after all, refers back to Schoenberg! I told you how impressed I was by those questions of variation and repetition which occupied Schoenberg's keenest thoughts. In *Concert for Piano*, I decided to apply that principle of variation and repetition, and then innovation and invention of new forms, to the entire work, that is, to the ways of composing. But as the work advanced, I was forced to invent more and more graphisms to solve my problems. It was all done by chance operations, to avoid slipping into uncontrolled improvisation. So, the arrangement of notations on a given page later appeared to convey a certain visual interest. Still, it was only the result of a certain work, and within that work, of my faithfulness in following through to the end the plan I had drawn up for myself, which was to apply, with the help of chance operations, Schoenberg's distinctions.

D.C.: Nonetheless, the more one advances into your work, the more notation becomes a 'causal' writing. It indicates not what must be achieved, but the starting point, the act to be made. If you write fifteen to

[1]Yes; at Basel, this year, in front of one of his works. (John Cage: footnote of 1972.)
[2]And of these, I prefer those which contain no figurative element. (John Cage: footnote of 1972.)

twenty supplementary lines above the upper range of the piano, the performer will indeed have to go look somewhere east of the keyboard for an object to strike. Does your writing for percussion share any of the responsibility for this fixed idea of 'gestural' notation?

J.C.: When I was writing music for percussion, I simply wrote notes to designate the quite different sounds we were able to collect. We constantly changed sounds and the notation merely served as a way of doing it. Shortly thereafter, my writing again became entirely conventional. There were no more notes to be interpreted each time in a different way. But once I developed the prepared piano, notation became a way to produce something. So words were no longer enough to indicate the result. First I had to inscribe the grid of the transformations to be effected inside the piano, and show how to attack the keyboard, but the performer no longer had the impression that he would be able to hear the piece immediately on the first reading, the way it was going to sound.

D.C.: And how did you notate your first 'electronic' works? I am thinking not only of Imaginary Landscapes, *which you worked on at the Cornish School in Seattle, just before the war, but also of your accompaniment music for* The City Wears a Slouch Hat, *Kenneth Patchen's broadcast in Chicago for CBS in 1941.*

J.C.: You know, all that was rather simple. I wrote those attempts just as I had written my percussion scores, with notes and the words which were indispensable for sketching a description of the sounds.

D.C.: Then it was only later that you specially developed your writing techniques?

J.C.: In 1958, a score like *Concert for Piano* served as a sufficient cause for me to seek the greatest diversification possible. [As I mentioned before, there was also my concern with pushing some of Schoenberg's ideas to their limit.] But this non-homogeneous side of my notations also came from the idea of the possible mixture of all notations.

D.C.: They are, in fact, graphic collages! That shows up again in your book Notations. *Without retranscribing the 'playing instructions' that the composer customarily places at the head of his score, you reproduce all possible writings, just classifying them in alphabetical order. It is a book for graphologists.*

J.C.: I added a few comments, in the form of quotations more or less in the margin, which in principle had nothing to do with the musical examples themselves. I completed this task with the collaboration of Alison Knowles, and following the *I Ching*'s indications. It told us how many words we had to write, and in relation to which subject. The *I Ching* also called for remarks from other composers, and specified how many words they should write.

D.C.: And where did you get the idea for such a work?

J.C.: First of all, there was an attempt to procure money for the Foundation for Contemporary Performing Arts. That institution had received some funds, even the bulk of its resources, from the sale of paintings that many painters had given us. The idea was that artists who produce finished products, like painters or sculptors, naturally have access to money, while those who produce works that must be performed, like music, dance, theater, need money and lose money at each performance or production. Performance artists, the artists whose objects are operations to be achieved, therefore received, for several years, money from the Foundation, thanks to those gifts from our painter friends. The day came, however, when we had almost exhausted the generosity of the painters, and we had to find some other subsidy. Several suggestions were made. And I thought of assembling a collection of manuscripts that could be sold. That way, the musicians would in a sense be helping themselves. I have not yet sold that collection, but I hope that it will happen soon.[1]

So I gathered what I myself happened to possess, and I began writing to all the musicians I could think of and many replied with great generosity. I'm still adding to my collection. One of the last works I received was a previously unknown musical project by Marcel Duchamp. It was given to me by Teeny Duchamp and begins with the hypothesis of a freight train of which several cars pass under a loading funnel; the train takes on no coal or liquid, only notes. That brings about a distribution of notes in different octaves, and the production of new scales of musical sounds.

D.C.: The preface of Notations *contains an illuminating comparison on the way you envision music and also existence in general. I want to talk about the aquarium.*

J.C.: Yes, I started out with the idea that in a clasic aquarium each type of fish is enclosed in a little compartment with its name in Latin above it. While in more recent aquariums, all the species mingle together and it becomes impossible to decide, when a fish passes in front of you, exactly what name you should call it. So, I allowed myself a few extrapolations which suit not only my book, where the most varied notations (ranging from the most meticulous exactitude to a total absence of notation) co-exist if only through alphabetical order, but which also suit music as I envision it, and the entire whole of society where segregation – and I believe this strongly – must eventually be eliminated.

D.C.: What McLuhan says about the electronic age's need to overcome the segregation of people reminds me of your aquarium. Today, music no

---

[1]The collection has been deposited at Northwestern University though it remains to be purchased. (John Cage: footnote of 1980.)

longer conceives of itself as isolated.

J.C.: We have more than just ears.

D.C.: And that again raises a problem familiar to aestheticians: that of correspondence between the arts.

J.C.: I don't believe very much in 'correspondence.' It seems to me that instead there is dialogue. That is, that the arts, far from communicating, converse among themselves. The more foreign they are to each other, the more useful the dialogue.

D.C.: That applies perfectly to your collaboration with Merce Cunningham! Have you known each other long?

J.C.: Yes, since about 1936. That was in Seattle. He was a student of Bonnie Bird, who had a dance class at the Cornish School. I was Bonnie Bird's composer-accompanist.

D.C.: That was when you were conducting your percussion orchestra?

J.C.: But I didn't accompany the dancers with my orchestra! There was no room for the orchestra. In the theater, the dancers used the stage. There were no wings. To make a space for the piano, we had to remove the first row of seats. Those conditions brought about the development of the prepared piano. But I often would ask dancers to leave the theater and play in my percussion orchestra. And Merce was one of them. And then it became obvious that he was going to devote his life to dance. So, he left Seattle, to join the Martha Graham Company, of which Bonnie Bird had been a member. And from there, he went to New York – long before I did.

D.C.: You lost touch with him?

J.C.: We didn't begin working together until 1943. And it was I who encouraged him to leave the Martha Graham Company, to try his own wings. It's not that I didn't like Martha Graham's work. In fact, I liked some of her dances a great deal, one of them in particular, *Celebration*. But the works she produced became more and more literary. There was a series of works on Emily Dickinson, etc., and I was opposed to all that literature. So I suggested to Jean Erdman and Merce Cunningham that they leave the Martha Graham Company, and they put together a program for the two of them for which I wrote the music. Since then, I have never stopped working with Merce Cunningham. I have composed a lot of music for him, and I have been responsible for his Company's music. At present, as I have explained to you, I share my responsibilities with David Tudor and Gordon Mumma.[1] Thus, we are never separate. I participate in nearly all of his tours.

[1] Currently, together with David Tudor, and Martin Kalve and Takehisa Kosugi. (John Cage: footnote of 1980.)

D.C.: *The communion of spirit between you should be complete. However, I retain this word 'dialogue' to characterize your rapport with him. From one ballet to another, your music changes completely; but, with Merce, you get the impression you're rediscovering figures, or even established and codified styles. So when you see the films devoted to Merce Cunningham, and when you compare them with his ballets — which was the case in Paris last season — you say to yourself that the dancers work in such a precise, such an exact manner that nothing unforeseen happens any more.*

J.C.: Yes, but there you are, facing the unavoidable difference between dance and music, between the movements of a human body and the 'dance' of sounds.

D.C.: *We're not completely in the aquarium any more?*

J.C.: If two sounds bump into each other, there is no problem; in the case of choreography, a slightly violent collision between two dancers may prohibit one of them from continuing to dance. You have to consider the opposition between utility — this time I am using the word in the sense of a necessity you cannot avoid — and aesthetic experience. This opposition doesn't exist, or no longer exists, in music; it maintains its rigidity in the case of the dance. Thus music offers us the model for a life disengaged from all utility. While choreography is an example of what must be done in order to live with utility. I would, however, like to stress a relatively unknown aspect of Merce's action — and, I must also say, of my own. Our common ideas have led many younger dances and choreographers to reject the vigorous technique which he himself maintains at all costs. And when he sees what these dancers and choreographers are doing, Merce is often tempted to question the extreme discipline he always maintains, even now, in his troupe. Well, I believe that it is very important that he has insisted on preserving this discipline — as far as he is concerned. Why? Because energy at its highest level, energy that can be expressed by the movement of the human body, will not burst forth unless the dancers have had the courage to train themselves with extreme meticulousness. He says that over and over again. And he's right.

D.C.: *Nonetheless, there are in his repertory, dances which are more relaxed and loose than others.*

J.C.: That is true, certain dances are strict. Others are more open. I must still say that Merce Cunningham's ideas, although not always the same as my own, are very close to mine. Whatever the circumstances, we have always been able to work together with complete freedom. That was possible precisely because we share the same views.

D.C.: *You and Merce have reflected a* sense of space *which is lacking in much contemporary dance. Did Merce Cunningham get that sense from you, and how did he get it?*

J.C.: We didn't reach autonomy from the very first. Of course, it's an idea which has always haunted me. The independence of two different arts comes about through the space around each. And space is what we are always lacking. Better to have too much of it than not enough. But I will answer you by telling you how, in 1952, at a festival at Brandeis University, Leonard Bernstein introduced the first ballets using *musique concrète*. He asked Merce Cunningham to perform twice in one evening a dance on a series of extracts from the *Symphony for a Single Man*, by Pierre Schaeffer and Pierre Henry, because of the strangeness of the music. Merce, in fact, arranged for two completely distinct choreographies: one, a solo, the other for seventeen dancers. And as some of the dancers were relatively inexperienced, he asked them to limit themselves to performing acts from everyday life. But it's difficult to find where you are in this music because in general it lacks a regular beat. So, the dancers received a score which was all their own and did not follow the music. The music stopped imposing anything at all on the dance. That was in 1952; since then, Merce and I have had many occasions to renew that experience. We were in agreement each time in recognizing dance's, as well as music's, right to space, which simply assumes the possibility of simultaneity. Anyway, Merce Cunningham has freed dance from its subservience to what it is not. That is what allowed us to continue working together, that is, to meet each other.

D.C.: Then, before anything else, dialogue is space?

J.C.: Certainly. Since 1952, the dancers, at least those in the Company, no longer expect some sort of synchronization of action to sound. We share the same time ... But this sharing is no longer hierarchical. Above all, rehearsals before performances can take place separately.

D.C.: You mentioned 1952 as being a particularly significant year for Merce Cunningham and his dancers. But at the Museum of Modern Art you talked about another, perhaps even more important, event, which also dates from 1952, in which Merce Cunningham participated a good deal, and which you organized — the first happening at Black Mountain College. There you gathered together in a free exchange not only two but all the arts.

J.C.: The idea was in the air. Merce Cunningham had for a long time been interested in the problems of assembling heterogeneous facts that can remain without interrelationships. For the Black Mountain show, my idea had been to treat the surrounding objects, including the different activities of the artists, as sounds. So I had to find a way to multiply those 'sound sources.' On the other hand, I was intrigued by Schwitters' descriptions of Dada theater in a book that had just been published. And I had read Artaud. Thus we decided to divide the audience into four triangles whose peaks would be directed toward an empty center. So free spaces were arranged everywhere. And the action wasn't supposed to occur in the center, but everywhere around the audience. That is, in the four corners, in the gaps, and also from above. There were ladders, which you could climb to read poems or to recite texts. I climbed up there myself and delivered a lecture. There were also poems by M. C. Richards and Charles Olson, piano by David Tudor, films projected on the ceiling and on the walls of the room. Finally, there were Rauschenberg's white canvases, while he himself played old records on an antique phonograph and Merce Cunningham improvised amidst and around all that. The whole thing lasted forty-five minutes.

D.C.: Wasn't that leaving music for theater?

J.C.: But my music was already theater. And theater is only another word for designating life.

D.C.: Your Theater Piece *of 1960, however, bears a title which hints that it is not exactly music.*

J.C.: The score of *Theater Piece* gives the performers a series of numbers which apply to actions. These actions pertain to things to which the performers themselves are willing to relate theatrically. So, on the basis of what they decide to work with as actions and props, the participants themselves make music out of the piece, an audio-visual production, a 'theater piece', etc. They do what they do. But there's no way they can perform without making sounds.

D.C.: In your happening at Black Mountin, you had set up in the same way a precise group of 'theatrical' actions to be run through.

J.C.: Yes, it was a very 'compartmentalized' piece. I needed a lot of chance operations to find all those specifications. The division of the audience, which took into consideration the absence of a stage [as Artaud points out], allowed people to see each other, since everything was turned toward the center, as in a theater-in-the-round. But things happened at points around the audience. So, as far as what was being presented to the audience, everything had been fixed. Now I no longer operate that way.

D.C.: What do you do?

J.C.: First of all, I prefer to avoid having the public in a fixed position. There are seats so that people who are tired can rest, but we make sure that the seats don't impede the audience's freedom to move from one place to another. And not only may the people move around in the hall, but outside as well. They are free to leave when they wish.

D.C.: *You go beyond what Artaud had envisioned.*

J.C.: What *The Theater and Its Double* taught me was the notion of a multi-dimensional theater. We were all greatly influenced by Artaud at Black Mountain. Tudor had not only done his work on René Char and Mallarmé, but also on Artaud, whom Mary Carolyn Richards had just translated. For the happening, the length was dictated by the time it took to read my lecture.

D.C.: *What subject did you talk about?*

J.C.: It was a lecture with long silences. I don't recall whether it was my *Lecture on Nothing* or my *Juilliard Lecture*; it must have been my *Juilliard Lecture*, the one that was subsequently published in *A Year from Monday*. I put on a black suit. I climbed to the top of the ladder, which was on the edge of the square made up of the four triangles of audience. I used very precise time brackets notated and placed in the framework of the forty-five minutes of the entire duration.

D.C.: *Did all the participants have to conform to such strict programming?*

J.C.: From the point of view of the length of time brackets, yes. And there was superimposition of these distinct ones. But of all those elements, dance, of course, was the most free. Merce Cunningham moved about in the aisles between the triangles of the public, and he could change positions as he wished, in front of, in, and behind the audience, and around all of us. As for David Tudor, he was entirely free in the choice of his pieces, but, like the others, he had to conform to the time limitations.

D.C.: *What do you think of the subsequent flowering of happenings in response to your Black Mountain show? Was it a well-defined artistic genre, the gathering of elements coming from several arts? You yourself talk less about happenings than about events, mixes, reunions ... Why?*

J.C.: As far as I'm concerned, I believe that music alone only very rarely manages to introduce us to life. When we live, we see, we smell, we touch, we exercize our body every moment. We must cite McLuhan on this subject, what he says is true. Now, I don't see a great need for classifying all these efforts. The titles have little importance. In each case, it is a question of developing a form of theater without depending on a text. It is as simple as that – for me at least. Obviously, words can enter into these happenings. But the principal thing is that they not begin with a text or try to express its aesthetic qualities. That was what Artaud had already envisioned.

D.C.: *Can your work, then, be differentiated from that of a Kaprow, a Higgins, or that of the Fluxus Group?*

J.C.: In the case of Kaprow or Higgins, intentionality is present. If something unexpected happens, in their eyes it can only signify an interruption. They make true *objects* of their happenings. I, on the contrary, am committed to letting anything happen, to making everything that happens acceptable.

D.C.: *Can you give me some examples of a happening that returns to the object state?*

J.C.: I attended the production of a play by Dick Higgins in Chicago. While it was progressing, a young man in the audience got up and climbed onto the stage. Finally, he stood on his head in the lotus position. Dick Higgins, who was performing on stage, immediately stopped the action, went quickly towards the young man and pushed him over. He could not tolerate an external intervention, even though it was well to the side of the stage; his work could not accommodate anything else at all. I witnessed a similar audience reaction during a performance of the Merce Cunningham Company, at Saint-Paul-de-Vence. But there, the intervention was more serious, because there was the risk of physical danger to both the members of the audience who were on stage and the dancers. In Higgins' case, his intentions were interrupted, but not, in reality, what he was doing.

D.C.: *But what do you think of the activities of the Fluxus Group? And those of the Korean Nam June Paik?*

J.C.: I am not very familiar with *Fluxpieces*; I believe it has something to do with distributing directions to the audience concerning the most varied actions. But I know Nam June Paik, and I can talk about him. His work is fascinating, and rather often frightening. Now I would think twice before attending one of his performances! He generates a real sense of danger, and sometimes goes further than what we are ready to accept. But it is very interesting. He has made an hour-long film without any images at all. All you see is the dust on the film itself and on the lens of the projector. For a whole hour! But it changes all the time, and it is extremely interesting. He has also produced some extraordinary things on television, and now on video. But I have a grim memory of him from the happening in Cologne, at Mary Bauermeister's ...

D.C.: *The Homage to John Cage?*

J.C.: Yes. Nam June Paik suddenly approached me, cut off my tie and began to shred my clothes, as if to rip them off of me. Just behind him, there was an open window with a drop of perhaps six floors to the street, and everyone suddenly had the impression that he was going to throw himself out of the window. Fortunately, he was content with leaving the room, but we remained dazed, immobile, and terrified for some time.

Finally, the telephone rang – it was Paik calling to say that the performance was over!

D.C.: Still in the realm of happenings, what did you produce after your experiments of the years 1952 to 1960? What about Reunion, *for example?*

J.C.: The idea of *Reunion* was to bring together many distinct sound systems, each activated by a different composer. And the word *Reunion* signified that the composers, who had always been separated, could now come together and make music in common. The first performance took place in Toronto in 1968. David Behrman, David Tudor, and Lowell Cross were there. Each had his own sound sources and systems, that is, means of modulation and amplification and loudspeakers. All these systems were active, each one of them connected to squares of a chess board that Lowell Cross had wired electronically; movements took place on the chess board, then outside the chess board. The chess board acted as a gate, open or closed to these sources, these streams of music. The first time, it was Marcel, Teeny Duchamp, and I who played. Our game affected all the sound sources, but it was not one itself.

D.C.: It was Duchamp who taught you to play chess?

J.C.: I was his very poor student. One time, exasperated, he said to me: 'So, don't you ever want to win?'

D.C.: I can only think of one effort comparable to yours: that of Stockhausen in Darmstadt, I think it was in 1967, but before Reunion. *Stockhausen assembled twelve composers, and each one's sequences intermingled with and followed each other, as in* Reunion. *Except Stockhausen remained the* maestro *because he had imposed an* a priori *plan – on the different scores. It certainly was no chess match! More probably a happening for composers. With something in mind.*

J.C.: Yes, the chess game contains a finality in itself, since the object is to win. But if the game is used to distribute sound sources, and therefore to define a global sound system, it has no goal. It is a paradox, purposeful purposelessness.

D.C.: But that paradox doesn't presuppose a renunciation on your part of all control.

J.C.: There is, obviously, control over what happens. But that control is a function of uncertainty. You never know what the performing composers are playing. And you have no idea of how the game will develop.

D.C.: That is already the theme of one of your most famous works, the Imaginary Landscape No. 4 *of 1951.*

J.C.: Yes, the radios were certain to produce very different kinds of music. The actions of the performers and the juxtaposition of twelve sets should have provided for completely unforeseen auditory encounters. A brief story about that work: people say that at its first performance, in 1951, nothing happened, because it was too late at night and we couldn't find anything on the radios. In fact, there were all sorts of broadcasts! Still, I have always been attracted by those sonorities that someone else wants, and that are immediately distorted and transformed to fit into the sphere of goallessness. It's not exactly a collage. It's a way of opening up to the absence of will. In the case of the *Imaginary Landscape*, I had a goal, that of erasing all will and the very idea of success. So I composed a work. I had foreseen perfectly well the fragility of that work! And once again, contrary to what people had expected (and to what each person reports ...), the radios did their job that evening quite satisfactorily. So you see, I sometimes manage to bring about pure processes.

D.C.: *Still, you exercize relative control over what happens in* Reunion.

J.C.: But not in *33 1/3*. All this title says is the speed of a long-playing record. When we first presented it, we had a dozen phonographs and almost two hundred fifty records at hand. When the audience entered the hall, they found no seats to sit on. There were only tables, around the room, with piles of records, and loudspeakers distributed throughout the space. It very quickly became obvious to each member of the audience that, if they wanted a little music, they would have to produce it themselves. For a long time, I had been looking for a way to bring about what people call audience participation. But I don't want people to sit down at the piano if they have not studied it. On the other hand, you can let everybody handle a phonograph.

D.C.: *Doesn't that absence of intention still come as a blow to the audience – or the performers?*

J.C.: At the time of the performance that I am telling you about, there was actually a rather elderly man who was visibly bothered by hearing so much music at the same time. It sounded like a *Musicircus*! Then, and this is the only time I ever saw something like this, he began to go around the room taking off the records and turning off the phonographs one by one. But he couldn't take two steps before someone put on another record!

D.C.: *Have you had other ideas for getting the audience to 'participate' in the performance.*

J.C.: *Newport Mix*, for example – a demonstration of a type that seems slightly less 'musical.' In a sense, it resembles theater more than music. People were invited to dine in a restaurant which is a yacht anchored in the Ohio River. On each invitation, the guests were each asked to bring a tape loop. Nothing was specified, except that without a tape loop, no one would be admitted. Many people came without a loop. But we had prepared the necessary equipment for making loops, and before entering, each person was obliged to record his own. And everything had been arranged to allow the tapes to circulate everywhere, around the tables and above ...

D.C.: That brings us back to the Rozart Mix *and the 1970 Music Weeks in Paris.*

J.C.: The important factor, in these works that use tapes, is that the sounds obtained don't result from predetermined choice. I set a minimum of eighty-eight tape loops for the *Rozart Mix* because with such a number of loops, you can't keep up a willful control of what music will appear on a given tape. What is important is to make the situation complex. People won't really begin to participate unless the situation is already complex. The role of the composer is to prepare the elements which will permit the situation to become complex.

D.C.: The notation becomes very simple ...

J.C.: That depends on the circumstances. As you know, the score of *Rozart Mix* is just the correspondence between Alvin Lucier and myself – it is our letters on *Rozart Mix* which have been photocopied. On other occasions, in particular in the case of *Variations V*, I wrote the score *after* the work. This score simply contains remarks written after the performance, not to describe the work, but to explain to those who might want to play the work how to go about it.

D.C.: Doesn't that end up being a description of what was put together after the fact, as in the case of some electronic studio works?

J.C.: Not exactly. I'm talking about remarks, not descriptions. And I determined by chance operations not only the number of remarks, but the number of words in each remark ... I had some difficulty adjusting to those requirements.

D.C.: Is the notation part of the work? Is it unique to the work?

J.C.: In the present case, it is a sort of poetry on *Variations V* – a prolongation of the work. But what do you mean when you ask if it is part of the work?

D.C.: I had in mind Kostelanetz's formulae on 4' 33". For him, each piece of inferential art includes not only the object, the piece itself, but the whole of the commentaries that can be made on it. The score, the written trace, and also the mental traces are all drawn into the wake of the work, all became work. Including commentaries, criticisms, etc.

J.C.: [The notation of *Variations V* may pass for inferential notation.] But the audience that attends *Variations V* is not obliged to know the score. And you must not confuse my remarks on the first performance, which serve as guidelines for a second performance, with criticisms. There is no judgement involved!

D.C.: *You just orient the reader.*

J.C.: I explain.

D.C.: *But your explanation doesn't lead back to what took place. You substitute variation-notation for repetition-notation.*

J.C.: You could say that I am still faithful to Schoenberg!

D.C.: *Your notation tends toward indeterminacy.*

J.C.: Yes, and the extreme manifestation of this form of notation would be no more notation at all!

D.C.: *Isn't that what free jazz proposes?*

J.C.: We're going to have to talk about that! Everyone tells me that jazz is *free* today. But when I listen to it, it always seems to me to be confined within a world of ideas and musical relationships.

D.C.: *But that's not all there is in free jazz …*

J.C.: In most jazz compositions I hear an improvisation that resembles a conversation. One musician answers another. So, rather than each one doing what he wants, he listens with all his might to what the other one is doing, just to answer him better. And what is called free jazz probably tries to free itself from time and rhythmic periodicity. The bass doesn't play like a metronome any more. But even then, you still get the feeling of a beat. It remains 'music.'

D.C.: *Sometimes. But sometimes, too, it moves away …*

J.C.: Perhaps, but I want to tell you about an experience from a few years ago that I had with a jazz group in Chicago. They told me so many times that they admired my music that I agreed to participate in one of their sessions. They asked me to listen to them, and then to tell them what I thought they should do to move in a direction which would suit me. They grouped themselves on the stage and acted as I just described to you. They began to listen to and answer each other. At first I thought that if they started by separating and moving around the room, everything would work better. I advised them not to listen to each other, and asked each one to play as a soloist, as if he were the only one in the world. And I warned them in particular: 'If you hear someone starting to play loud, don't feel that this obliges you to play louder yourself.' I repeated to them that they should be independent, no matter what happened. Well, at the rehearsal, everything went along quite well. It was what you might call successful free jazz! And they were very pleased with what happened. Unfortunately, when they had to face an audience, no matter how much they walked around them, they started taking up their old habits of conversing and answering again. It is very difficult to liberate yourself so quickly!

D.C.: And in the musicircuses, do you find that the musicians have freed themselves from their habits – in particular, the habit of conversing?

J.C.: In Paris, I noticed that some groups fell silent when they noticed that other groups were starting to play. That's in fact exactly what happens in jazz, except that in *Musicircus*, the effect was the opposite. However, in the two musicircuses which we produced in the United States, each group really worked in an independent manner. No one worried about his neighbor. The result was amazing. But if you stick to concentrated attention, or if you retain the principle of discourse, musicircuses may not be of any interest at all.

D.C.: You revert to a concert situation.

J.C.: In Paris, the listeners were faced with the problem of becoming virtuosi and producing their own circus!

D.C.: They were expecting a work ...

J.C.: People always think that there is something to understand. They imagine that the composer really had something in mind.

D.C.: And when they attend a Merce Cunningham ballet, they are unable to admit that at this point in time you don't know what the dancers are doing.

J.C.: But the contrast between the freedom of sounds and the non-freedom of the dancers should give them the idea that a ballet is an encounter, a collision, and not just a unison.

D.C.: It seems to me that at the Museum Event *of a few years ago at Saint-Paul-de-Vence, or more recently when the ballet* Canfield, *with music by Pauline Oliveros, was performed, the public began to feel that collision, they were shaken ...*

J.C.: Yes, at Saint-Paul-de-Vence, people followed the dancers into different rooms of the museum. Others gathered around me on the terrace. Little by little, it became fluid. Did you really find the spectators more relaxed for *Canfield*?

D.C.: You set the example of movement. You would leave the room, and the musicians would communicate with you by radio. The sound continued although it wasn't noticeably connected to your actions. And the dancers on stage were obviously quite unconcerned with what was going on around them ... Yes, I think it was successful. There was no attempt to fix attention on any one thing.

J.C.: No more discourse. Instead, there was electronics.

D.C.: *In your eyes, isn't electronics the saving grace for rock and roll?*

J.C.: If we're talking about rock, everything changes! Electronics has transformed everything in it. Jazz was hung up on its traditions; but in rock, the traditions are drowned in sound. Everything becomes confused – it's wonderful! And the performers seem to be all in agreement... They are alive! While in jazz, they get bored. Jazz is a linear form; not rock.

D.C.: *But there's no escaping the beat, especially in rock!*

J.C.: But that regularity disappears if the amplification is sufficient. You no longer have a rhythmic object in front of you shaken like a rattle. You are inside the object, and you realize that this object is a river ... With rock, there is a change of scale: you are thrown into the current. Rock takes everything along with it.

D.C.: *The effect on the listener of some of your works,* Variation V *or* HPSCHD *for example, is rather similar. Certain moments, like during the performance of* Song Books *at the Théâtre de la Ville, remind me of what first struck me in* Canfield*: immersion in an ocean of sound. Yours or Pauline Oliveros' music takes on a dimension of waves breaking into foam. You feel caught up in a battle of the elements, in a tempest ...*

J.C.: I'll make a date with you for *Thunderclaps*! You'll be caught in a *real* tempest.[1]

[1] See the footnote on p. 212. (John Cage: footnote of 1972.)

SEVENTH INTERVIEW

Cheap Imitation: beyond indeterminacy

The presence of others in music

Homage to David Tudor

The plurality beyond the ego

The current situation in France

Pierre Boulez

Individualism

Love and tranquility

Devotion to Satie

The subject of the *Song Books*: Satie and Thoreau

Life at Stony Point

Mycology

Drugs and family feeling

D.C.: Given what you said about the indeterminacy *of a certain number of your works, to what extent do you feel it applies to your work in general? Aren't you subverting your own practice of indeterminacy when, in* Cheap Imitation *for example, you return to a more traditional mode of composition?*

J.C.: *Cheap Imitation* really stands in complete contrast to my indeterminate works. It has a beginning and an end. It has three parts. Well, that's all a result of my great love of Satie. In a strict way, the work follows sometimes the melodic line, sometimes the accompaniment of Satie's *Socrate*. Perhaps I could be blamed for my devotion to Satie. But I would never renounce it. In the rest of my work, I'm in harmony with myself – because of what we might call a kind of continuity – in the quest for an ever more radical indeterminacy. But *Cheap Imitation* clearly takes me away from all that. [So if my ideas sink into confusion, I owe that confusion to love.[1]]

D.C.: After so many risky experiments, don't you feel a need to get back to firm ground, *even if that means some sort of tradition?*

J.C.: I would say instead that what may be making my present position puzzling in your eyes is that you're not thinking of the whole of my work. This view of the whole, I feel, leads to the observation that I have never written except for individuals, for specific persons. I have only very rarely written for symphony orchestras. Generally speaking, everything I have written has been intended for soloists. Or for small groups. First came my compositions for my own percussion orchestra – for musicians with whom I was working and whom I trained. I wrote my music for two pianos once I had met Fizdale and Gold in New York. I composed *Sonatas and Interludes* because I had Maro Ajemian in mind. Everyone can play them; but the work in itself remains a portrait of Maro Ajemian. A black rose giving as much the impression of being asleep as of being awake ...

[1]Performed without a conductor, *Cheap Imitation* does not, however, remain an object. The work returns to itself to *make itself*. It becomes a current, a flux. Even the rhythm is better. And the 'confusion' I felt in 1970 today seems to have diminished. As soon as there is no one in charge of things, there is passage from object to process. I will come back to this later on. (John Cage: footnote of 1972.)

D.C.: Your two piano works are portraits of Fizdale and Gold?

J.C.: I consider them as elegant, not as Fizdale and Gold themselves, but as certain neo-classical scores that they like to play – and that elegance is surely a distinct feature, not at all comparable to the characteristics of my other works.

D.C.: There was also David Tudor ...

J.C.: And his extraordinary virtuosity, and his competence, and the meticulousness with which he has always resolved all sorts of technical problems ... Yes, that fascinated me. But what made him what he is for me is his spirit, or his personality – I don't know what word is appropriate here.

D.C.: 'Firm ground', then, means other people? David Tudor, for example?

J.C.: In all my works since 1952, I have tried to achieve what would seem interesting and vibrant to David Tudor.[1] Whatever succeeds in the works I have done has been determined in relationship to him. In my opinion my most significant production, the one I like to think will always hold some interest for him, is *Variations II*. When I composed *Music of Changes*, David Tudor applied himself completely to that music. At that time, he *was* the *Music of Changes*. And then, after a few years, that identification disappeared – because it is in David's nature not to repeat what has been done – because he must always go forward. That's why he no longer plays the piano, except on certain, very rare occasions. What strikes me is his devotion to electronic circuits both audio and video ... But we have already talked about that. Still, I must stress that to this day he has always accorded to this work, which is his very own, the same respect that he devoted to the work of composers working outside his own preoccupations. David Tudor was present in everything I was doing ... Today he is present in himself. And I am truly very happy about that.

D.C.: You counted very heavily on David Tudor's presence for the Song Books, *at the Music Weeks in Paris ...*

J.C.: When I was commissioned to do the *Song Books,* I knew that not only Cathy Berberian but also Simone Rist would be performing them. So, and I admit this, I forgot that I was composing for them ... and I composed for David Tudor! Which is stupid, since David doesn't sing![2] When I was composing *Aria* in 1958, I was around Cathy every day. I

[1] In 1974, I began writing the *Etudes Australes* with another pianist, Grete Sultan, in mind. Since 1977, I have worked closely with the violinist, Paul Zukofsky. That work, currently on the *Freeman Etudes*, continues. (John Cage: footnote of 1980.)
[2] Actually we have often sung together in Takehisa Kosugi's music for Cunningham's *Squaregame*. (John Cage: footnote of 1980.)

was able to write something that suited her. When I was composing for David Tudor, he would play what I was writing, and so it suited him. But Simone Rist . . . I didn't know *who* she was. I could only think of her as an instrument. For all I knew, she could even have been a better instrument than Cathy Berberian! Then, despite myself, I composed with David Tudor in mind.

*D.C.: **But** is composing always in reference to someone? Doesn't your indeterminate music aim at the anonymous . . .*

J.C.: It's true that I'm often asked what the role of the composer is today. What it is – or what it should be. And I answer, just as often, that I'm not the least bit interested in telling others what they have to do. I'm not a policeman! It bothers me even more that, in the *Song Books* as well as in *Cheap Imitation*, I acted exactly like I say others shouldn't.

D.C.: Is that a contradiction you really feel!

J.C.: Yes, but I still have excuses for it. I was commissioned to do *Cheap Imitation* by the Koussevitsky Foundation; they had been asking me for an orchestral work for a long time. Moreover, I was refused the right to arrange Satie's *Socrate* for two pianos;[1] in its place, I needed a score which would somehow be rhythmically identical with *Socrate*. Unfortunately, I was so infatuated with my imitation of Satie[2] that I decided to convert it into a work for orchestra, two birds with one stone. In fact, maybe even three! So, I willingly admit that between the *Song Books* and *Cheap Imitation*, I hardly fulfilled the role of the composer as I defined it elsewhere. To conclude my excuses, I would say that my problem is to place my ideas on the improvement of the conditions of life in this world in relation to my viewpoints about composition . . . My work has stopped being purely musical. I mix musical needs with social needs.

D.C.: Don't social needs lead you to short change musical needs?

J.C.: That would be odd. Remember that some of my recent works aren't written for their real performers, but for David Tudor, who doesn't play them!

D.C.: Doesn't that contradict what you call 'social' needs? You always write for a virtuoso!

J.C.: No, that's not it. My thinking on the present state of the world makes me write not for an individual or a particular person, but for many individuals and persons instead . . .

[1] I actually made the arrangement for a dance by Merce Cunningham. (John Cage: footnote of 1972.)
[2] Originally for piano solo, 1969, now also for unaccompanied violin (1977). (John Cage: footnote of 1980.)

D.C.: Yes, but you always come back to David Tudor!

J.C.: I do however believe that this tendency to write for many people and not for one alone is clear in *Musicircus*, in *HPSCHD*, in the *Newport Mix*, etc. They are not pieces for *one* virtuoso.

D.C.: But by multiplying your image of the performer, you run the risk of being disappointed, as you were, for instance, by the Paris Musicircus?

J.C.: That's a problem I haven't yet resolved. In the United States, the first two musicircuses came off in an atmosphere I felt to be harmonious with my ideas on world improvement. A lot of people working together without getting in each other's way. In France, the same idea fell prey to ... a sort of social constipation! How do you resolve this problem? Should I blame the Parisian public? Or myself? Is it that I know America, in the sense that I know *who* David Tudor is, while I don't know anything about France, or about what it's like to be French? I can't answer those questions. I would like to be able to say that all men, all over the earth, are but one and the same person ...

D.C.: But you can't.

J.C.: It's not that I want to deny the multiplicity and variety of individuals. But I cling to the idea that all those who are living now, wherever they are, are more or less subjected to the same information. More than once, it occurred to me that what seemed completely new to us in New York was commonplace in Zagreb, for example. Except, when I speak to the French, they answer me by culture, they cling to their culture as property, and they can't give up that property. It sticks to their skin. It separates them from other peoples with another culture.

D.C.: Does what you are saying apply to a man like Boulez?

J.C.: Probably. I told you how thrilled I was by his *Second Sonata*. Faced with a work like that, I couldn't help but be stupefied by its activism, by the sum of the activities inherent in it. I couldn't limit myself to traditional relationships anymore. I didn't understand that music, I felt it. After I left France, around the time Boulez wrote that *Sonata*, around 1952, I kept up a very long correspondence with him, which ended only when I began to work with chance operations. Boulez's letters interested me no end; I dare hope that my own letters didn't leave him indifferent! But he rejected outright any acceptance of the idea of chance. That wasn't a part of his views. Later came Mallarmé's posthumous *Book*, which could have brought us together again, since in the end Mallarmé too accorded primacy to chance. In fact, Boulez in turn threw himself into chance operations. But for him, chance served as a pretext for inventing the term 'aleatory.' I believe he established its present musical definition. Well, he used that word only to describe appropriate and correct chance operations, as opposed to those which seemed to him inappropriate or incorrect – mine! In fact, his chance operations fit into his compositions only as part of a drama. He very strictly distinguishes between determinate passages and 'aleatory' passages in the same composition. As a whole, it becomes a drama between opposites: determinate vs. indeterminate.

D.C.: And your conception of 'theater' is different?

J.C.: It's not dramatic. Even when I was in High school, I preferred speech to debate. It didn't bother me at all to talk, but it bored me to argue with people who contradicted me.

D.C.: Next to you, Boulez appears to be a 'literary' author. His theory of the parenthesis or italics owes a lot to Mallarmé. But there's nothing similar to that in your ideas on indeterminacy.

J.C.: I agree completely.

D.C.: You have already mentioned the impact of certain literary themes on your composition. But would you explain it again — this time in relation to Boulez?

J.C.: Joyce, you know, is my principal source of inspiration. There was also Gertrude Stein. And, since college days, I have always greatly enjoyed Eliot, Pound, and Cummings. Joyce and Stein,[1] however, remain the most important to me.

D.C.: But Boulez has likewise referred to Joyce. As much as to Mallarmé.

J.C.: The difference is that I continue to admire Joyce to such an extent that I would never say that my work is 'Joycean'! You know my concern for richness and complexity ... Well, I can very well see how much I could criticize everything I have done from that double point of view, by comparing it with Joyce. *Nothing* I have composed up until now comes from Joyce, because in richness and in complexity, none of my works can be compared to his.[2]

D.C.: 'Culture,' as you understand it, doesn't wait around to be used as justification.

J.C.: And, above all, I'm certain that culture, as it is understood in France, will soon crumble into dust because of what McLuham calls electronic technology. Or rather – *it will evaporate, and fall again,*

[1] And Pound. (John Cage: footnote of 1980.)
[2] Since 1976, I have been occupied with *Finnegans Wake*. Besides several *Writing Through Finnegans Wake* I have made *****, ***** *Circus on ***********, a means of translating any book into music, and, with the technical assistance of John Fulleman, my realization of it, *Roaratorio, an Irish Circus on Finnegans Wake.* (John Cage: footnote of 1980.)

perhaps polluted — but usable everywhere, in other circumstances and by other peoples.

D.C.: Listening to you, it would seem that literature may be 'utilized' by the musician. But he doesn't have to bow down before it.

J.C.: I believe in particular that all the thoughts of all 'cultures' – in the ethnological sense of the term – and all the experiments ever attempted and ever recorded are going to come together, unite, and intermingle. They will form a climate with scarcely any focus. Thus you'll be able to use it differently each time. Repetition won't exist any more.

D.C.: Then it's ultimately repetition, the sense of a refuge in tradition, that you detect in European composers?

J.C.: [And I also feel that in Europe, you have always tended to take shelter under your cultural umbrella. People don't like cultural fallout – they believe true cultural purity is possible. That's probably an illusion.]

D.C.: 'Purity' equals isolation, compartmentalization. And also individualism?

J.C.: Yes, but you probably think I'm an individualist when I compose for specific people! But that's not the case. To bring all these ideas together, let me say that I would be happy to continue being a composer in two ways. First, I hope to go farther, much farther than in the past, in unleashing processes and activities not controlled by any authority whatsoever.[1] That is the idea of the *project* – I plan on getting more and more participants involved in my efforts. And giving less and less orders! That is the quantitative side which, as you know, interests me much more than the qualitative side.

And there is a second point. I would like to be able to continue writing for individuals. But there's no sense in writing for someone if that someone doesn't want you to write for him. So I'll write for me ...[2] In the short run, that might turn into an investigation of language. I told you how interested I am in the problems of language. And how much I like to talk. Perhaps I'll even start singing!

D.C.: When you talked about Cheap Imitation, *you spoke of* love. *Do you mean that the* tranquility *which otherwise plays a central role in what you value – referring to Indian aesthetics – can ultimately become an obstacle for you? Don't you have to sacrifice tranquility for love?*

J.C.: But I don't feel that I've sacrificed anything at all.

---

[1]An example (which I have already mentioned), would be *Cheap Imitation* – for orchestra without conductor. (John Cage; footnote of 1972.)
[2]Even though I'm sixty years old and arthritic, I manage to play *Cheap Imitation* for piano solo myself. (John Cage; footnote of 1972.)

D.C.: Isn't there a bit of egotism left in tranquility? In your oscillation between determinate and indeterminate works, isn't there a vestige of this kind of problem of precedence between these two terms, love and tranquility?

J.C.: You mean that the indeterminate work preserves a kernel of egotism? As far as my imitations of Satie are concerned, what I had to do was to transcribe Satie. The circumstances were not dependent on me. I only accepted a task of this kind because of my devotion to Satie and Merce Cunningham's dances. If I continue or prolong it today, it is still in that spirit of devotion. But tranquility is evident on the surface of this work because everything that happens in it does so through chance operations. I have no plans for or worries about the physical result, the outcome, or the end. In fact, I'm very curious to know what will be produced. I'm very curious because I don't foresee it. Obviously, *Cheap Imitation* lies outside of what may seem necessary in my work in general, and that's disturbing. I'm the first to be disturbed by it, and that can undermine tranquility. Nevertheless, I doubt that there is any conflict or struggle for precedence, as you put it. I'm disciplined enough not to have a fit because of that. Circumstances led me to a detour, that's all. But this detour will definitely have interesting repercussions ... and not necessarily on a musical level.[1]

D.C.: Is it because of Satie that you detoured – I won't say reverted – towards a more traditional form of music?

J.C.: It was because of my devotion to him.

D.C.: And where does that devotion come from?

J.C.: Well, I love Satie's humor just as I love Chuang-tze's. It resides not in his music, but in his words.

[1]The first performance of *Cheap Imitation,* (with 24 of the work's 96 parts) was scheduled for the beginning of May, 1972, by the Gaudeamus foundation, the Dutch musical organization. The conductor was Jan Stulen, and the musicians had been specially chosen from among the Mobile Ensemble. When I arrived at The Hague, on the day arranged for the performance, I discovered that the musicians were only on their first day of rehearsal! The work proved to be too difficult for that single session. That evening, however, instead of the expected first performance, we performed a *first public rehearsal* of the first movement.... We were supposed to repeat the work the next day, at another concert. On that second evening, we successfully managed to perform two movements, still in the form of a rehearsal, and still without a conductor. That second public rehearsal at least taught me that my two and a half years on that piece had not been in vain, and that I had written a beautiful work which obliged the musicians in the orchestra to listen to each other – something they rarely do ... The Gaudeamus Foundation was so embarrassed that they arranged for the work to be performed – and this time really presented for the first time – about a month later as a part of the Holland Festival; I was formally assured that all the preparations for this performance would be arranged. However, when I arrived in Holland a month later to attend the final full rehearsal, I discovered not only that it was again just the *first* rehearsal, but also that *most of the musicians had not even taken the trouble to look*

D.C.: But you appreciate Satie's music, and not just his titles?

J.C.: I admire his sense of psychology. His music reflects exactly my theory of aesthetics. There are none of the bursts of energy or climaxes we usually associate with Beethoven. And what I consider equally remarkable is the feeling of similarity that comes to mind when you examine any composition having parts – any three. Moreover, what's also incredibly striking is that between those three pieces and any three others there can be hardly any feeling of rapport! You see, Satie felt to an unparalleled degree the need to renew himself. But to me in turn, that need seemed completely new. Since I discovered that, I always start everything over again from zero. In fact, there isn't anything that Satie could have written, or that he could have said, that wouldn't make me absolutely enthusiastic. Even today, I never come to the end of Satie. Just like the mushrooms.

D.C.: How's that?

J.C.: After twenty years of picking mushrooms, I tell myself that I'll probably get bored looking for others. But each year, when I go back into the woods in the Spring or in the Summer, I find new ones. It's as exciting as the first time! Well, it's the same thing with Satie. Mme Salabert recently sent me the posthumous works of Satie that she published. I was crazy about them. Besides, around the time I wrote *Cheap Imitation,* I was composing other imitations of Satie. These became part of the *Song Books.* Each time I finished one, I forced myself by means of chance operations to write the next one differently. Thus I tried to imitate pieces of Satie in many different ways. I finally found one, based on his posthumous chorales, that pleased me. The piece I ended up with amazes me as much as if it were by Satie. You're wondering how I did it ... I just took the chorale and placed directly over the printed score a transparency with staves giving each half-tone the same amount of space. The staff Satie used was obviously conventional and

at the score! Jan Stulen had been replaced by a pupil of Boulez who, at the beginning of the rehearsal, asked me 'I believe that this work has three movements; is that correct?' After a few miserable little attempts to play the first phrases, I interrupted the rehearsal, and told the musicians what I thought about the deplorable state of the society in which we live – not just musical society. I added that I was withdrawing the work from the program of the concert planned for that evening, and that I congratulated myself for having come up with, in the composition of *Cheap Imitation,* something capable of opening the ears of orchestra musicians. I had offered them something with which to make music, and not, as is practiced today, something with which to scrape together a little money.

I am convinced that they play the music of others as badly as mine. However, in the case of *Cheap Imitation,* there are neither climaxes, nor harmony, nor counterpoint, in brief, nothing which would enable the musicians to hide that absence of the slightest devotion which characterizes them. One must take care not to reproach individuals for that absence of devotion – whether they be musicians or simple vacationers throwing their garbage in the streams. We must hold the present organization of society responsible for this. That is the raison d'etre of revolution. (John Cage; footnote of 1972.)

consequently any major third was written as close together as the minor third adjoining it. This obscures the space between the two on the paper. With my new staff, just by tracing Satie's melodic contour onto it – at no matter what angle, even randomly – I was able to obtain a new melody – a microtonal melody. It's not an imitation, it's a rubbing! Yet, it's rigorously something else entirely ... a discovery.

D.C.: Let's return to the genesis of the Song Books. *Is there a relationship between Satie and Thoreau?*

J.C.: I'm not sure there are many. But I picked out the most obvious ones in particular. Neither Satie nor Thoreau were ever married. Each was greatly preoccupied with symmetry: Thoreau, with the forest reflected in the lake; and Satie, with rhythmic structure ...

D.C.: I heard that you attributed the numbers that fill up Satie's note-books to calculations for future works. But couldn't they have been just grocery bills?

J.C.: That's what Darius Milhaud maintains.[1] He thinks that I'm wrong to see rhythmic structures in those figures. But I carefully examined these columns of numbers at the Conservatory Library, and I noticed that they resembled the ones that I myself was using to calculate my rhythms. And I also verified the figures myself. If you want to analyze a Satie piece, you have to end up with notations like that. So I'm right, and Milhaud is wrong.

D.C.: So on the basis of those observations, you feel you can talk about Satie's use of symmetry?

J.C.: In Satie's case, that symmetry definitely provides a tranquil continuity. And if we then couple the word tranquility to Thoreau, we end up with a very satisfactory equation.

D.C.: Even with the railroad track at Walden that so infuriated Thoreau?

J.C.: He rebelled against the fact that people could own something without possessing it. He thought he possessed their land more than the owners did. Had he been able to read Wittgenstein, he would have paraphrased the philosopher by saying that possession lies in use!

D.C.: Isn't Stony Point a little like Concord? Not in the sense of topo-graphy, but from the point of view of what you were trying to achieve there. You were a city-dweller, but one day you just left New York. And you, who are terribly irritated by insects, discovered all the charms of the country ... Weren't you following Thoreau's example by becoming in turn a man of the woods?

[1]*Cf.* Darius Milhaud, *Ma vie heureuse.* Editions Pierre Belfond: Paris, 1973.

J.C.: I certainly wasn't conscious of it at the time, but when I recently recognized the parallel, I started reading Thoreau's *Journal* and couldn't put it down. Yet, the community we formed doesn't exactly conform to the life Thoreau imagined and practiced. To parallel Thoreau's attitude today, we would have to construct urban communities! For everything has changed ... I like Claes Oldenburg's image of himself as a sort of urban Thoreau!

D.C.: But you don't feel that you can apply that comparison to yourself?

J.C.: I don't live just at Stony Point.[1] I now have an apartment in New York. And I have become ambivalent about country life. I'm not that young anymore, I have trouble climbing hills or carrying anything heavy because of my arthritis. So, for the moment, I have decided to spend the Winter in the city and the Summer in the country. But I lead a terribly itinerant life. For me, in fact, there is no Winter or Summer. I travel during every season. I can't say that I really live anywhere anymore. The only stable thing is my work, which I carry with me in my briefcase; and I can work in just about any setting. At one time I used to walk a lot in the woods, but now, I have little opportunity for that. I was very fortunate to be able to live in the country in 1954, albeit at a time when people were not really aware of what I was doing – at a time when they weren't interested in my work yet. That left time for me to discover the mushrooms.

D.C.: Do you answer every letter and phone call?

J.C.: I accept everything that comes. I force myself to remain faithful to my idea of the fluidity of all things. I wouldn't be what I am without the telephone, I'm caught up in the movement of technology. Its natural that I take part in it. If I tried to separate myself from social life, from existence by requests and replies, that would mean that I was opting for determinacy. My contradictions don't go that far. I try to remain open.[2]

D.C.: Was Stony Point a way to isolate yourself, to close the door?

J.C.: Initially, we didn't want to be an artist colony separated from the world. We didn't even want to be all of us artists. But it so happened that those who tried the experiment were, for the most part, interested in art or various crafts. The process of selection became rigorous in itself! We began, in fact, by creating something that resembled a music center ... around five musicians, a potter, a filmmaker, a painter, and a sculptor ... Today, that has all changed; there are other people with us, and I

[1]See the footnote at the end of the 'Dialogue with John Cage.' (John Cage: footnote of 1972.)
[2]However, I am at present assisted by Artservices, an organization established in Paris and New York by Bénédicte Pesle. In New York, Mimi Johnson, and in Paris, Ritty Burchfield take care of many details of correspondence, reservations, etc. Without their support, I would be at my wits' end. (John Cage: footnote of 1972.)

don't know what they do. There are even some whom I don't know at all. Their idea, which doesn't please me very much, is that the number of inhabitants in the community should be increased to the maximum. That leaves me sceptical. On the other hand, the country is so much cheaper and so beautiful ... I feel a little like I'm being pushed out of Stony Point, but at the same time I'm very tempted to stay there. And, alas, the truth is that I'm becoming an absentee landlord, exactly what disgusted Thoreau. I have become an owner who doesn't use what he possesses. In our age, that's a transgression of morality. I have become immoral.[1]

D.C.: Fundamentally, you don't seem to be too favorably inclined towards an experiment of that kind. Were you disappointed by life in a community.?

J.C.: I wouldn't go so far as to say that. Our community was nonetheless quite unique. Paul Williams, who was behind Stony Point, was a student at Black Mountain, and his father was an inventor. And a successful inventor! He made more than a million dollars. While Paul was at Black Mountain, he was interested in minimal architecture – producing comfortable dwellings at the lowest cost. He left college to get married, and with his wife Vera, who was also a student, he wanted to establish a community starting with people from Black Mountian. So he asked us where we would like to live. Most of us had urban activities, and so we couldn't live too far away. I myself lived in New York, and I wanted to continue leading a city life. So, at first we said we would like to live as close as possible to New York. He started looking and proposed a large choice of very different properties to us. We opted for one of them. Same thing for the kinds of houses – each of us had to choose. Then everything was arranged and built. And we agreed to reimburse Williams over a period of thirty years for the houses and the land. You see, there was no question of escaping urban existence, nor of an organized life ...

D.C.: Nothing comparable, then, to a hippie commune?

J.C.: I will say, though, that all of the couples who in 1954 were married have separated since then. And all the couples who come to the community and stay there end up separating. In reality, our community is a community for separation. It sometimes happens that people who have separated find someone to remarry within the community; sometimes they find them elsewhere.

D.C.: A while ago you mentioned the mushrooms that you were free to collect. That's at least one merit of this community.

[1]Since I have left the community, I am content with renting a house in the middle of the forest, near a river (also in Rockland County) during the summer. (John Cage: footnote of 1972.) And now I live the year round in an old department store in the middle of Manhattan. (John Cage: footnote of 1980.)

J.C.: When I left New York for Stony Point, it was like a revelation! I had never taken seriously Suzuki's remark that there is no Zen life except outside the city. Well, the mushrooms allowed me to understand Suzuki. Rockland County, where Stony Point is located, abounds in mushrooms of all varieties. The more you know them, the less sure you feel about identifying them. Each one is itself. Each mushroom is what it is — its own center. It's useless to pretend to know mushrooms. They escape your erudition. I have studied mushrooms a great deal ...

D.C.: *It seems that you collected the best private library in the United States on the subject,[1] and that you were one of the founders of the Mycological Society in New York ...*

J.C.: Yes, and if I say that mushrooms defy our efforts at classification and inquiry, it is because I have often had the opportunity to experience this. One day, during a morning walk in a forest in Vermont, I got sick after eating a mushroom that I normally ate cooked and that raw, proved to be poisonous. This particular time, I hadn't yet eaten anything that day and the mushroom was raw. I was sick for twelve whole hours. But I was able to tell my friends not to get too alarmed. I knew that it wasn't a deadly mushroom. Another time, I confused the poisonous hellebore with skunk cabbage, and I nearly died from it.

D.C.: *Artaud wrote about peyote. Have you ever considered using hallucinatory mushrooms?*

J.C.: No, never. Last autumn, in California, I tried a marijuana cigarette. Then a second one. No effect at all! They told me that this was normal, and that you have to continue. A girl got me to take a toke of hashish, and that didn't do anything to me either. Then they left me alone. Drugs don't interest me.

D.C.: *Have you observed the effects of drugs on other people?*

J.C.: There are all sorts of effects. LSD can awaken creativity, other drugs can lead to suicide. I have seen it all — good and bad. In general marijuana is better than alcohol. Marijuana calms young people down, it often produces appeasing ideas. With alcohol you never see the sense of fraternity and non-ownership that many hippies seem to achieve with marijuana.

D.C.: *Can't you get addicted?*

J.C.: Not to marijuana. They smoke it when they have it. Myself, I am a

[1]In 1971, I gave it to the University of California at Santa Cruz. (John Cage: footnote of 1972.)

slave to tobacco,[1] much more than young people are to marijuana. Perhaps it's because they're not slaves that they have learned how to help one another.

D.C.: *Do you see a real difference between what they do and what adults do?*

J.C.: One day when I was in Virginia, going from one university to another, I came across a hitch-hiker and I picked him up. He was a hippie. He was going from Texas to Pennsylvania, and all along the way, at each stop, he discovered friends whom he didn't even know, but who supplied him with everything he needed. When I was young, that didn't exist, there was no fraternity.

D.C.: *There was the sense of family ...*

J.C.: But today the family is everywhere. The sense of fraternity remains unbroken even if you leave the group. That's great. And it's not a question of religion, but an attitude of open welcome that's part of daily life. In the past, we were alone. Today, that's no longer true. More and more people have given up being alone.

---

[1]No longer. Some years ago, six or seven, I thought of myself as two people, one who knew that I had stopped smoking, the other who was unaware of that fact. Whenever the latter picked up a cigarette, the former started laughing, and didn't stop until he put it down. (John Cage: footnote of 1980.)

EIGHTH INTERVIEW

Visual effects and film music

Image and sound in *HPSCHD*

Recording *HPSCHD*

The Paris *Musicircus* and the meaning of organization

On order and disorder; Stockhausen and Christian Wolff

On Xenakis

Japan and its music

On musical art as an invitation to nobility

The discipline of listening

Towards a Fulleresque university

Against the economy and making a living

Crimes of 'action' and employment

D.C.: A while ago, you were talking about Cheap Imitation *and the old ladies you were going to scare with it. Given the reception your* Musicircus *received in Paris last October, I wonder if you don't think that France is a country of old ladies?*

J.C.: No, there were a lot of young people at the *Musicircus*, and it was wonderful! And one of them told me, at the end: 'Come back, and we'll make the revolution with you.'

D.C.: But when any one group monopolizes the microphone, the situation can't be very revolutionary!

J.C.: At the gathering at Les Halles, I was particularly distressed by the absence of visual activity. We could have had a lot of films. But at the last moment, the arrangements for a projector fell through. That's what created the impression of total motionlessness as you walked around the circus. Everything would have been presented differently if there had been film.

D.C.: Many of your scores allow for cinematographic or visual effects. But you haven't composed much for film ... Didn't the score you did for the film on Calder's mobiles win a prize?

J.C.: Yes, in 1951, at the Woodstock Film Festival. That's strictly speaking my only film music.[1] I also composed *Music for Marcel Duchamp* for the Duchamp sequence in Hans Richter's film *Dreams That Money Can Buy*. You could also compare my Calder music to the piece I wrote earlier for the CBS Radio Workshop, *The City Wears a Slouch Hat*. In 1942, I thought of using the noises unique to each place in the most realistic way possible. These were urban noises, which I treated not as sound effects, but as materials for music. I wanted to produce a musical continuity which would also be directly linked to the subject of the text by means of the naturalistic character of the sounds used. In the case of *Music for Marcel Duchamp*, I limited myself to writing a piece based on a particular rhythmic structure which filled the exact amount of time of the sequence devoted to Duchamp. The spirit of my music was

[1]In 1971, I composed *WGBH-TV* (for composer and technicians), which is also a 16mm film. (John Cage: footnote of 1972.)

what I considered the most appropriate to the images I had seen. But I was also aware how poor the piano and the metallic noises sounded when recorded. So I decided to prepare the piano to make it sound better and to avoid any fluctuations in resonance – which often occurred at that time in recordings. For the Calder film – my last attempt in that field – I used a combination of two approaches: using environmental sounds 'musically'; and composing a specific piece appropriate to the subject of the film. At certain critical points of the structure, I tried to achieve an absolute synchronization of music and image. But once I had finished my work, other cuts were made which reduced that effort to nothing, so the music no longer corresponds to the images with the same precision I had at first desired and later achieved. Nevertheless, I had tried in that film to play on the parallelism between image and sound, which had not been the case in my earlier efforts.

D.C.: You talked about environmental noise in The City Wears a Slouch Hat. *Was there an equivalent in* The Works of Calder?

J.C.: In the middle of my film on Calder, I used sounds from Calder's studio itself – the sounds of the mobiles bumping into each other, or the noises of a single mobile with parts bumping or brushing against one another, etc. – and I used them as is, following the general pattern of *The City Wears a Slouch Hat*. I composed this middle section after the piece for prepared piano that I mentioned. And I found it so extraordinary that I considered cutting out the piano piece and filling the entire film with just the sounds of the mobiles alone.

D.C.: How do you achieve the 'visual' aspect of your more recent scores like HPSCHD?

J.C.: I've already talked about the first year spent composing that work. We spent the second year recopying the computer data, transcribing it into 'manuscripts' and arranging the details for performing it in Assembly Hall, the immense theater at the University of Illinois, which is a circular space, surrounded by a sort of corridor with glass walls. I had always admired that hall, and imagined that it would be a wonderful location for a concert, or rather, for a musical event. I was able to obtain the collaboration of Ronald Nameth, a film maker from the Art Department, and Calvin Sumsion, who later collaborated with me on the series of lithographs and plexigrams called *Not Wanting to Say Anything about Marcel*. Nameth took charge of gathering the films. Because the space was so immense, we were able to project films from several spots at once. The music, as I have said, was planned according to a division of the octave into equal steps – five to fifty-six per octave. That reminded me of a microscope, so I thought a telescope would be a fitting symbol for the images and suggested to Nameth that most of the films be about space travel. NASA easily provided us with about forty of them. [We also obtained about a hundred animated cartoons.] And in addition to the eight film projectors, we had eighty slide projectors with about 8000 slides. Many of the slides also dealt with space travel, some were of biomorphic forms, ink figures, details of complex or abstract forms, etc. There was a great variety. But the central theme was interplanetary travel. The audience was completely free to move around amidst all that abundance of films and slides. They could sit down, or walk around. About 6000 people came, but the hall could have held fifteen to twenty thousand. Consequently, everyone always experienced a great freedom of movement, since it was possible to change the sound *and* visual dimensions of the event at any moment simply by turning or going in one direction instead of another.

D.C.: How was the sound dispersed?

J.C.: Each of the fifty-two different tapes were broadcast through its own channel through loudspeakers positioned high around the entire perimeter of the hall. In the middle of the hall was a very large space around which each of the seven harpsichords sat on its own separate platform. In the center, Calvin Sumsion placed semi-transparent screens. These didn't completely block the images of the films and the slides but allowed them to interact with different images on other screens. By standing under the screens, you could follow this meta-morphosis of each image through space. The sound of the seven harpsi-chords, projected into space by the seven loudspeakers in a way criss-crossed this interplay of image and light. The crowd moved around in complete freedom, and at times people spontaneously started to dance, thus adding their own theater to the whole global theater they had been given.

D.C.: And do you think that the recording of HPSCHD *captured that complexity – at least in terms of the sound?*

J.C.: I mentioned that there were fifty-two tapes corresponding to the fifty-two divisions of the octave. Because the recording was to be in stereo, we used only three solos, one on the first channel, one on the second, and David Tudor's on both channels equally. We went to a studio in Chicago specially equipped for mixing eight tapes at a time, and there combined the fifty-two tapes without too much additional distortion! We simply superimposed the three solos onto this mixed-down tape. By combining more and more of the tapes thanks to this technique of successive mixings, we were able to achieve the feeling of complexity caused by the superimposition of sound events. Seventeen tapes mixed together gave us chamber music. When, say, thirty-four tapes had been combined, the result had the density and quality of an orchestra. But all fifty-two tapes together sounded like something never heard before – it was truly unheard of! This record resembles the recording of *Cartridge*

Music in that it could not have been produced live – the result indeed relies on the facilities of a recording studio.

D.C.: On the other hand, the Paris Musicircus *stood out because of its simplicity.*

J.C.: From the point of view of the spectators' mobility, the two events aren't comparable. In Paris, you couldn't move. But I especially noticed a rather disagreeable difference from the point of view of sound. The voice of a director, broadcast over the entire loudspeaker system, ordered the crowd to leave the stage. It could very well have been a government imposing itself on a situation which, in itself, rejected all organization! They also asked me several times to go up onto the central stage. I deliberately refused to do that, because it would have focused attention, provoking the exact opposite frame of mind from the free and unfocused one which I was counting on. Unfortunately, that focus came shortly thereafter, once the audience had enthusiastically responded to the appearance of the acrobats. Then they reverted to the all too familiar context of a spectacle.

D.C.: Would you agree that French society is a 'spectacle' society?

J.C.: I would prefer to think that the form that the *Musicircus* took in Paris depended less on French culture, strictly speaking, than on the external, physical circumstances. On the one hand, the absence of suitable technology; on the other, space inadequate for the turnout ...

D.C.: Wasn't there also some misunderstanding as to the organization, or rather, disorganization that you wanted? Your suggestions were hardly followed at all!

J.C.: I believe that that's the root of the problem. And I refuse to be personally implicated in it. I had nothing to do with organizing the two American musicircuses – I was happy to just throw out an idea. But both times, in Illinois and in Minneapolis, someone was there to assume the role of a utility. Not someone who acted like a director, saying 'Don't do that,' but who acted in a way that facilitated the work of others.

D.C.: A stage manager.

J.C.: I know that it's difficult to draw a line between the activity of a well-contained utility and that of, say, a policeman. But I'm sure that the difference exists and that it can be sensed. It's really a question of recognizing how important the difference is and not letting it escape.

D.C.: Can you define it?

J.C.: You need the same kind of organization for a musicircus as for a world's fair. Let's start from the beginning. When you go to the world's fair, you first enter an immense parking lot. Such a huge parking lot that it might be very difficult for you to find your car again when you're ready to leave. In Montreal, they solved that problem nicely. They labelled each section of the parking lot with the emblem of a different animal. It was easier to remember whether you belonged in the kangaroo, the snake, or the tortoise section. And they decided to use animals rather than words because people were coming from around the whole world and couldn't be expected to understand a given language.

D.C.: At the Musicircus *we each wore a little likeness of John Cage pinned to our lapel!*

J.C.: The problem at the *Musicircus* was having about thirty groups perform on seven different stages. It was a scheduling problem. Or you could say it was the problem of a person who goes to a restaurant, only to find it already full. And his problem is aggravated by the fact that the guests are already spilling into the kitchen. What you find here is the absence of a utility. And that's what happened at the *Musicircus* at Les Halles. The central platform was supposed to be used by several groups of performers, not just one. It ended up being occupied by the audience. That's why I consider that term *constipation* to be perfectly pertinent!

D.C.: So it's difficult to 'organize' without appearing like a policeman ...

J.C.: You have to know how to use numbers – how to turn them to your advantage. I explained to you how each of the *HPSCHD* tapes had been precisely programmed and calibrated by the computer. It represented total organization, extreme coherence in terms of the program. At one point while we were re-recording tapes on top of tapes, starting perhaps with thirty-four tapes together but certainly reaching it when all fifty-two were superimposed, all order disappeared. Disorganization can result from the accumulation of organizations having fine differences.

D.C.: In the 'open work,' too, the composer makes the whole flexible by increasing the rigor of each detail. In Stockhausen's piece XI, the pianist must execute very detailed little groups, but in a global ordering that remains entirely up to him. Yet, despite my admiration for Stockhausen, I'm convinced that he cannot be aware of all the possible sequences. Don't you run the same risk given your idea of accumulating various orderings of detail to achieve a global disorder?

J.C.: No, because your objection to Stockhausen's work only deals with the question of sequence. A kaleidoscope juxtaposition of fixed fragments can't have anything more than merely ornamental value. What's more, you can't free yourself of the order the composer intended by simply shuffling still recognizable groups. At best, that technique can only give the impression that the work remains unfinished on a temporal level – but even that's uncertain. But everything would change, if, instead of playing the eleven groups organized by the composer one after the other, you played them all at once! All eleven at once wouldn't be so bad! And one hundred and eleven of them together would be even better! Then, we wouldn't have to worry about relapsing into a predetermined organization!

D.C.: When we last discussed Stockhausen's idea of continuum, you disagreed that a work could at once be determinate and indeterminate ...

J.C.: Yes, if 'at once' implies a global vision of the structure of the work, taken abstractly as an essence, as something very general. That is too often what the conventional composer does, whether or not he composes serially. He automatically situates himself outside of time in some imaginary space. Then, obviously, it would be very flattering for the composer to feel that his work involves both the determinate and indeterminate, and everything in between. But that view of things eliminates the strangeness unique to indeterminacy. If you accept the idea of a continuum, you reduce indeterminacy to a more or less perfected variety of determinacy. You forget that there's a jump from one to the other. And how do you make this jump? My answer is to let time act. Don't stick to an overly distant and overly dominating vision of the work which must include this and that, thus excluding various other elements, etc. Don't think of the work outside of time. Instead of controlling possibilities, instead of letting them emerge only in succession, break their linearity and run them simultaneously, immediately and all at once. As in *HPSCHD* or the *Musicircus*, you should let all the various orderings emerge and connect freely: non-linearity makes them cancel each other out. Then all you have to do is to maintain that non-linearity, and that is the role of the 'utilities.' The 'utilities' insure non-order, freedom. Without the 'utilities,' on the other hand, you'll fatally relapse into order, into linearity. Tyranny and violence fall under the heading of linearity. Indeterminacy, as I conceive it, is a leap into non-linearity. Or into abundance.

D.C.: But even amidst the abundance of HPSCHD, *isn't there still this duality of determinacy and indeterminacy? And isn't it also detectable in the* Musicircus? *For although everyone continually walked around, anyone could concentrate for a moment on a particular group or soloist. And he would probably recognize that a vocal or instrumental figure normally belonged to a particular tradition. But we were supposed to listen to the whole. And that whole, no matter how confused and multidimensional it might have appeared, was nonetheless apprehended in turn as a thing, as a unity. There was linearity in this whole.*

J.C.: Perhaps. But what you discovered was not the unity of a fixed figure, but that of a tremulous 'non-figure.' That is what I call multiple unity. It's not the unity of a multiplicity or diversity. I mean that the plurality of the groups is not eliminated by the impression of a superindividual unity. You don't revert to a duality of figure and background, or determinacy and indeterminacy, etc. You remain *between* one and two. You can't choose, because everything comes at once – there is temporal simultaneity. That's what Suzuki calls non-dualism – but we have already talked about that.

D.C.: So, you would criticize Stockhausen's music in much the same way you criticize Boulez's. Since it aspires to a continuum between immobility and mobility, it is a dramatic music.

J.C.: Well, when Christian Wolff appears to oscillate within this same double principle of determinacy and indeterminacy, he too seems to be heading towards drama. He has some sounds that must be played in a set manner, but he also calls for others that can be replaced at will. But in Stockhausen, on the level of conflict, everything is willed. It's even more than drama, it's tragedy as there must be determinacy or indeterminacy, one or the other. While in Wolff's music, there is freedom. It doesn't matter if carefully defined sounds can be combined with sounds unforeseen. All of these sounds can intermingle. In Stockhausen's music, one particular idea is increasingly accented until it becomes clear, so clear that we become preoccupied with it and lose track of the sounds themselves. In Wolff's music, there is nothing but sounds. No set ideas, but a fruitful means of eliciting an unexpected continuity.[1]

D.C.: Whence your distinction between chance resulting from an equal distribution of events – which is Xenakis' idea of chance, scientific chance – and chance resulting from inequality, thus necessarily uncontrollable and devoid of fixed ideas. Xenakis talks about the beauty of music in terms of the intelligence it conveys. Christian Wolff and even you reject everything that comes from the intellect. Yet, as soon as there is equality, there is an idea.

J.C.: I must, however, confess that I don't know Xenakis' work very well. I have really listened to only two pieces by him. One, *Nomos Alpha*, was a solo for cello; the other, a piece performed on Swedish Radio, seemed to me to be a work for tape. It used a lot of sounds, especially in the higher frequencies. I wonder if Xenakis is that far away from what I'm trying to do – not of course in what he says, but in what he achieves. For I remember well the pleasure Yuji Takahashi told me he felt while playing Xenakis' *Herma and Eonta* on the piano. He told me that he liked two kinds of music – music that had too many notes, and music that didn't have enough.

D.C.: Has Yuji Takahashi played your works?

[1]These thoughts are in relation to Wolff's early music, as are those that follow, and not his more recent work. I admire the recent music too but not its concern with power, with political subject matter. (John Cage: footnote of 1980.)

J.C.: Yes.

D.C.: *And in which category did he classify you?*

J.C.: With the musicians who use too few sounds. Xenakis was in the category of musicians who use too many sounds. Now, my music contains even more sounds than Xenakis'. And I wonder what Takahashi must think, for he played my *Sonatas and Interludes*, which doesn't seem to fall into either extreme!

D.C.: *In general, Japanese musicians seem to receive you very favorably. Toshi Ichiyanagi's work owes a lot to you. And in* The Bride *and the* Bachelors, *Calvin Tomkins describes how Sofu Teshigahara, a master of Japanese floral arrangement, invoked 'blessings upon the avant-garde activities of Mr. Cage and Mr. Tudor' at the special service held in your honor in 1962 at the Grand Shinto Shrine of Ise.*[1]

J.C.: Indeed, I did go to Japan on two occasions with David Tudor, and we have many friends there. From a musical point of view, I think that what we played for them gave them the chance to discover a music that was their own – rather than a twelve-tone music. Before our arrival, they had no alternative other than dodecaphony. Neo-classicism was not really accessible to them, because it would have meant a simple return to their classicism. In fact, our music, that is, the music David Tudor played for them, was the only music that could afford them an appreciation analogous to their appreciation of traditional Japanese music, something they couldn't find in the different modern musics. So we deserve a small part of the credit for the fact that contemporary Japanese music features elements similar, although not identical, to those of ancient Japanese music.

D.C.: *Can you give an example of that?*

J.C.: Just a few weeks ago, I had a very odd experience in a Japanese restaurant in New York. In this restaurant, there was a tape recorder playing Japanese music. Usually, rhythm is stressed, and I don't particularly like it. I prefer Korean music. In terms of Japanese music, I prefer *shakuhachi* music, the flute suits me better than the *koto*. We were conversing as usual while the music was playing. Little by little, during the gaps in our conversation, I realized that the silences included in this music were extremely long, and that the sounds that occurred were very different from each other. I was surprised by my discovery, because the extent of the tape was absolutely unusual, it was very long. And I had never run across that in traditional Japanese music. This piece wasn't destined uniquely for Japanese listeners, but for the entire universe, exactly in the manner of the music that Wolff writes and

[1]Calvin Tomkins, *The Bride and the Bachelors.* London: Weidenfeld and Nicolson, 1965; and New York: Viking Press, 1965. p. 69.

plays. In fact, it wasn't very much different from a work by Wolff. There were sounds, which floated in an immense space, a space of time – and doubtless also in space in general – coming from all parts of space at once, so it seemed to me. Wolff's pieces certainly convey that explicitly. But here there was only one tape-recorder. Everything was coming from it. And it was very, very beautiful. I was unable to recognize any tempo, any periodicity at all. All I was able to identify was the arrival of a few sounds from time to time. I was transported to natural experiences, to my daily life, when I am not listening to music, when sounds simply happen. There is nothing more delicious!

D.C.: *A few years ago, at the International Congress of Aesthetics in Amsterdam, a Japanese professor explained some of the features of Zen music, using gong sounds recorded in a temple as an illustration. He wanted to prove that Zen music is addressed to the body, to the abdomen, and not to the head or to the ear, and he thought it appropriate to repeat each sound three times. After the talk, the president of the session asked him if the number three played a specific role in Zen. The bewildered lecturer had to explain that the gong sounds were played back three times for the purposes of demonstration! In Japan, people don't listen to them as organized sounds, but as sounds in their own centers, unrelated and not counted.*

J.C.: When you listen to sounds that share a periodic rhythm, what you hear is necessarily something other than the sounds themselves. You don't hear the sounds – you hear the fact that the sounds have been organized. Zen cultivates this flowing back towards non-organization, that is, towards sounds as such, for and in themselves.

D.C.: *I'm afraid that the 'average' listener can hardly measure up to that aspect of the direction you take.*

J.C.: Music as I envision it ... But here, I must admit the difficulty. It is at one and the same time a pedagogical music and a music of 'reality' which takes for granted that pedagogy has been thrown out, finished, we've graduated, a music, that is, that's an invitation to something I'd like to call *nobility*.

D.C.: *In what sense? Are you in some way referring to Nietzsche?*

J.C.: No. 'Nobility' is an expression that I take from the Buddhist tradition. To be 'noble' is to be detached, at every instant, from the fact of loving and hating. Many Zen stories illustrate that nobility. To help you understand what this is all about, I would say that the absence of nobility occurs, in a performer, for example, when, instead of behaving faithfully by doing what he is asked to do, he decides that what he has to play is unworthy of him. He has heard it said that this music is indeterminate, left up to chance, etc. – and refuses to play. Or else, the performer may decide that everything is good, that anything goes, that it is enough to play any way at all. I must tell you now about my quarrels with Leonard Bernstein's orchestra for the New York performance of *Atlas Eclipticalis*![1]

D.C.: The absence of nobility, to tell the truth, appears to be a rather widespread phenomenon.

J.C.: We run the risk of falling into it each time we do no more than subject things to our likes and dislikes.

D.C.: Every time, in short, that we make a judgement based on taste.

J.C.: That's it. Every time we practice aesthetics! I write by using chance operations to liberate my music from every kind of like and dislike. I believe that I am not mistaken in observing a lack of nobility in a musician when he refuses to understand that.

D.C.: You have only defined the absence of nobility. What about nobility itself?

J.C.: For the Buddhists, there exist both sentient beings and non-sentient beings, according to whether or not they have sense perceptions. But to be sentient and non-sentient are not modes of existence which can be hierarchically arranged. One is not better than the other — or rather, both have the same — infinite — value. It is to this equality that the Japanese refer flower arrangement and the tea ceremony. Thus, my music could perhaps appear perfectly contemptible to a particular critic, or to a particular musician. Or to a particular performer! For a Westerner, my music is a non-sentient being. You can do anything you want with it. I, on the other hand, consider it rigorously equal to a sentient being. If people rejected me, if they beat me up, I would complain, because I'm sentient. But if they reject my music, if they do it violence, what would I, *I who am not my music*, have to complain about? I'm not complaining about anything. But I observe an attitude which is the exact opposite of nobility. My music is not a sentient being, and it is not I. I have nothing to say. But it's not less than I am. It deserves to be treated like a human being. No matter how miserable it may be, it's worthy of that much compassion. You wanted a positive definition of nobility? It's treating all things equally. And having equal feelings toward all beings, whether sentient or non-sentient.

D.C.: That's a definition which is strangely reminiscent of 'serenity' — Gelassenheit — Meister Eckhart's definition. That Gelassenheit, which includes lassen, *'letting be,' is also defined by Heidegger as an 'equality of soul with regard to things.' But in what sense would you refer to nobility*

[1]Cf. the footnote on the Orchestra of The Hague in the seventh interview. (John Cage: footnote of 1972.)

in a listener, for example? Is it enough to abdicate all will in the presence of what happens?

J.C.: Not necessarily. If you go to India, you'll see that, far from remaining without will and without reactions, people listening to traditional music *participate* in that music. They don't remain indifferent. Their nobility manifests itself by letting the sounds be, at the same time that they move back and forth, make gestures, nod their heads, sway, breathe in a way that is itself an art. The Spanish manifest comparable nobility by their way of living music – punctuating it with shouts and special noises. With us, I think nobility must consist in being as calm as possible and letting the other listeners be themselves. As well as the sounds!

D.C.: The Indians believe there is an art of listening, and yet, concerts are foreign to the music of the Orient.

J.C.: You won't find there what in our culture flourishes under the name of 'amateurism.' There, music is – or was, for that's no doubt in the process of changing – a way of life. There is no less social dignity in the fact of being a listener than in that of being a performer. Moreover, composers themselves are the performers (the performers are the creators) and not composers who simply condescend to play their own music. You don't listen to the performer, but to the sounds. [Nobody goes to any trouble for a virtuoso – but they would for a *raga*.]

D.C.: So then, it seems that we should look to the Orient.

J.C.: But I don't really look to the Orient at all. My position is not to *impose* a certain attitude on Western listeners, but to persuade them that there are sounds, and that those sounds, whatever they are, are worthy to be heard.

D.C.: Just before Christmas vacation in 1970, I was supposed to give a class at the University of Paris VIII, but some other class was entrenched in the classroom that had been assigned to me. They refused to leave, but as we couldn't find another classroom we ended up joining them. In the same room two languages were at work. I was talking about Messiaen and the rival class was discussing Mao Zedung. Since I was talking rather loudly, the students in the other group stopped trying to compete and started to read the text in unison. They phrased their reading so clearly that the musicians stopped listening to me and began to improvise around this 'raw' background sound with their flutes and chairs. This lasted an hour and resembled one of your events ... Although no one learned much about Mao or Messiaen, I thought the experience was far from pedagogically empty. What do you think?

J.C.: That's the beginning of Buckminster Fuller's university! In *Education Automation*, he suggests that the university should become an open space, capable of embracing very different activities. The buildings themselves should not be divided up on the inside, so you could teach every subject at once in the same space. Each student could choose freely what suited him, rather than being shut off into a single course at a time. That seems to me to be the real experience of every-day life in its most general sense. You only have to walk around in a city. What happens there is equivalent to classes or professors who leave us alone to study what we want.

D.C.: *So the art of listening becomes essential.*

J.C.: Yes, and there wouldn't be any more classrooms, or concert halls, for that matter! I'm convinced that we can apply this art of listening to all domains. Personally, I chose to start with music. But music itself is only a word. Why should it be limited to this or that specific field? The entire world must be made into music. Or into a Fuller university.

D.C.: *But if you remain within the traditionally accepted definition of the word* university, *your perspective would probably tend to eliminate all classical teaching ...*

J.C.: I don't see why a professor should have to teach his students what he already knows, or what he knows how to do. This is all the more true for teaching music. Since the professor knows how to do what he knows how to do, since he's already supposed to know the discipline he's teaching, that ought to be enough! There's no reason at all for the students to follow the same path. They shouldn't repeat, they should invent something else!

D.C.: *Yes, but we generally acknowledge that people are in a university in order to learn a profession.*

J.C.: Well, if the university is truly teaching a profession, and if the student is seriously interested in learning that profession, then he'll probably succeed in a situation that also includes many other things. And if, from one place or another, a lack of seriousness arises, *a fortiori*, attention will be free to shift to something else!

D.C.: *I admire this line of reasoning ...*

J.C.: I know that the freedom I am talking about is far from prevalent. The universities are way behind. For the most part, they still don't understand the need to avoid worrying about making a living. There shouldn't be anything but *experimental* universities, 'noble' universities, detached from all preoccupation with employment. When they leave the universities, students are directly exposed to the economy, that is, to organization. But in the name of this encounter with the economy, each person is forbidden to multiply his interests. At the University of Illinois, they have begun to try to remedy that state of affairs. There are no course requirements. They are working on establishing equivalency exams and eliminating prerequisites. I think a student should be able to stay a student as long as he wishes!

D.C.: That's a challenge to the all-powerful economy.

J.C.: Certainly. The economy[1] must be eliminated, and politics, too.[2] We shouldn't let it rule us, we should rethink it so that it will free instead of limit us. But you have to start by liquidating the most anachronistic of dogmas – the profit motive. It's perpetuated by the universities, which thereby become the slaves of organization and government. The employment dogma – making a living. The economy hinders us from treating technology as a 'utility.' It becomes the medium of organization. It exalts property. It makes it different for all those who won't devote themselves to making a living to live in a suitable way. That's what employment is; we should get rid of it!

[1]By 'economy,' here I mean money. (John Cage: footnote of 1972.)
[2]By 'politics,' here I mean power. (John Cage: footnote of 1972.)

NINTH INTERVIEW

'Zero time' and silence

Work and play

Against the rules

The 'celebration'

Works to come

Keeping score between order and disorder

The *I Ching* and microbiology

Abundance

Quantity and quality

Living in the world

The role of money

Everything has already been thought

About interdisciplinarity

The interior life of an ashtray

About *Variations VII*

Electroencephalographic music

Surrealism and Dada

Rhythm and *irrelevance*

D.C.: You were talking about our getting rid of the profit motive and employment. That, of course, would be ideal. In reality, we are self-employed and active. We go on living. Through your work, you yourself provide an example of the most painstaking work. Can you clarify your own 'motive' — which aims towards the non-act — on a more technical level? What role, for example, does time *—as you conceive it in your latest scores — play?*

J.C.: That reminds me of a comment that the composer Robert Ashley once made during an interview I had with Roger Reynolds. He said that music was *any kind of temporal act whatsoever.*

D.C.: And theater? Anyway, when you performed in Gordon Mumma's Configuration *last July, your participation was musical as well as theatrical. It was called 0' 00", in contrast, it seems to me, with 4' 33", which is a more conventional musical work in the sense that it marks its own temporal limitation, a time signature. How would you define this 'zero time' characterizing your latest works, which complicates the distinction between music and theater, without erasing its 'musical' aspect?*

J.C.: 'Zero time' exists when we don't notice the passage of time, when we don't measure it.[1]

D.C.: So we should be in *zero time all the time, so to speak?*

J.C.: Sometimes we are, and sometimes not. I mean that when I work on the piece you mentioned, or 'in' that piece, I am indeed 'in' zero time.

D.C.: 'In' zero time, there's no room for measurement. If I understand you correctly, measure is a variation of the 'profit motive' you want to eliminate.

J.C.: Naturally, but that doesn't stop me from working, from doing what my work requires. The difference is that I am no longer working towards an envisaged end, that is, in line with the economy.

---

[1]This expression 'zero time' comes from Christian Wolff. He was the first to use zero time in his compositions, concurrently with clock time. (John Cage: footnote of 1972.)

D.C.: The Peters catalog entry 0' 00" bears the subtitle, 4' 33" no. 2. This then is your second silent work?

J.C.: Yes, and I have still another.

D.C.: That's rather intriguing. How do you manage to differentiate among them?

J.C.: The first one, *4' 33"*, involved one or several musicians who made no sound. The second one, *0' 00"*, indicates that an obligation towards others must be fulfilled, in a partial or complete manner, by a single person. The third one involves gathering together two or more people who are playing a game in an amplified context. A bridge or chess match, or any game at all can become a distinct – another essentially silent – musical work.

D.C.: You said 'a distinct' work? That presupposes that the work already exists …

J.C.: Yes, in nature, and at every moment. 'Distinct' means that there is amplification. It's a work on a work – like all my indeterminate works! I say that it's essentially silent because I believe that it allows the silence of a game of chess to appear for what it really is: a silence full of noises.

D.C.: It can't appear exactly as it is, since it's amplified.

J.C.: That's how I *act,* with the aid of technology.

D.C.: Then your 'action' consists in choosing a particular situation: the game.

J.C.: But my music isn't a game. I don't like the idea of a game, if by *game* you mean rules and measurements. In *Homo Ludens,* Huizinga demonstrates quite well that games are an affair of rules, and that these rules lead to separating the world of the players from the rest of the world. I chose the situation of a game, but not because I consider my music to be a game. In fact, I could have chosen any other situation as well.

D.C.: Rules reflect the economic world?

J.C.: Of course. What interests me isn't the rules, but the fact that those rules change. That's why I don't believe that my art is a game. I try to change the rules or eliminate them each time. A game, on the contrary, depends on following those rules. But first of all, of accepting them. That is why in my work, when you get right down to it, I have nothing to do with games. I prefer invention.

D.C.: But for Buckminster Fuller, for example, the concept of the game is fundamental.

J.C.: He's dealing with a world game involving a strategy for the 'utilities'. He's changing the rules of all the games which to date have gone by the names politics, economics, organization, etc. Moreover, I don't see why we shouldn't organize what needs to be organized, that is, the 'utilities'. We need an organization on that level. Not elsewhere. When I myself need a 'utility', like the irregular clock in my *Concert for Piano,* I organize it. But that's specifically to change the normal rules of the game in a piano concerto.

D.C.: In the Concert for Piano, *the conductor fulfils the 'utilitarian' function of disordering time. In 0' 00", the title disorders time. But in your third silent work, the time of the game, which is relatively ordered, is disordered by amplification, which allows the uncontrollable sonorous dimension of the game of time to appear 'beneath' the time of the game!*

J.C.: Rather than talking about a 'game of time', I would prefer to say that what counts is what occurs, and that what occurs has to do with *celebration,* and not with game.

D.C.: Celebration? *You used that word in* Silence, *where you speak of 'celebrating the fact that we possess nothing'.*

J.C.: Precisely. We aren't the ones celebrating, it's *what occurs that does the celebrating.*

D.C.: Let's talk about Atlas Borealis, *the project which, I believe, is to complete what you began in* Atlas Eclipticalis. *When you composed* Atlas Eclipticalis, *you wrote it as the first line of a haiku.*

J.C.: The allusion to the haiku comes from one of my Japanese friends, Hidekazu Yoshida, who suggested that I consider the first line of each haiku as referring to nirvana, the second to samsara, the third to a specific individual action – which, however, is completed through non-action. So I planned *Atlas Eclipticalis* as the first line of a haiku that included *Variations IV* as its second line, and *0' 00"* as its third line. *Atlas Borealis* is a different work. It was suggested to me by Marshall McLuhan. He asked me: 'Why don't you make a piece using the Thunderclaps from *Finnegans Wake?*' We have already talked a little about the *Ten Thunderclaps.* I would like to have some equipment made that would be attached to the throats of the chorus members so that when they sing the *Thunderclaps,* their sound would fill up the envelopes of actual thunderclaps.

D.C.: For the reader, I would like to quote the first of these 'thunderclaps', which appears in the third paragraph of the first chapter of Finnegans Wake: *'bababadalgharaghtakamminarronnkonnbronntonnerronn-tuonnthunntrovarrhounawnskawntoohoohoordenenthurnuk!' Other than chorus, what instrumentation will you use?*

J.C.: There will be an orchestra – probably a string orchestra – with perhaps a few wind instruments near the end. *Atlas Borealis* will be composed in the same way as *Atlas Eclipticalis,* from astronomical maps. But the string instruments, like the chorus, will use special equipment with microphones to transform the sounds actually emitted so that they fill up the envelopes of rain falling. More and more rain will fall as the piece unfolds – rain falling on water, on earth, on metal, etc., in relation to the history of civilization, as McLuhan has pointed out. Since the *Thunderclaps* of *Finnegans Wake* describe the various stages of the history of human civilization, and in particular, of technology, the last thunderclap will represent the electronic technology of our era. At that stage, rain may no longer fall on anything whatsoever, but simply sound in the air – and that is why I will perhaps make use of wind instruments in the last section.[1]

D.C.: If I can judge by your description, your finished product will be a gigantic choral, symphonic, but most of all, electronic poem...

J.C.: ... On the history of civilization, as it has been taught to me by McLuhan, and especially Buckminster Fuller!

D.C.: What you just said about your last Thunderclap *reminds me of McLuhan and his ideas on an electronic environment. But how has Fuller inspired you?*

J.C.: But Fuller talks about that too. I remember the years 1949 and 1950 when I met him at Black Mountain. One day he told us that the wind around the earth always went from west to east. There were people who went with the wind, others against the wind. Those who went with the wind went to the East and developed an Eastern type of thought; those who went against the wind went to Europe and developed European philosophy. And he suggested that the two tendencies met in the United States, and that their meeting produced a movement upward, into the air.

D.C.: What is this movement into the air? Spiritual ascension?

J.C.: No, the invention of the airplane!

D.C.: And you, following McLuhan, would probably add the electronic era ...

J.C.: But that was also in Fuller's thinking. My *Thunderclaps* will attemt to make all that clear.

D.C.: So your music is going to become more and more Fulleresque?

[1]In June, 1972, at the Encuentros of Pamplona, I sang the *Mesostics re Merce Cuningham.* The concert took place in the Sala de Armas of the Ciudadela, albeit on the ground floor of this old abandoned citadel open to the winds. The wind started whistling through the mikes ... The effect, which the audience undoubtedly perceived, was surprisingly close to what I hope to achieve in the *Thunderclaps.* (John Cage: footnote of 1972.)

J.C.: When I was writing the preface to *A Year From Monday*, I realized that I was referring in my writing more and more to Fuller. And I wondered if I were in some way misrepresenting his thinking, since many people feel that his work represents a very high degree of order, while mine tries to give rise to a high degree of disorder. You might therefore think that the two were opposed. I myself was worried that he would think I was undermining his own enterprise. At the time, I happened to be in Cincinnati, and fortunately, he was in southern Illinois. I paid him a visit and examined with him each of the quotations or mentions of his work in *A Year From Monday*. And I asked him if he saw any opposition between his order and my disorder. He replied that there was no problem! I couldn't repeat to you the details of his commentary, which involved constructing a theoretical model of the non-opposition between order and disorder – a model which I didn't understand too well. In reality, he has the soul of a builder and the mind of an architect; I sometimes have trouble following him. But essentially, I believe that I am completely faithful to his ideas. Later, I met an English architect, Critchlow, who was interested not only in Buckminster Fuller's ideas, but also in the *I Ching*, like me. He constructed a model linking the *I Ching*'s sixty-five hexagrams to Fuller's Dymaxion. Using a model, he was able to produce another for the compatibility between order and disorder.[1] His explanations were likewise mathematical, and again, I confess that I didn't understand very much of it.

D.C.: *Joseph Needham thinks that Chinese science has influenced the development of Western science to a greater extent than you would ever imagine. Yet, is that enough to validate a confrontation between the* I Ching *and certain aspects of modern mathematics?*

J.C.: I'll give you another example. Do you know Gunther Stent? He's a molecular biologist at the University of California at Berkeley. He wrote a book first called *The Coming of the Golden Age*, then *The Golden Age*. And that work records a certain number of his observations concerning the hippies in the San Francisco area. He is perfectly aware of the recent developments in microbiology, *and* in art and music. We were both invited to a symposium on world prospectives which was to be held during the winter of 1968-1969, or maybe 1967-1968, in the Yucatan.[2] When I met him, he gave me the proofs of his book to read. Leafing through those proofs, I came across a genetic table, a table of the division of DNA and other molecules, which, as you know, determine our personality according to current microbiology. Well, I immediately recognized

[1]Douglas Messerli's collection of his poems, *Dinner on the Lawn*, is prefaced by this remark of Gertrude Stein: 'I am inclined to believe there is no difference between clarity and confusion.' (John Cage: footnote of 1980.)

[2]The complete proceedings of this symposium have now appeared: C.H. Waddington, *Biology and the History of the Future*, Edinburgh: Edinburgh University Press, 1972. (John Cage: footnote of 1972.)

the *I Ching*! It contains sixty-four elements, and includes trigrams which combine into hexagrams. Thus our personalities result from chance operations – *just like music!*

D.C.: *How far does this correspondence to the* I Ching *go?*

J.C.: I mentioned to Stent what the genetic tables in his book made me think of. But I'm not at all an academician, and could not go very far with my explanations. So Gunther Stent, who was himself quite struck by this discovery, turned to one of his friends, a poet I believe, who is quite an expert in the exegesis of the *I Ching*.[1] This person, who lived near Berkeley, used his interest in the *I Ching* in the same way that Critchlow had been able to combine his interest in Fuller with his interest in the *I Ching*. Well, that poet was able to complete what I had suggested, and he gave Stent the broader details of the structure of the *I Ching* – which permitted Stent to clarify theoretically the arguments in favor of this correspondence between the *I Ching* and microbiology. These arguments are, it appears, decisive.

D.C.: *Does that mean that you wouldn't hesitate to refer to contemporary science to legitimate certain aspects of your course of action? I would have thought you would agree with Jean Wahl that we cannot rely too much on contemporary science, since it is less true than future science!*

J.C.: But I'm not interested in relying on science. What I meant by telling you about the connection between the *I Ching* and contemporary science was that we haven't the grounds to refuse anything at all. I'm not seeking to eliminate possibilities, but to multiply them. Look at what's happening at Wesleyan University. They have built new auditoriums for works that require a framework completely different from what the old theaters could offer. During the same period, they developed a School of Oriental Music. They organized what are now called the Curry Concerts, with Indian music, Indian food, Indian dances, Indian costumes, etc. And since they built several auditoriums, you may choose each evening from among Indian music, Western chamber music, electronic music, rock, etc. Just as in Tokyo where you may have your tea to Beethoven, to ancient Japanese music, to Debussy ...

D.C.: *I still wonder if Fuller's direction isn't in fact ambiguous. Won't Fuller's golden age of technology seem terribly static? Shouldn't ideas that value progress also value dynamism?*

J.C.: Fuller points out that up until now we have only obtained mediocre results, and that the deplorable use we have made and are making of our technology is linked to our will to dominate. When I talk about my own

[1]Harvey Bialy. Cf. Stent, *op. cit.* (John Cage: footnote of 1972.)

music, it's not because I believe it belongs to me. I know perfectly well that I don't possess it. Likewise, techniques only interest me if I don't possess them. If I don't try to control them to make them the instrument of a politics or of a thirst for possession, then I can use them freely. I can have them or not, they deprive me of nothing. Now, I have to take into account the fact that I have or don't have my glasses, that I do or don't have central heating or an elevator. I have the television and the media, I have the computer. All that can go completely unnoticed. I can use them without thinking about them all the time! Color television gives us colors that aren't true, and at first we think about it. We won't think about it anymore when, through progress, we forget the difference between televised image and real event. You call that a static age. I would say that we obviously already have, in nature, the colors that television will recreate. We will soon be able to discover those colors on our screens. Then we will use television much more naturally, as if it didn't exist. In general, we are not able to consider technology in a *natural* way because we aren't accustomed to our environment. The future will be no more static than the past. We are already in *stasis*!

D.C.: Doesn't Fuller's thinking cheapen real struggles and real disorders like those recorded in History?

J.C.: Fuller also advises us to keep everything that comes to us from the past, so that we may compare the future, all the richness of the future, with the poverty of the past. So, the true history of humanity is perhaps the history of technology ...

D.C.: But I can't seem to resolve this problem: how can we conceive of a reconciliation between acting – order – and non-acting – disorder – even in Fuller's perspective?

J.C.: I was led to non-acting and disorder by the Orientals. Well, the Orientals don't have our problems. They are infinitely closer to the environment than we are. They'll accept electronic technology more easily. Look at Japan! And China, already! As for India, I promise you surprises ... The Japanese acquired the most modern technology of the world while they have retained Zen. They had order and disorder. That doesn't mean that their order is the right one; but they are beginning to enter the era of simultaneous order and disorder. All we ourselves need to do is to abandon our ideas of competition and competitiveness – which is the essential way of *non-acting* – for an infinity of possibilities to open up. Fuller very rightly says that the goal is to escape the idea of a goal. That's what I'm trying to accomplish in my field: an ecological music. A music that would permit us to inhabit the world. And I mean the whole world, and not just a particular part of the world. The world in its entirety, and not separate fragments or parts of the world. The world recognized at last for what it is. We must construct, that is, gather together what exists in a dispersed state. As soon as we give it a try, we realize that everything already goes together. Things were gathered together before us; all we have done is to separate them. Our task, henceforth, is to reunite them. To do so, we must live in a new way, perhaps not in conventional houses anymore, but in nomadic or mobile houses; in the deserts, in the oceans, on the tops of mountains. Rockets will enable us to live in the skies. [I try to make my music show us that we *already* inhabit our environment. I try to suggest a new kind of listening for this new living in the world: not a music for you and me, but a listening which will recognize, as of now, the fact that there will be seven billion people in the year 2000, and twenty billion in 2060!]

D.C.: How can we not fear over-population?

J.C.: You fear it only because you believe there is an entire segment of humanity that goes to sleep hungry. And you are afraid that this phenomenon will get worse. I believe that I agree with the basis of your thinking: we must assure each person the basics of life. But, in my opinion, we will only manage that by realizing that we are all here together. Not separate. Every authority, be it political or economic, that we have asked to formulate the problem – let's not even talk about finding answers yet! – represents techniques of separation. Until recently, our only thought has been to separate ourselves. What awaits us, what we are already experiencing is the fact of being together. So, we must first break ourselves of the habit of asserting our individuality and our values alone. Only by retreating from these values can there be something like a humanism. And this humanism presupposes the acceptance of over-population! We should accept the idea of humanity residing in a global village. As long as we can't understand that – and governments, politicians and economists will never help us there – there will be no way of giving each other what we need.

D.C.: Yes, but doesn't giving everyone what he needs impoverish the whole?

J.C.: On the contrary! Needs are not a vital minimum! They also and especially include abundance! No one must have to do anything else at all. That's non-action!

D.C.: What do you think of the role of money at the present time? And how do you think we can get rid of the social divisions which rely on money?

J.C.: Currently, money is an aspect of, or even the reason for, the existence of government. As far as I'm concerned, governments exist only to protect the rich against the poor. And for itself: to become richer than the neighboring government. That is why we have so many wars! And that is also why we have all these riots, and the other illnesses of contemporary society. What is surprising in the United States is that robbery has become a more common phenomenon than rain. And people have long ago realized that it is impossible to protect a house against burglars. I have friends who are victims of robberies an average of three times a month. Well, do you think all these robberies are simply the result of bad education or deplorable temperament? Or race? There are all these robberies because the robbers must at all costs make some money and they have no other way to do so than to take objects from other people and sell them. Gordon Mumma recently told me that all his electronic equipment had been stolen three times this year. His equipment particularly excites the envy of thieves because it is very easy to resell. He added that with all those repeated robberies, he has lost all sense of ownership. His attitude is not one of distress, but rather, of recognition. What led him to this sense of non-ownership, of non-property, was not having read my books, but having been systematically robbed!

D.C.: And what role has money played in your personal experience?

J.C.: As a child, I had a passion for music. My parents were upset. They knew from previous family experience that music was not a profession, that it was insufficient for making a living. They tried everything – without success – to discourage me. They did everything. My father's financial situation continually fluctuated, and so he tried to convince me of the extreme importance of money. He felt very deeply, I believe, a desire not to see me suffer as he himself had suffered. Despite this, I never could take money seriously, except, of course, when I had too little of it – really not enough. When I went to New York, around 1943, I didn't have a cent. I was completely broke. Of course, that didn't last. But I lived like that with an extraordinary feeling of freedom. I have never forgotten how liberating it can be to live without a single cent! But soon, of course, I felt famished – and I told myself that I should do something. Just at that moment, the novelist Steinbeck, who was one of our friends,[1] came to New York and invited us to lunch at the 21 Club – the famous club on 52nd Street. A single meal at that club cost $100! It made us feel badly to eat for $100 ... Life would have been so much simpler if we could have used that money instead of eating it! But in any case, I had chosen to adopt the behavior of one who is interested in music, not in money. So I forced myself to earn money only when I really needed it. On that occasion I had none at all. I wrote to some friends in Chicago to tell them I was in a bad situation and that I absolutely needed money, and they sent me something like $50, I believe.

Ten years later, when I was writing the *Music of Changes*, I likewise found myself without a penny. I told myself that it would be better to look for a job. That's what I did. I spent two or three days trying to find

[1]Xenia and I were still married. (John Cage: footnote of 1980.)

someone who would hire me. I found nothing. So, I decided not to look anymore, but to do my own work – and, if necessary, to die as a result. Before plunging entirely into the *Music of Changes*, I sent out a lot of letters to all the people I knew, offering to sell them shares in the earnings I would make with *Music of Changes*. And I used a slogan: 'Would you like to be rich when you're dead?' Thanks to that stratagem, I collected $250. But it took me nine months to finish the *Music of Changes*! And during that entire period I really had very little money. My father and my mother were always generous to me. Each time they were able to help me, they did so. Fortunately, later I was in a position to help them in turn, when they were in need. My financial situation has improved, and in the last few years of my life, I have really been able to come to the aid of my mother and my father. But that obliged me to learn how to make money, whether I needed it or not. I can live on very little, I am even easily at ease with very little money. But I learned to earn it.

D.C.: Does that mean that you're satisfied with your status – and the fate of artists in general!

J.C.: You can never be sure of the revenues which your rights as an author will give you. It depends, obviously, on the sales of your books or scores, and performances, which can increase or diminish. Right now, the amount I earn has rather strongly increased. In the past, I made $250 a year, while I have now reached almost $3000 a year. With nothing but the rights to my books and music, I think I could provide for my own needs if I chose to withdraw to some isolated corner of the globe. I could live in a Mexican village, or in a backwoods area of North Carolina, but I wouldn't be able to pay for all the trips I take. What permits me to do that is my activity as a lecturer. The prices of my lectures have increased. I ask more now in order to reduce the number of lectures that I'm obliged to give. I need a lot of time to be able to continue my work, and the increase in my fees was the only way for me to spread myself a little less thin. But between the lectures and the concerts, I manage to earn more than I really need. So, there is the Cunningham Dance Foundation, which invariably needs money, and to which I give what I can every year. I also donate money to good works organizations and to the Civil Liberties Union.

D.C.: Are there any institutions that spread the ideas of Buckminster Fuller, for example, and that you aid in some way or other?

J.C.: I admire very much the work of the *Whole Earth Catalogue*, which directly diffuses Buckminster Fuller's ideas. It closely resembles a department store catalogue … but it concerns books and objects which are or will be fundamentally useful in the society to come. 'Utilities.' Everyone, on their communities, can read this catalogue and find all sorts of ideas in it. I'm happy to say that my work, *A Year From Monday*, is included in that catalogue.

D.C.: But this idea of a catalogue, of an exhaustive inventory, surprises me. The world as you describe it according to Fuller will not be closed in on itself. It will be open to abundance, to non-linearity, to the richness of everything that presents itself. Can we envision cataloguing it? And doing so from this moment on?

J.C.: When I explain to you the modesty of my real needs, or the sense of poverty that the burglars provoked in Gordon Mumma, I don't think that I'm going against the meaning of abundance. It doesn't consist in possessing everything, but in possessing only what you really use. The catalogue doesn't imply that there's a limit to our possibilities, it simply indicates what's necessary. Let me surprise you even more by mentioning Gunther Stent again, for he thinks that the essential work, concerning ideas in all domains, both in the sciences and in the arts, has been done already. There's no need to work anymore in the field of fundamentals. We still need to arrange a bunch of details, but they're just details. And once we have a new attitude towards organizing 'utilities,' we'll be able quite simply to be content with our actual situation. On the level of ideas, everything has been thought; all the fundamental discoveries have been made. And in the domain of music, Gunther Stent thinks that music as it exists at present, now that sounds themselves have been recognized as free, spares us any supplementary work on the basics. That doesn't mean that we don't need to compose new music, but new ideas on music are no longer necessary.

D.C.: Messiaen considers music to have reached its harmonic ceiling, and to be approaching a rhythmic equilibrium. And you said you were not in disagreement with Leonard Meyer's belief, based on your work, that the present and future state of music is a period of stasis.

J.C.: We henceforth find ourselves in a situation where the old overlaps the new and interferes with it. In a sense, everything is finished, everything has been discovered and tested. Of course that doesn't mean that from this moment on we are in a golden age. But we have gathered the essential ideas which will allow us to live in that new era.

D.C.: Isn't that a theme borrowed from the nineteenth century?

J.C.: Is that so important? [Look at David Tudor. By producing feedback between audio and video circuits, isn't he in the process of bringing some of Scriabin's spiritualist tendencies to fruition? Scriabin's disciples thought a correspondence existed between man's various senses. They are very much concerned with establishing a rapport between a particular pitch and a particular color. Scriabin and his followers were only a few of the people in the last century, and in the beginning of this century, who shared the same belief.]

D.C.: And even after the beginning of this century. Again it's impossible not to mention Messiaen!

J.C.: [All that was carried out on a spiritualist rather than technological level. They made the obligatory references to the reigning psychology, judgements, tastes, memories, etc. Today, all that's no longer necessary. We have technology. It's useless to cling to those ideas anymore. For I'm sure that through David Tudor's circuits, we will very quickly reach a complexity sufficient for any sound whatsoever to produce any color whatsoever. We will accomplish what Zen philosophy teaches: you can't talk about the distinction between cause and effect, because in the universe everything causes everything else.]

D.C.: *But again, couldn't this stabilization, this stasis of ideas, lead to an impoverishment?*

J.C.: On the contrary, I have been talking about abundance. I believe that what we can reasonably expect, within this state of stasis, is the interpenetration of those arts and those sciences which, up until recently, have grown hierarchically, and individually, kept separate for the purposes of simplification and pedagogy. We can expect that all those disciplines will henceforth intermingle in a climate very rich with joy and – I am purposely using an expression frequent in Japanese texts – bewilderment.

D.C.: *So you're betting everything on interdisciplinarity?*

J.C.: It is definitely an important acquisition on a very practical level, I have no doubt if I can judge by certain universities I know. At the University of Illinois, they plan to generalize the system of courses so that they can be given by a professor from outside the discipline in question who has no competence in the subject. In other words, cross-fertilization will soon become general practice, even in the most academic circles. A scientist will be asked to speak to musicians. The results could be much better than if they were left in the hands of another musician.

D.C.: *What you have to do is divert technical ideas or objects from their function.*

J.C.: In any case, it seems to me that, if you can manage to transfer them into other domains than those for which they were created, like music for example, scientific methods of investigation would truly take flight ...

D.C.: *Could you give me an example?*

J.C.: Look at this ashtray. It's in a state of vibration. We're sure of that, and the physicist can prove it to us. But we can't hear those vibrations. When I went into the anechoic chamber, I could hear myself. Well, now, instead of listening to myself, I want to listen to this ashtray. But I won't strike it as I would a percussion instrument. I'm going to listen to its inner life thanks to a suitable technology, which surely will not have been designed for that purpose. But at the same time, I'll be enhancing that technology since I'll be recognizing its full freedom to express itself, to develop its possibilities.

D.C.: In one of your Variations, *didn't you make a similar attempt to deal with sounds beyond the threshold of perception?*

J.C.: Yes. We know the air is filled with vibrations that we can't hear. In *Variations VII*, I tried to use sounds from that inaudible environment. But we can't consider that environment as an object. We know that it's a process. While in the case of the ashtray, we are indeed dealing with an object. It would be extremely interesting to place it in a little anechoic chamber and to listen to it through a suitable sound system. Object would become process; we would discover, thanks to a procedure borrowed from science, the meaning of nature through the music of objects.

D.C.: That reminds me of Alvin Lucier's success in capturing and transforming electroencephalographic noises into 'musical' sounds. The experiment was done again in Paris by Pierre Henry. Are you familiar with these attempts? It seems to me that that's very similar to listening to an ashtray.

J.C.: Absolutely. I know Alvin Lucier's work, especially since I assisted him at the first performace of his *Music for Solo Performer* – which took place on the evening when we first performed *Rozart Mix*. I myself attached a good many electrodes to the composer's scalp. The performance involved generating alpha waves by closing his eyes and performing other movements. The result of Alvin Lucier's cerebral activity was sent through several loudspeakers situated around the room, each coupled with a resonating object. For example, speakers were placed on a kettledrum, a gong, or a trash can. The result was great diversity in sound due to the different set-up and location of each speaker. When a given activity was fed through one speaker, it sounded differently than the same activity fed through another speaker, because of the difference in resonance. The audience was greatly impressed by the aspect of 'participation mystique' that the piece seemed to promote – a rather natural effect, since each listener was quite aware that he, too, had a brain! And if electrodes had been attached to his skull, the result would have been an equally moving music. [What interested me in this work was the fact that, because of the situation, the performer didn't have to have any particular skill at all.]

D.C.: I'm sure that you must have been filled with wonder faced with the surrealistic aspect of these encounters between improbable, ridiculous objects: electrodes and trash cans, hospitals and concert halls.

J.C.: Certainly. But I must say that I've never really appreciated Surrealist works. Critics who in general link my activities with Dada are not mistaken. But I've noticed that the Dada of 1920 had a much deeper need to break with everything that had been done, to create emptiness, than the Dada of 1950.

D.C.: People mention neo-Dadaism when they discuss you ...

J.C.: Another superfluous label! If they say I'm neo-Dada, I'll arrange somehow to free myself from that category. All that came from painting. When I began composing, I also began painting. I didn't continue, but I felt very attracted to abstract expressionism. I was brought back to representation by Rauschenberg and Johns, and since they were then labeled neo-Dadaist, I suppose, due to lack of imagination, the critics couldn't find anything else to apply to me.

D.C.: Music doesn't so easily lend itself to classification under pictorial categories.

J.C.: In any case, I felt closer to *musique concrète,* which is still representational, than to electronic music, which was immediately thought to be abstract. But beginning with the *Song of the Adolescents,* Stockhausen himself launched into 'representation'!

D.C.: Then you don't even consider yourself an heir to Dada!

J.C.: [Listen, Satie was much more Dada than I am. *Vexations* is a Dada piece!] But I didn't approach it that way at all. I felt it a duty to make it heard.

D.C.: Alvin Lucier's Music for Solo Performer *is certainly non-repetitive, rather the reverse of* Vexations ...

J.C.: Yes, and that reminds me of the definition of rhythm I made up one day. Rhythm is not at all something periodic and repetitive. It is the fact that something happens, something unexpected, something *irrelevant.*

When I compose, I don't try to interrupt that irrelevance, that freedom from being controlled, which characterizes the sounds I encounter. My music basically consists in bringing into existence what music is when there is *not yet* any music. What interests me is the fact that things already *are.*[1]

---

[1]Upon reading these pages, I believe that I can clarify my views on the Dada and Surrealist movements, around which part of this interview centered. What followed Dada, Surrealism, was social in thought or intention (André Breton), individualist in fact. What followed Johns and Rauschenberg, Neo-Dadaism, in short, what today has taken the place of Surrealism, is social from the outset and through and through, because it is an art which deals for example with industrially produced tomato juice cans. Now, if I were obliged to choose between Surrealism and Dada, I would naturally choose Dada. And if I had to prefer one Dadaist above all others, I would keep Duchamp. After which, of course, I would liberate myself from Dada. (John Cage: footnote of 1972.)
As did Duchamp. (John Cage: footnote of 1980.)

TENTH INTERVIEW

John Cage's list of the ten most significant books

The importance of Norman O. Brown

Sexuality

On Neo-Taoism

The equivalence of music and ecology

Ecology and the establishment

The music, equilibrium and Harmony of everything

On Henri Pousseur's meliorism

Beyond subjectivity

Globalizing music

Revolution and synergy

D.C.: A few years ago, you composed a list of the ten books which had been most important for you. Would you at all modify that list today?[1]

J.C.: What I'm reading these days is Thoreau's *Journal*; a week ago, it was Kauffman's treatise on mushrooms. That mushroom book motivates me to observe nature, and thus, to better appreciate Thoreau. I think Thoreau must be included in a new list.

D.C.: He was not in the old one.

J.C.: I had included Buckminster Fuller. But I said I had not yet read him! Today that's no longer true. I would keep him, of course. And I would definitely add McLuhan.

D.C.: Does any one of McLuhan's books seem particularly significant to you?

J.C.: There is an article that I rank above all his books. Its title, *The Agenbite of Outwit*, is a paraphrase of James Joyce, and it was published in the first issue of a magazine called *Location*. In it McLuhan develops an idea which is perhaps essential to all his work: whatever happens surges forth everywhere at once. You can't live in just a partial way, but totally. You must rid yourself of all specialization. Art, for example, is everywhere, so you don't have to get rid of it. This text by McLuhan seems truly significant to me. It must be added to my list.

D.C.: You included Alfredo Casella's work on Cadence. Would you keep it?

J.C.: I reread it recently. Today its importance is questionable. During the thirties, it was indisputable. You can see how much the situation has changed.

[1]Gertrude Stein (any title): Alfredo Casella (*The Cadence*): Luigi Russolo (*The Art of Noise*); Sri Ramakrishna (*Gospel*); Ananda K. Coomaraswamy (*The Transformation of Nature in Art*); *Huang-Po Doctrine of Universal Mind*; Chuang-tze (*Writings*); Franz Pfeiffer (*Meister Eckhart*) translated by C. de B. Evans; Buckminster Fuller (any book); C.H. Kauffman (*The Agaricaceae of Michigan*). Cf. John Cage's *List No2*, in *John Cage*, edited by Richard Kostelanetz, New York: RK Editions, 1970 and London: Penguin Press, 1971. Pp. 138-139.

D.C.: And Joyce?

J.C.: He would be on my list today.

D.C.: And Brown?

J.C.: I especially love *Love's Body*, and I have told you why. When I was busy composing the *Song Books* one morning, I suddenly started thinking of Norman O. Brown so strongly that I called him and told him what I was doing. He replied: 'I'm doing the same thing: composing hymns.' I would also add Ira Einhorn, another writer who is involved in similar projects – he is currently writing songs – and who frequently corresponded with both Brown and me. He lives in Philadelphia, and a few years ago, wrote several pamphlets worth of material on the misery of contemporary society. He is a polemicist of great breadth. Now, he is devoting himself to songs because he puts great emphasis on what could be called positive activity. He believes the most powerful revolutionary force will derive from the most positive rather than any negative attitude.

D.C.: So we add Einhorn and Brown?

J.C.: Brown provides a sense of ecology, not just in ideas, but in life. He defines the complementarity of opposites, the soul and the body, for example, as a real reunion. And he considers language the force that operates this reuniting of opposites. He would restore to the world, and to life, words like *to eat, to consume, to defecate* – traditionally banished from language as it has always been locked in an artificial spirituality. Brown is really very important.

D.C.: There is one subject we haven't yet discussed but that a discussion of Brown inevitably introduces: sexuality.

J.C.: In our Mycological Society, I used to plan lectures instead of excursions and weekend field trips during the Winter, because when the countryside is covered with snow, it's impossible to gather mushrooms. One of the monthly lectures I had scheduled dealt with the sexuality of mushrooms. We had invited a specialist from Connecticut, who had cultivated a certain species of mushroom, a Coprinus, in very large quantities to study their sex. In his lecture, he taught us that the sexual nature of mushrooms wasn't so very different from that of human beings, but that it was easier to study. He explained that there are around eighty types of female mushrooms and around one hundred and eighty types of males in one species alone. Some combinations result in reproduction, while others do not. Female type 42, let's say, will never reproduce with male type 111, but will with certain others. That led me to the idea that our notion of male and female is an oversimplification of an actually complex human state.

D.C.: *Then we should multiply, rather than minimize, this dichotomy.*

J.C.: Yes, in the sense that the Japanese don't limit this consideration to two opposite sexes, but extend it to rocks, flowers, the moon, etc. I have recently learned that plants respond to the affection you show them! They can almost tell you exactly who cares for them! And they won't grow if they're not loved.

D.C.: *That's why my rubber plant is less healthy than my philo-dendron ...*

J.C.: As for human beings, Margaret Mead wrote recently, that the fact that we live longer would give one the chance not to go on loving forever one other person but to change around, just naturally. We wouldn't stop loving each other, but the flexibility and adventure of our erotic emotions would increase.

D.C.: *To return to your list of the most important books, it includes a very large number of books devoted to Oriental traditions. You include Gertrude Stein, of course, and Luigi Russolo, but also Meister Eckhart, and in particular Ramakrishna, Coomaraswamy, the* Huang-Po Doctrine, *and Chuang-tze. Would you change any of that?*

J.C.: You can keep everything – but keeping in mind that I now feel closer to Huang-Po[1] and Chuang-tze than to Indian philosophies. People sometimes think that all my Fuller and McLuhan ideas have definitively 'liberated' me from my youthful passion for the East and the Far East. But the *Huang-Po Doctrine* is quite literally applicable to an ethics of the Global Village! I feel closer to Chuang-tze today than ever before![2]

D.C.: *But then, how much faith can we have in your foreword to* A Year From Monday *where you assert the unity of your course of action? In fact, you jump from one doctrine to another and combine your ideas at random ... eclectically! You pilfer a little from McLuhan and Fuller, then a little from Zen. That all points to an essential versatility which – still according to the critics – shouldn't occupy too much of our attention.*

J.C.: And there's also my foreword to *Silence* on Zen ...

D.C.: *... Where you effectively absolve Zen from any responsibility for your activities – but only after you attribute to it the initial impulse for taking the steps you have taken.*

---

[1] *The Huang-Po Doctrine of Universal Mind*, by Hsi Yun, transcription P'ei Hsiu. (John Cage: footnote of 1972.)
[2] In 1971, I began a methodical study of the writings of Mao Zedung. He hoped to free the Chinese mentality from certain Confucian ideas; I realized that his theses are perfectly compatible (cf. especially his text on contradiction) with those of Zen and Chuang-tze. (John Cage: footnote of 1972.)

J.C.: All that means is that it's impossible to naively believe in Zen in the middle of the twentieth century, as if nothing had changed! But Zen perhaps has more depth than that – that's also what I meant, and it would be useful to open our eyes to what the technological universe means. We'll never understand it unless we adopt an attitude at least related to that of Zen.

D.C.: *Your attachment to Taoism is a little less explicit, although no less real. Still, there will probably always be a few good minds who will nonetheless hold against you your attraction for what Cyril Connolly called the corruption of the 'live-and-let-live' attitude ...*

J.C.: Yes, if they remain the slaves of action and logic.

D.C.: *On the surface, I see it as a sporadic longing for a kind of erudition that fortunately will never be yours. But beyond that, you seem to be lamenting a behavioral incompatability forcefully transposed onto a moral level. Your critics often portray themselves as moralists.*

J.C.: But that's not very important. It will pass ...

D.C.: *Is your Taoism really that of Chuang-tze? Wouldn't it rather be more closely related to that of the great commentators of the third and fourth centuries, Hiang Sieou and Kouo Siang? They, in fact, bring a decisive correction to the doctrine of Chuang-tze, by asserting that Tao is* nothing – *literally nothing: a* nihil absolutum – *which leads to a pluralism to which you seem to be very close. Let me quote you this passage: 'We can say that Tao is anterior to things. But Tao is nothing. Since it is nothing, how can it be anterior to things? We do not know what is anterior to things, but things are produced continually. That proves that things are spontaneously what they are ...'*[1] *What do you think?*

J.C.: That's a splendid idea! Yes, it's very beautiful. Remember the ashtray we were talking about yesterday. We wanted to enclose it in a little anechoic chamber. Well, thanks to this idea, we can have a multiplicity of anechoic chambers, containing not just ashtrays but anything we want. And we can listen to these various objects all at once! That's going to be wonderful! But, in fact, it is already our daily experience. We're surrounded by all this multiplicity ... And our attention – I'm using this word only because it comes from Thoreau and because we can use it in Brown's sense – or our appetite, if you prefer, is going to increase. We will become more and more capable of experiencing things, of having our own experiences. It's true that we are becoming more and more impatient and voracious in our desire for the very different things we have always wanted and in greater quantity. And just as McLuhan realized, this will all happen at once.

[1]Dunstheimer translation in Fong Yeou-Lan, *Précis d'histoire de la philosophie chinoise.* Paris: Payot, 1952. P.231.

D.C.: And consequently we could never categorize your thinking.

J.C.: That is, since Tao, the ultimate term, is *nothing* or *Nothingness*, we could also conclude that we shouldn't become mesmerized by the difference and that *there is no* ultimate term. Thus, no system.

D.C.: So, in the end, we shouldn't be hypnotized either by a systematically constituted music that doubly exploits nature or the elements?

J.C.: You mean that music is always *becoming*, and that it always becomes *something*, and that this is not necessary, because that something already exists?

D.C.: Right. I was thinking about your silent pieces. Aren't they superfluous, since the noises of nature already *exist?*

J.C.: The aspect of nature with which we are the most familiar – and this familiarity is almost painful – is that we, as a human species, have endangered nature. We have acted against it, we have rebelled against its existence. So, our concern today must be to reconstitute it for what it is. And nature is not a separation of water from air, or of the sky from the earth, etc., but a 'working-together', or a 'playing-together' of those elements. That is what we call ecology. Music, as I conceive it, is ecological. You could go further and say that *it IS ecology.*

D.C.: Then it indeed ceases to exist as a separate entity?

J.C.: But it has never existed as a separate entity, except in the imagination of 'professional' musicians. It has always opened onto nature, even when it was structured 'in the opposite direction.' The problem was that people paid all their attention to its construction. Today we can diversify our attention, and construction no longer hides the ecology from us.

D.C.: But if we transpose this reasoning using a Marxist vocabulary, we obtain the criticism you most commonly receive. Your music and your attitude are too 'reactionary', they only aim at specifically ecological changes. Thus, your insistence on ecology is suspect, since it is answerable to ideology. Why? Because by pretending to defeat attention and its economy, and by refusing to accept essential musical forms, you in effect distract *your listeners. You divert them from the 'true' debate, which is political and economic. You serve the* establishment. *You, and all your circus ideas, are the clown of reactionary tendencies!*

J.C.: In a Marxist sense, wouldn't you have to say that the texts of *Silence* are reactionary because they concern individual experience? While those from *A Year From Monday* are progressive because they concern society? If I were to assume a Marxist point of view, I wouldn't see them as reactionary at all. But then, we should return to the qualifier 'reactionary' applied to *Silence*. Because what led me from a consideration of individual experience to a consideration of social experience was not so much the social nature of music as McLuhan's idea that contemporary society itself is an individual! And an individual who, according to Brown's terminology, and not Marcuse's, requires psycho-analysis.

D.C.: Let me borrow a few lines from a critic of Chinese Buddhism, a Confucian who was a sixteenth century philosopher, Wang Chu-Jen. They seem fairly clear in relation to our problem: 'The Buddhist pretension of not having any attachment to phenomena demonstrates that Buddhists are attached to them. And the fact that we, Confucians, do not pretend to lack attachment for phenomena shows that we are not attached to them ...'[1] From a Marxist point of view, an amalgam of Buddhism (or Taoism) and Confucianism can be forged. If the Confucians are 'reactionaries' although they are not 'attached to phenomena' – which doesn't stop them from fighting for the established order – then the Taoists and other Buddhists are even more so. Under the banner of foiling tradition and institutions, they reinforce and confirm them – albeit a contrario. *On the lowest level, people do say – as they did the other day in an article in* Musique en jeu – *that Cage is nothing but a reactionary!*

J.C.: Alas! This whole argument seems only good for confusing the debate, which involves tilting the scale from one side to the other. But we must indeed take care that the scale is *the same* in both cases: between attachment and non-attachment, and between Confucians and Buddhists. It cannot be convincing, precisely because it is only an argument ... verbal criticisms, good for exciting the intellect. But if you look at reality, you realize that, in both cases, Confucius and Zen, there is a compatability of attachment and non-attachment. So, to find the true differences, you must go a little farther with your analysis! ... And take into account what is really happening. The Taoists have been important enough in the history of China for anyone at all to know, if only superficially, that this history doesn't consider them reactionaries *a priori*; and the same must be said of Chinese Buddhism. Now, I would say that those who wield that language, reactionary or progressive, do so in the name of power! The difference between them and me is that they want the power for themselves, and thus they want to maintain it. While myself, not only do I not want it, but I want to destroy it. When I really began making music, I mean, composing 'seriously', it was to involve myself in noise, because noises escape power, that is, the laws of counterpoint and harmony. When I spoke about Schaeffer, I said that noises had not been liberated but had been reintegrated into a new kind of harmony and counterpoint. If that were the case, that would mean that we had only changed prisons! My idea is that there should be no more prisons. Take another example: Black Power. If blacks free them-

[1]Fong Yeou-Lan, *op. cit.*

selves from the laws whites invented to protect themselves from the blacks, that's well and good. But if they in turn want to invent laws, that is, to wield power in exactly the same way as whites, what will the difference be? There are only a very few blacks who understand that with laws that will protect them from the whites, they will just be new whites. They will have come to power over the whites, but nothing will change. During the period of harmony and counterpoint, there was good and bad, and rules to support the good against the bad. Today, we must identify ourselves with noises instead, and not seek laws for the noises, as if we were blacks seeking power! Music demonstrates what an ecologically balanced situation could be — one in which whites would not have more power than blacks, and blacks no more than whites. A situation in which each thing and each sound is in its place, because each one is what it is. Moreover, I'm not the one who's inventing that situation. Music was already carrying it within itself despite everything people forced it to endure.

D.C.: And I cannot help but relate that situation to the sense you have of Harmony — in the tradition of the Classical Taoists.[1] There is no harmony of treatises on harmony!

J.C.: Yes, I conceive of Harmony in that way, and not in the 'Western' manner. And I think that it rather widely surpasses music — but that music is, today, a route toward Harmony, and a necessary route. Harmony is what we can today picture in terms of ecology.

D.C.: But confronted with this Oriental sense of Harmony, we must understand the optimism it supposes. You have confidence in nature. You think that by letting it act, equilibrium will be re-established.

J.C.: Exactly.

D.C.: Are you familiar with Eugen Herrigel's book on archery? Jean Paulhan — naively in some people's eyes — said that it would soon become as important as Descarte's Discours de la méthode.

J.C.: I liked that book very much. I was reading it at the time I met Hidekazu Yoshida. And when I spoke with him about it, he told me that there was at least one fact the German philosopher had forgotten to mention. There is an archer in Japan who is considered a master, an extraordinary archer, but who has never been able to hit the bull's eye, even in broad daylight!

D.C.: That reminds me of your reaction when you saw the garden of the Ryoan-ji for the first time.

---

[1]Mao Zedung in turn talks about the 'Great Harmony' to designate a future state of humanity in which the exploitation of man by man will have disappeared, but not the contradiction. (Daniel Charles: footnote of 1972.)

J.C.: I was amazed when I found myself facing that garden, and my impression was that the rocks could well have been in any position whatsoever. A lot of art critics and philosophers give you the impression that the rocks are exactly in the right place. These people go through a lot of calculations, they make a blueprint of the garden, and they end up demonstrating that the equilibrium and harmony of those fifteen stones on a base of sand could only have been obtained in one single manner – the one that was used.

D.C.: *Then what is really an* a posteriori *observation tries to pass itself off as the discovery of a law ...*

J.C.: Yes, a law of nature and beauty! But I had exactly the opposite impression. I was in New York with Hidekazu Yoshida, the Japanese friend we just mentioned. And I told him that, in my opinion, the rocks could easily have been put anywhere at all. Then, he simply smiled, got out of my car, went into his hotel, and brought me back a present: a tie.[1]

D.C.: *That story is the perfect counterpart to your 'happening' with Nam June Paik!*

J.C.: In happenings, I don't find that particular sense of Harmony that never diminishes but only grows stronger when things are free to be what they are.

D.C.: *Others criticize your undertakings by maintaining that, in the final analysis, the real objects you use in your work as a composer, your electronic instruments, are* not even *objects. You probably wouldn't be adverse to that idea. But it takes on a critical value from Henri Pousseur's perspective, for example, when he terms your music a gigantic process of degradation. You encourage entropy. What you are doing is then even more dependent on poor art and empty lots, in short, on Beckett's trashcans, than on the sophisticated technology you pretend to use. In fact you use it in the wrong way. He's accusing you of leading straight to a miserable – both meanings – art.*

J.C.: My intention is to let things be themselves. Now, what does that mean, letting things be themselves or not approaching them except as they are? [Pousseur's project, if I understand correctly, would consist in negating entropy, and multiplying information. It would involve improving the status and quality of all the sounds in the universe. In my opinion, that is an overly ambitious project.] I prefer to see things as they are, and to see what good they contain. I have never heard a miserable sound, not one! I have never heard a sound that made me think of decadence or putrefaction! I believe that Pousseur must be alluding to what certain critics call the 'result'. Quite often, people have

[1] I do not wear ties anymore. (John Cage: footnote of 1972.)

expressed the opinion that my activity was very interesting, but nothing more, that I was a philosopher and not a musician, that the 'results' I obtained were not all that great, in short, that I would do better to continue dreaming and abstain from composing. That would mean that, instead of giving each new sound its own meaning, you should rather worry about legislating what that meaning should be. [To improve my musical status, they suggest I get high or take acid! Well, I see nothing in marijuana or LSD. I've tried marijuana before and it didn't do anything. It didn't change sound at all!] Sometimes when you concentrate on the result to be obtained, you don't get anything at all. Sounds are not the same as results!

D.C.: Henri Pousseur also talks about the other side of the objection. Under the guise of eliminating subjectivity, while pretending or imagining that you are destroying subjectivity, aren't you in fact surreptitiously reintroducing it? You think you're adhering to the discipline of the Zen thinkers, you say that the ego is an illusion — but in saying that, aren't you the victim or instrument of a more subtle egotism? Above and beyond your protests of innocence appears an even more fearful will for power — because it is disguised and advances behind a mask. So, you become a candidate for Nietzsche-style demystification. What do you think about that?

J.C.: I think that I have the right — and, in fact, the need — to be myself, as long as I live! As if I were a sound. But I try to keep this fact of being myself *for myself*, that is, I try not to impose it on others. In a restaurant, I'm perfectly free to choose chicken instead of meat. What I perhaps did not stress enough, when I made this comparison at the Museum of Modern Art, is that the one use of the ego I should not undertake under any pretext would be to force others to choose chicken![1] If I choose chicken, I show my preference to others. And in a sense, I indeed have to do so. But I never wish my preferences to be imposed on anyone else. And that's what links me the most closely with Duchamp and Thoreau. In both of them, as different as they may be, you find a complete absence of interest in self expression. Thoreau wanted only one thing: to see and hear the world around him. When he found himself interested in writing, he hoped to find a way of writing which would allow others not to see and hear how he had done it, but to see *what* he had seen and to hear *what* he had heard. He was not the one who chose his words. They came

[1]Now, however, after, say, four years of following the macrobiotic diet, my health has so greatly improved that I would seriously advise almost anyone who would lend me an ear to make a shift in diet from animal fats to vegetable oils, to exclude dairy products and sugar, to 'choose' chicken only if it actually is a chicken, that is, free from injected hormones, agribusiness, etc., to eat fish, beans and whole grains, nuts and seeds, and vegetables with the exception of the *Solanaceae* (potatoes, tomatoes, egg-plant, and peppers). (John Cage: footnote of 1980.)

to him from what there is to see and hear. You're going to tell me that Thoreau has a definite style. He has his very own way of writing. But in a rather significant way, as his *Journal* continues, his words become simplified or shorter. The longest words, I would be tempted to say, contain something of Thoreau in them. But not the shortest words. They are words from common language, everyday words.[1] So, as the words become shorter, Thoreau's own experiences become more and more transparent. They are no longer his own experiences. It is *experience*. And his work improves to the extent that he disappears. He no longer speaks, he no longer writes; he lets things speak and write as they are. I have tried to do nothing else in music. Subjectivity no longer comes into it. And there is no artifice in this effort.

D.C.: In your Interview with Roger Reynolds, *you do appeal to subjectivity. Robert Ashley had just concluded, from what you had said previously, that time, temporal action, is the ultimate definition of music. Then, you went on from that to the equivalence of music and theater, and from that, to the idea that experience becomes 'markedly more subjective'. If one person is struck by the sound and another by some other aspect of the same piece, you would say the situation one was within was theatrical. But at the same time, you invoke each person's 'subjectivity' more strongly than ever before by saying that each one of us is supposed to feel what suits him.*

J.C.: Yes, but you know we're no longer dealing with a composer's *style* or subjectivity. The 'subjectivity' in question here is no longer that of an ego. It is that of the listener, the observer. It designates instead the Self of Zen, the Self as the celebrated Koan implies it: 'What was your Self before your birth, and before you knew good and evil?' We are not dealing with the 'subjectivity' of Western philosophers, which always needs 'objects'. We are dealing with what each person is in the depths of himself: a Self, not reducible to an ego. If you put the problem of the nature of that Self to a Zen-Buddhist, he would probably answer it with *Nothingness* or *Nothing*. The Self is not an ego; it is rather the fact that each of us is at the center, is the center of the world, without being an ego. The Self is what *I* do not impose on others. It is not a kind of 'subjectivity', but a reference to something which comes much before that and which – beyond that – allows that 'subjectivity' to be produced. It is a reference to the Nothingness that is in all things, and thus also in *me*. It would be more appropriate here to invoke, as I did concerning Suzuki, the soul's *Base,* Meister Eckhart's *Grund*. Or society!

D.C.: So it's also an invitation to plurality or multiplicity. Your experience is one thing, mine is different. The works signed 'John Cage' don't

[1]See also what Mao Zedung says about literature in his Yenan texts. (John Cage: footnote of 1972.)

belong to their author. They are just as much what you make of them as what I make of them, because you are there and I am here.

J.C.: I agree completely. There's no reason to fetter the plurality of situations and perceptions present in our meeting; it's irreducible. But you also realize that we must put these different attitudes and situations together. We're not communicating, but we are conversing. It's a global situation in which we are engaged, but not as egos. It is the situation of the Self: each is that Self. That's what I mean by a 'subjective situation'.

D.C.: Then your music would be the most universal phenomenon imaginable?

J.C.: Ultimately *I* don't write for this person or that person, but *I* try to create the conditions for a generalized interpenetration. Sounds would become identical to us and we should identify ourselves with sounds. [The result will be a generalized permeability.]

D.C.: Then what about the objection that you appeal to an extremely limited audience? Any Marxist critic could reproach you with your inability to thrill the masses. Your concerts interest only a petit-bourgeois fraction of intellectuals or students. Blue collar workers, shop keepers, farmers, and probably a lot of other people, too, aren't at all interested in your music.

J.C.: [You know, I started out on a small scale. I have told you about those lectures during my heroic period. I've made no fortune with my music, and I have only very slowly won an audience.] In the fifties, I'd get one hundred and twenty-five listeners per concert. Little by little, I became more famous. In Darmstadt, they began to wonder if one day they wouldn't have to take me seriously. After 1958, that changed. Now, I've drawn at least 5,000 for the *Musicircus* in Illinois, and surely more for *HPSCHD*. Some estimates put the audience at over 9,000. [It doesn't seem to me to be important to reach a particular audience rather than another. It's more effective to get musicians to understand the basis of their own effort. They'll surely end up telling everyone else.] Now, it's true that my music, in contrast to some others, is prepared to confront the overpopulation of the year 2000. But when that time arrives, we'll no longer need simple individual composers. By then, sounds will be enough, entirely sufficient for and in themselves. I hope my music will help us in accepting the importance of ecology. But I have no illusions about the role I'm to play in this realm. It will probably be a rather humble role. The ecology, I firmly believe, can assert itself all by itself.

D.C.: You foresee no imminent revolution?

J.C.: But the revolution won't have just one single cause!

Revolutionaries might touch it off, but they won't be doing it all alone. It is unimaginable that one particular attitude alone would be able to unleash what you envision under the name *revolution*. I believe instead that the revolution is in the process of unrolling right before our eyes on all levels – and that we aren't aware of it. Take credit cards; they signify the imminent disappearance of money. It's a part of the revolution, yet we don't perceive it. Instead we think it's a ruse of the bankers to make us spend more. What's surprising is that this ruse, if in fact it is a ruse, has succeeded so well in surpassing it's original purpose, without ever creating the aura of confidence that bankers normally require before freely disseminating credit cards like they're doing now. Capitalism won't wait for the revolutionaries to bring about its collapse ...

D.C.: That's a risky statement!

J.C.: Not really. Protest movements could quite easily, and despite themselves, lead in the opposite direction, to a reinforcement of law and order. There is in acceptance and non-violence an underestimated revolutionary force. But instead, protest is all too often absorbed into the flow of power, because it limits itself to reaching for the same old mechanisms of power, which is the worst way to challenge authority! We'll never get away from it that way!

D.C.: And how will we get away from it?

J.C.: Through synergy. Buckminster Fuller has demonstrated how much an alloy can surpass in effectiveness – that is, in rigidity and resistance – the sum of its components. The revolution will be an alloy! If we protest, we fix our attention on a qualitative change. This can obviously be done, but through one single point, or a few precise points. What is decisive is quantitative change. The revolution as envisioned by the revolutionaries can be non-selective only in appearance. [In reality, it remains value-oriented,] that is, it presupposes, in the short or long term, a selection, a qualitative decision. Synergy, on the contrary, deals with assembled elements of different qualities which gain worth only through their accumulation. The quantitative point of view can contribute what quality refuses. By letting 'bad' elements proliferate, you need not expect a general deterioration of quality, but a radical change which makes quality appear as an unacceptable limitation. When I wanted to make my piece on plexigrams in homage to Marcel Duchamp, *Not Wanting to Say Anything about Marcel Duchamp*, I wanted 'to say nothing about Marcel'. I used 1,428 pages of a dictionary, dividing them with the help of the *I Ching* into 64 groups. I divided these groups by chance using the *I Ching* to obtain first words, then letters, and finally, fragments of letters. By combining these fragments with the 261 typographical possibilities I had been given, I was able to obtain a whole of great richness.... Despite the poverty that someone interested in quality alone would see in this bunch of typographic characters or letters or isolated fragments. For his qualitative mind would never allow each of those elements to be apprehended in its simplicity, for what it is. On the other hand, quantity is a determining factor of simple upheaval.

D.C.: Then the revolution will necessarily be global and synergetic?

J.C.: It already is.

D.C.: But will it be capable of affecting all aspects of existence? Will the nine emotions of Indian aesthetic thought stop being 'permanent'?

J.C.: I think your question touches on a private matter – that is, it needs to be asked of each one of us. I don't see why the possibility of those emotions has to be toned down, especially when you remember that each one has several dimensions itself. The highest form of the erotic, according to the Hindus, for example, is devotion, and it doesn't seem to me that the revolution can take place on many levels without devotion. For a student to be able to study, in the very broadening of a revolutionary situation in the sense I mean it, he will always need devotion! I likewise think that tranquility will remain at the center of all these emotions – that tranquility that we could call non-violence, and that Satie described as 'interior immobility'. For there will continue to be tranquility at the heart of heroism – that is, acceptance of everything that occurs – at the heart of the erotic – that is, in its highest aspect, devotion. We will always have sorrow – the loss of something loved, or the gaining of something not desired. I don't think we'll ever be able to want to be free of this 'private' experience of emotion.

D.C.: Yet you conceive of this revolution in terms of the fall of the ego. Won't it therefore bring along with it the decline of everything 'private'?

J.C.: You can imagine it as being similar to the way new music makes you feel a very profound, universal, and yet personal change in how you experience time. I remember having talked about this problem one day in Hawaii. I referred to Charles Ives' *One Hundred and Thirteen Songs*. At the end, there is a text in which Ives envisions time from the viewpoint of a man seated in his armchair[1] smoking his pipe. He looks at the hills, and the dawn. You might object that this experience has nothing in common with how someone listening to Bach considers time. But in fact, it signifies the individual and personal creation of one's own music. That seems to be a satisfactory definition of the revolution. And one which doesn't hurt anyone.

D.C.: One of the forms of subjectivity certainly consists in wanting to be separate from others, and to want to situate oneself in relation to others by

---

[1]Sitting on a porch in a rocking chair. (John Cage: footnote of 1980.)

criticizing them. What has struck me in our interviews is that, out of all the musicians we have discussed, you have not maliciously criticized a single one, while so many of them take the liberty of attacking you ... I admire this silent response to all your critics. By hardly ever defending your ego as a sufficient originality, you avoid that mediocrity which would attack its opponents with bitterness and spitefulness — the hallmark of the ego. And of a false revolution.

J.C.: My deepest desire regarding contemporary music is to hear it all. Not successively, but all at once, at the same time. Everything together! But perhaps that's a perverse wish ... Who knows if we'll do it even when we have the necessary technology? That technology doesn't exist yet? Well, long live the technology to come!

Afterword to the French Edition

When we first started recording our conversations, I had some difficulty answering Daniel Charles' questions in a lively manner. It's that my interviewer is not only a musician but a philosopher, too, and one who has devoted himself seriously to the study of my writings, my music, and my activities in general. But he is also a university professor and French. As an academician, then, he naturally submitted my remarks to the so typically French requirement summed up by the expression: 'Clarify that.' (On second thought, is that so bothersome? I once answered a journalist from Illinois who asked me to put all my philosophy into a nut shell: 'Get out of whatever cage you find yourself in.') It was, I believe, on the third or fourth day of our interviews that I admitted my discomfort: I explained to Daniel Charles my uneasiness when confronted with any attempt to construct a discourse which started from certain premises in order to draw conclusions from them. Afterward, our dialogue became easier and more fluent. But also less organized. It became clear to each of us that we were no longer getting anywhere – inasmuch as it was a question of preparing a book destined for French readers. So Daniel Charles offered to re-examine these recorded conversations later. He would redistribute my remarks, insert interpolations based on my texts or letters to him, add here and there more scope to my statements by supporting them, if necessary, with the writings of others, etc. According to him, a real book – a collage rather than a word-for-word transcription – could quite easily result from our meetings. And such a book would have a good chance of generating interest.

As I think this work does. I insisted on twice reviewing it entirely myself. The second time, I found it even more interesting than the first time. First of all, because it contains a lot of information that can be found nowhere else. Secondly, because it can respond to the concern, demonstrated by Daniel Charles, of defending my positions against the attacks which are today common currency in Europe, and, oddly enough, in France. But this book satisfies me, too, because what I was able to read in these pages on my work assures me that it remains *questioning* – that is, always alive. We are continuing to wander. Among these wanderings – and *in the middle* of them – here, all of a sudden, is a release. Or an opening.

John Cage